The Arab Spring

About the Author

HAMID DABASHI is the Hagop Kevorkian Professor of Iranian Studies and Comparative Literature at Columbia University. Born in Iran, he received a dual Ph.D. in Sociology of Culture and Islamic Studies from the University of Pennsylvania, followed by a postdoctoral fellowship at Harvard University. Dabashi has written twenty books, edited four, and written over a hundred chapters, essays, articles and book reviews. He is an internationally renowned cultural critic, and his writings have been translated into numerous languages.

Dabashi has been a columnist for the Egyptian *Al-Ahram Weekly* for over a decade, and is a regular contributor to Al Jazeera and CNN. He has been a committed teacher for nearly three decades and is also a public speaker, a current affairs essayist, a staunch anti-war activist, and the founder of Dreams of a Nation: A Palestinian Film Project. He has four children and lives in New York with his wife, the Iranian–Swedish feminist Golbarg Bashi.

THE ARAB SPRING

The End of Postcolonialism

HAMID DABASHI

Zed Books

LONDON | NEW YORK

The Arab Spring: The End of Postcolonialism was first published in 2012
by Zed Books Ltd, 7 Cynthia Street, London N1 9JF, UK
and Room 400, 175 Fifth Avenue, New York, NY 10010, USA

www.zedbooks.co.uk

Copyright © Hamid Dabashi 2012

The right of Hamid Dabashi to be identified as the author
of this work has been asserted by him in accordance with
the Copyright, Designs and Patents Act, 1988.

Designed and typeset in ITC Bodoni Twelve
by illuminati, Grosmont
Index by John Barker
Cover design: www.kikamiller.com
Printed and bound by CPI Group (UK) Ltd,
Croydon, CR0 4YY

Distributed in the USA exclusively by Palgrave Macmillan, a division of
St Martin's Press, LLC, 175 Fifth Avenue, New York, NY 10010, USA

A catalogue record for this book is available from the British Library
Library of Congress Cataloging in Publication Data available

ISBN   978 1 78032 224 7 hb
ISBN   978 1 78032 223 0 pb

In memory of
Edward Said and Magda al-Nowaihi
who are not here to see it
— and for
Joseph Massad and Noha Radwan
who will see it through

Contents

Acknowledgments

To write a book about a world historic event as it unfolds needs a certain degree of audacity, which I have to attribute to my enduring rootedness in the Arab world, with friends, colleagues, comrades, and students at home from Morocco to Egypt to Lebanon, Palestine and Syria, and from Bahrain to Qatar, Saudi Arabia, and Yemen, without whose trusting camaraderie and collective wisdom I would never have dared to put pen to paper (or fingers to keyboard) and write this book.

The writing of this book is my way of joining my brothers and sisters in Tahrir Square chanting their slogan *al-Sha'b Yurid Isqat al-Nizam*, 'People Demand the Overthrow of the Regime'. I have taken that slogan and run with it, as it were, from one end of the Arab world to the other – articulating ideas, sharing hopes and fears, categorically investing in the aspirations of the heroic uprisings of Arabs from Africa to Asia. That sense of solidarity would not have been possible were I not blessed with friends who have made me feel at home in the Arab world.

The running commentaries of Azmi Bishara and Fawwaz Traboulsi, two towering Arab intellectuals, on the unfolding Arab Spring have been constant sources of enduring insight and critical intimacy with the Arab world. I have followed their thinking in the past, and particularly during the initial unfolding of the Arab

Spring. Over the years I have benefited particularly from Fawwaz Traboulsi's sharp wit and exquisite knowledge of Arab politics while in the gracious company of his kindness, generosity, hospitality, and camaraderie – and to him and his wife Nawal Abboud goes my sincerest gratitude.

Other dear friends in Lebanon – Mariam Said, George Saliba, Suzanne Elizabeth Kassab, Ahmad Dallal, Samah Idriss, Rasha Salti, Mervat Abu Khalil, Saleh Agha, Mai Masri, and the one and only Abu Said in particular – have for decades made me feel at home in Beirut and beyond in the rest of the Arab world. I am blessed by their friendship – and mere words cannot describe my indebtedness to their generous spirits.

A new generation of Arab intellectuals, for me best represented by Joseph Massad and Marwan Bishara, has had a deeply rooted investment in the unfolding Arab revolutions, and their writings at once reveal, guide, and warn its spirit. Noha Radwan, fresh from Tahrir Square leading the cause through the Occupy Wall Street Movement in Auckland, California, and Lamis K. Andoni, watching the Arab Spring unfold like a hawk, have in their collegial conversations and essays been major sources of insight about the historic uprisings. I am honored by their friendship and guided by their wisdom.

I am grateful to Wassan Al-Khudhairi, the director of Mathaf, the Arab Museum of Modern Art in Doha, Qatar, and her colleague Deena Chalabi, for graciously hosting me in Doha at a crucial moment in the course of my writing this book.

A special note of gratitude is due for my dear Elia Suleiman, the ingenious Palestinian filmmaker whose revelatory cinematic visions and precious friendship have been sources of much inspiration for me over so many years. I am graced by his friendship.

In Spring 2011, dear friends Peyman Jafary and Farhad Golyardi graciously hosted me in Europe for a series of talks in the UK and the Netherlands, where I delivered the initial lectures from which this book eventually emerged. I am grateful to them for their kind and generous hospitality and enduring friendship. While in London and long after, Daryoush Mohammad Pour has been a constant source of friendship and insight into the workings of our troubled but hopeful times. I am blessed by his friendship.

At SOAS, the School of Oriental and African Studies in London, I have learned much from my conversations with my friend and colleague Gilbert Achcar.

Dear friends and colleagues Said Amir Arjomand, Ervand Abrahamian, Ali Mirsepassi, Ahmad Sadri, Mahmoud Sadri, Farzin Vahdat, Reza Afshari, and Hossein Kamali, in both the manner and matter of their intellectual rectitude, are exemplary models of trust and confidence. My dear Columbia friends and colleagues Mohsen al-Mousavi, Wael Hallaq, Mamadou Diouf, Mahmood Mamdani, Sudipta Kaviraj, Sheldon Pollock, Partha Chatterjee, and Timothy Mitchell are unending sources of learning and inspiration.

Ferial Ghazoul, Samia Mehrez, and Sun'allah Ibrahim, all connected to me through my late friend and colleague Magda al-Nowaihi, have at various times hosted me in Cairo with uncommon hospitality. Their gracious company has always been inspiring.

To Anissa Bouziane goes my deepest gratitude for her enduring friendship and her grace and confidence when hosting me in a major conference on cultural dialogue in Rabat and Casablanca.

Joseph Massad has been instrumental in connecting me to friends and colleagues at Birzeit University and elsewhere in Palestine. Traveling in Palestine I have been much indebted to Annemarie Jacir, Hany Abu Assad, Riham Barghouti, George Khleifi, Najwa Najjar, and Mohammed Bakri. I am grateful for their kind, generous, and indispensable guidance and friendship.

My former student, now colleague, Rebecca Joubin and her late husband Monkith Saaid, the exquisite Iraqi artist who passed away without his art being much known or deservedly celebrated in his homeland Iraq or the rest of the Arab world, have graciously facilitated my trips to Damascus and the translation of my work into Arabic.

In April 2010, Elena Delgado, the director of the Museo de América in Madrid, kindly invited me to deliver a keynote at the Scientific Workshop of RIME (International Network of Ethnography Museums and World Cultures) that she and her colleagues had organized at their museum as part of the European Union's program of culture 2007-13. While in Madrid I also delivered a number of other lectures, including one at Casa Arabe. I am grateful to Elena Delgado, Omar R. Guzmán Ralat, Karim Hauser, and my dear old friend Sally Gutierrez for kindly hosting me and my eldest daughter Pardis, and for providing me with a congenial environment to think through this book.

My years of writing for *Al-Ahram Weekly* have been exceedingly precious experience for me, for which I am grateful to my good friends and editors Mona Anis and Rasha Saad, all of which was made possible and facilitated by my late friend and Columbia colleague Edward Said. I am exceedingly grateful to my Al Jazeera editor Nasir Yousafzai Khan for his good humor and gracious care in giving me a global audience in the Arab and Muslim world and beyond. Since the commencement of the Arab Spring, the Opinion page of Al Jazeera has been instrumental in teaching me how to articulate my own thoughts. Larbi Sadiki, Mark LeVine, Tarak Barkawi, Joseph Massad, Mahmood Mamdani, Marwan Bishara, Lamis K. Andoni, Sinan Antoon, M.J. Rosenberg, among others have been constant sources of insight and vision about the Arab Spring and related issues. The same holds true for the leading online venue of progressive writing on the Arab Spring, *Jadaliyya*. My sincerest gratitude goes to Anthony Alessandrini, Lisa Hajjar, and Bassam Haddad for their friendship and camaraderie.

In the summer of 2011, I taught a course on the Arab Spring at Columbia in which we navigated the various emerging contours of the uprising. I am grateful to my teaching and research assistant Golnar Nikpour and her diligence in helping me find sources and her invaluable role in leading our class discussions.

My wife and colleague Golbarg Bashi is a constant source of insight and inspiration about political issues from a solid humanist, feminist, and anti-racist perspective. I am blessed to have her by my side when I write, and grateful for all her wisdom.

I began to think seriously about this book while in London and in conversation with Jakob Horstmann. The outline of my argument has much benefited from our initial conversation and his steadfast interest in this book while an editor at Zed Books.

Three anonymous readers read the initial idea for this book and their kind guidance and approval of my thoughts offered me the chance to write more determinedly. I am grateful to them.

Words cannot describe my gratitude to my editor at Zed Books, Tamsine O'Riordan, and the instrumental role she has had in sculpting this book from more than two and a half times the number of words that I was supposed to deliver to her. I began writing the book based on an outline we had drafted, but then, carried away by my excitement, I wrote my way through a severe tendonitis. By the time I was done, I had written too much and gone off on too many tangents. Tamsine grabbed hold of my narrative, cut mercilessly but purposefully, and made my thoughts and sentences cohere. She is a gem of an editor, a blessing to any author who comes her way. To her, to my superb publicist Ruvani de Silva, and to the rest of the fantastic team at Zed goes my everlasting gratitude.

I am again indebted to illuminati for their excellent editorial and typesetting work during the final stages of the production of this book.

The Arab Spring took the world by surprise and generated much good will and solidarity around the globe during its dramatic unfolding. The writing of this book is much indebted to that global sense of awe, admiration, and solidarity with the Arab Spring. It is a blessing to have been at the center of so much goodwill.

Preface

'I am delighted that you are resolved and turn your thoughts from backward glances at the past toward a new understanding.' The young Karl Marx (1818-1883) was 26 years old when he thus began his short encomium 'For a Ruthless Criticism of Everything Existing' (1844), in the form of a short letter to Arnold Ruge, his co-editor of the newly established journal *Deutsch–Französische Jahrbücher*. As he wrote this letter, he was fully aware of a new historic understanding that was in the offing, which was necessary to make sense of a world unfolding in front of the young revolutionary. The declaratory letter was in many ways premonitory of the European Revolutions of 1848, also known as 'the Spring of Nations, or 'Springtime of the Peoples,' the euphoric uprisings that would later lead Marx with Engels to write the *Communist Manifesto* (1848), some three years before he thought the revolutions were betrayed and wrote *The Eighteenth Brumaire of Louis Bonaparte* (1851-52). But at this point Marx is ecstatic, prophetic, fiercely determined, and full of fire. He was witness to a European Spring very much as we are today to an Arab Spring. He wrote of Paris as 'the new capital of the new world,' as we do today about Cairo. The word 'world' or 'new world' is the most repeated trope in this letter. Marx knew he was at the threshold of a new world. With visionary determinism he declared: 'What is necessary will arrange itself.... I do not doubt, therefore, that all obstacles ... will be removed.' He saw not just the upcoming revolutions but also the counter-revolutionary forces that will try to derail them – as we do today, from Saudi Arabi and the Islamic Republic to the US, the EU, and Israel.

One must abandon all ludicrous postures of Monday morning quarterbacking and share with the young Marx his enthusiasm and feel the tenacious tonality of his voice and vision – for which he had no predetermined dogma or ideology. 'I am therefore not in favor of setting up any dogmatic flag,' he told his co-editor. 'On the contrary, we must try to help the *dogmatics* to clarify to themselves the meaning of their own positions.' He knew something was soaring in the air and thus he assured his colleague that 'we shall confront the world not as doctrinaires with a new principle: "Here is the truth, bow down before it!"' No: that would not do. Something else was necessary: 'We develop new principles to the world out of its own principles. We do not say to the world: "Stop fighting; your struggle is of no account. We want to shout the true slogan of the struggle at you."' None of that would do. He had his ears to the ground, and he was listening – to the Tahrir Square of his time. Something far more crucial was on hand: 'We only show the world,' he assured himself and his comrade, 'what it is fighting for, and *consciousness* is something that the world must acquire, like it or not.' On that note, he concluded with a bravura: 'Our motto must therefore be: *Reform of consciousness* not through dogmas, but through *analyzing the mystical consciousness*, the consciousness which is unclear to itself, whether it appears in religious or political forms.' Regarding that project, Marx promised, 'It will transpire that *the world has long been dreaming of something* that it can acquire if only it became conscious of it.' And then in a rare moment of high European Christianity: 'To have its sins forgiven mankind has only to declare them to be what they really are.'[1]

History may indeed, as Marx once frivolously put it, repeat itself (once as tragedy, once as farce) – but the world will not.

---

1. Karl Marx, 'For a Ruthless Criticism of Everything Existing,' in *The Marx–Engels Reader*, ed. Robert C. Tucker, 2nd edn (New York: W.W. Norton, 1978): 12–15; emphasis added.

The world keeps discovering, keeps inventing, keeps overcoming itself. In the Arab Spring, the world is once again pregnant with better and more hopeful versions of itself. The crescendo of transnational uprisings from Morocco to Iran, and from Syria to Yemen, are turning the world upside down. The task facing us today is precisely to see in what particular way our consciousness of the world is in the midst of transforming itself – by force of history. The world we have hitherto known as 'the Middle East' or 'North Africa,' or 'the Arab and Muslim world,' all part and parcel of a colonial geography we had inherited, is changing, and is changing fast. We have now entered the phase of documenting in what particular terms that world is transcending itself, overcoming the mystified consciousness into which it was colonially cast and postcolonially fixated.

In understanding what is happening in North Africa and the Middle East, we are running out of metaphors. We need new metaphors. Even the word 'revolution' – understood anywhere from Karl Marx to Hannah Arendt – needs rethinking. Such a new language of the revolution will cast the impact of 'the Arab Spring' on national and international politics for generations to come. These uprisings have already moved beyond race and religion, sects and ideologies, pro- or anti-Western. The term 'West' is more meaningless today than ever before – it has lost its potency, and with it the notion, and the condition, we had code-named *postcoloniality.* The East, the West, the Oriental, the colonial, the postcolonial – they are no more. What we are witnessing unfold in what used to be called 'the Middle East' (and beyond) marks the end of postcolonial ideological formations – and that is precisely the principal argument informing the way this book discusses and celebrates the Arab Spring. The postcolonial did not overcome the colonial; it exacerbated it by negation. The Arab Spring has overcome them both. The drama of this *delayed defiance* Arabs have now called their spring; and I will use the occasion to make a case for our having entered the phase of the end of postcoloniality, delivered from exacerbating a historic trauma.

Of the three terms circulating for what we have witnessed unfold from early 2011 – 'Arab revolutions,' 'Arab Awakening' and 'Arab Spring' – I have opted for 'Arab Spring' because it both marks the time of year it commenced and metaphorically announces a season of hope, trust, fecundity, and rebirth. Later on, when the Eurozone crisis and the American Occupy Wall Street movements had been termed the 'European Summer' and 'American Fall,' the world at large knew we had hit upon a winter of discontent. This is not to indulge in runaway metaphors that may be ahead of world-historic events, but to leave for posterity a sign of the sudden upsurge of hope in a better world that we were all reading in our midst.

The transformation of consciousness, and precisely not through dogma or violence, is the inaugural moment of discovering new worlds – not by willing what does not exist but by seeing what is unfolding. As I write, the Arab revolutions, each with a different momentum, are creating a new geography of liberation, which is no longer mapped on colonial or cast upon postcolonial structures of domination; this restructuring points to a far more radical emancipation, not only in these but, by extension, in adjacent socie-ties and in an open-ended dynamic. This permanent revolutionary mood has already connected the national to the transnational in unexpected and unfolding ways, leading to a reconfigured geopoli-tics of hope. That the Arab revolutions are changing our imagina-tive geography is already evident in the interaction between the southern and northern coasts of the Mediterranean in terms of modes of protest, with the spread of Tahrir Square-style youth uprisings evident from Greece to Spain, and indeed to the United States and the Occupy Wall Street movement – with even Aung San Suu Kyi comparing her campaign for democracy in Burma to the Arab Spring. These revolutions are not driven by the politics of replicating 'the West' – rather, they are transcending it, and thus are as conceptually disturbing to the existing political order as to the *régime du savoir* around the globe. The ground is shifting under the feet of what self-proclaimed superpowers thought was their globe. These variations on the theme of delayed defiance hinge on the idea that the revolutions are simultaneously a rejec-tion not just of the colonial oppression they have inherited but, *a fortiori*, of the postcolonial ideologies that had presented and exhausted themselves as its antithesis in Islamist, nationalist or socialist grand narratives.

The mystical consciousness our world has inherited hangs around the binary of 'The West and the Rest,' the most damning delusion that the European colonial map of the world manufactured and left behind, with 'Islam and the West' as its most potent borderlines. It is precisely that grand illusion that is dissolving right before our eyes. But that is not all: the challenge posed by these revolutions to divisions within Islam and among Muslims – racial (Arabs, Turks, Iranians, etc.), ethnic (Kurds, Baluchs, etc.), or sectarian (Sunni and Shi'i in particular) – has at once agitated and (*ipso facto*) discredited them. These revolutions are collective acts of *overcoming*. They are crafting new identities, forging new solidarities, both within and without the 'Islam and the West' binary – overcoming once and for all the thick (material and moral) colonial divide. The dynamics now unfolding between the national and the transnational will, as they do, override all others. The synergy that has ensued is crafting a new framework for the humanity they have thus embraced and empowered. Those dynamics are checked, to be sure, by counter-revolutionary forces that are now fully at work – and that have much to lose from these revolutions.

The world, and not just 'the Muslim world,' has long been dreaming of these uprisings. Since at least the French Revolution of 1789, the European revolutions of 1848, the Russian Revolution of 1917, since the British packed their belongings and left India in 1948, since the French left Algeria, the Italians Libya, the world has been dreaming of the Arab Spring. From the time the colonial world began lowering European flags, and as the postcolonial world was raising new ones, the world has been dreaming of the emblematic slogan, now chanted by people from one end of the Arab world to another: *Huriyyah, Adalah Ijtima'iyah, Karamah*, 'Freedom, Social Justice, Dignity.'

To pave the way for an open-ended unfolding of these revolts, the public space has been expanding for a very long time, and the political act is now being charged and redefined to accommodate it. But the public facade of unity across social classes and between different political tendencies, which has characterized the uprising from the very outset, has been and will continue to be fractured. But these fractures will expand the public space, not diminish it. That societal expansion of the bedrock of politics will not be along ideological lines. In the world beyond Christian dogma, people are not born in a state of sin, for this to be forgiven by way of communal declaration. As there is no original sin, there is no final forgiveness – and thus no grand illusion, no master-narratives of emancipation. The ideals remain open and grand, as they must, but demanding and exacting their realization require painstaking and detailed work by particular voluntary associations beyond the reach of the state – labor unions, women's right organizations, student assemblies – all by way of forming a web of affiliation around the atomized individual, thus protecting her, thus enabling him, to resist the ever increasing power of the emergent state.

The specter of that emerging state will keep the democratic muscles of these revolutionary uprisings flexing – for a very long time, and for a very simple reason. The world we have inherited is mystified (Marx's term) by the force fields of power that have at once held it together and distorted it. Fighting the military and economic might of counter-revolutionaries goes hand in hand with deciphering the transformed consciousness that must promise and deliver the emerging world. The colonial subject (now revolting beyond the mirage of the postcolonial state) was formed, forced, and framed as the object of European imperial domination, with multivariate modes of governmentality that extended from the heart of 'the West' to the edges of 'the Rest.' Europe colonized the Arab and Muslim world from one end to the other precisely according to the model of power by which it was itself being colonized by the self-fetishizing logic of capital. It was, by way of partaking in the making of the fetishized commodity, being alienated from itself as it was forcing that massive alienation on the colonial world. Postcolonialism was instrumental in conceptually fetishizing colonialism as something other than the abuse of labor by capital writ large. It is not, and never has been.

The postcolonial subject, which was none other than the colonial subject multiplied by the illusion of emancipation, was thus released into the force field of that very same colonial history on a wild goose chase of ideological certainty before and after political convictions. For more than two hundred years – the nineteenth and twentieth centuries – colonialism begat postcolonial ideological formations: socialism, nationalism, nativism (Islamism); one metanarrative after another, ostensibly to combat, but effectively to embrace and exacerbate, its consequences. As these postcolonial ideological formations began epistemically to exhaust themselves, the position of 'subalternity' (borrowed from Gramsci's initial formulation and mystified) travelled from South Asia and became a North American academic fanfare, before it was politically neutered and soon turned into the literary trope of a 'native informant.' Thus colonialism and postcoloniality combined to place the Arab and the Muslim (as its supreme and absolute other) outside the self-universalizing tropes of European metaphysics, where the non-Western (thus branded) was never in the purview of full subjection, of full historical agency. 'I am a Europeanist,' declared hurriedly the postcolonial theorist from 'the Department of English and Comparative Literature' – and rightly so. The world was thus sealed in a self-sustaining binary that has kept repeating, revealing, and concealing itself. Finally coming to full historical consciousness in terms of their own agential sovereignty and worldly subjection, 'the Arab' and 'the Muslim' are now exiting that trap, having identified it as the simulacrum of a renewed pact with humanity – beyond the European entrapping of 'humanism.' Arabs and Muslims in revolt have no crisis of the subject, no problem with their *cogito*.

'The work of our time,' Marx rightly declared at the end of his letter to Arnold Ruge, is 'to clarify to itself (critical philosophy) the meaning of ... its own desires.' Indeed – and in that spirit I write this book!

FRIENDS

The old word is dead.
The old books are dead....
We want a generation of giants.
Arab children,
Corn ears of the future,
You will break our chains,
Kill the opium in our heads,
Kill the illusions.

Nizar Qabbani (1923-1998)

INTRODUCTION

The Arab Spring:
The End of Postcoloniality

Towards the end of *Iran, The Green Movement and the USA* (2010), a book I wrote soon after the rise of the Green Movement in Iran in the summer of 2009, I promised to resume my story about the unfolding civil rights movement in Iran and its geopolitical consequences and repercussions in the region.[1] At the time of writing that concluding remark, and given the allegorical disposition of my narrative in that book, I meant that return more as a figure of speech rather than in the literal sense. Little did I know that world events unfolding ahead of us all would yet again occasion the urgent necessity of my picking up the story where I left off and thinking forward through the crescendo of events that have now engulfed the Green Movement in Iran, from Morocco to Syria and from Bahrain to Yemen (and beyond, from Kashmir to Senegal), and given it renewed significance and resonance. Extending my analysis of the Green Movement in Iran to the Arab Spring expands the horizons of the historical force field of a vanishing presence into a new – a renewed – liberation geography: the opening up of hitherto unknown horizons of our world and where it might go to achieve a better, more sustainable, and more just balance. As we achieve it, we need to be able to imagine it too.

1. See Hamid Dabashi, *Iran, the Green Movement, and the USA: The Fox and the Paradox* (London: Zed Books, 2010).

Such imaginings need both historical rootedness and an emancipatory defiance of the weight of that history. The link between the Green Movement and the Arab Spring – as variations on the same theme of delayed defiance of both European colonialism and its extended shadow and postcolonial aftermath – has reopened the gate of history, for a renewed consciousness.[2] By 'delayed defiance' I mean the sustained course of liberation movements that are no longer trapped within postcolonial terms of engagement and are thus able to navigate uncharted revolutionary territories. The Egyptian revolution has a central significance in this consciousness, for it is in Tahrir Square that the terms of a renewed pact with history resonates in the key slogan *al-Sha'b Yurid Isqat al-Nizam*, 'People Demand the Overthrow of the Regime.' This demand for the dominant 'regime' to be brought down is a reference not only to political action but, even more radically, to the mode of knowledge production about 'the Middle East,' 'North Africa,' 'the Arab and Muslim World,' 'The West and the Rest,' or any other categorical remnant of a colonial imagination (Orientalism) that still preempts the liberation of these societies in an open-ended dynamic.[3] The challenge the Egyptians faced in getting rid of a tyrant by camping in their Tahrir Square for eighteen days, with only one word (*Arhil,* 'Go!') hanging on banners over their heads, will resonate for a very long time, calling also for the rest of the world to alter the regime of knowledge that has hitherto both been enabling and blinded us to world historic events.[4]

The Future is Here

What we are witnessing unfold before our eyes – one might consider it a Palestinian intifada going global – is the moment of a

2. I have developed the idea of 'delayed defiance' as 'deferred defiance' in some detail in my *Shi'ism: A Religion of Protest* (Cambridge MA: Harvard University Press, 2011).

3. The origins of this binary consciousness ought to be traced back to the earliest encounters between Arabs and Europeans. In this regard see the classic work of Ibrahim Abu Lughod, *The Arab Rediscovery of Europe: A Study in Cultural Encounters*, with Introduction by Rashid Khalidi (Princeton NJ: Princeton University Press, 1963).

4. For an excellent early assessment of the Egyptian revolution and the challenge we face in reading it, see Asef Bayat, 'Egypt, and the Post-Islamist Middle East,' *Open Democracy*, 8 February 2011, www.opendemocracy.net/asef-bayat/egypt-and-post-islamist-middle-east.

delayed defiance, a point of rebellion against domestic tyranny and globalized disempowerment alike, now jointly challenged beyond the entrapment of postcolonial ideologies. The predicament of the Arab Spring nation-states was to be beyond the colonial and yet paradoxically lost in the presumptions of the postcolonial state when anti-colonial ideologies had paradoxically sealed and trapped manners and modes of emancipation. This was the moment we had been waiting for; yet we had not thought it would actually come about at any precise point or as a parameter in our own lifetimes. There is ecstasy present in the moment– not just in the revolutionary uprisings themselves, but also in attempts to fathom and narrate them, imagine, embrace, and define them. Indeed, the ecstatic moment is such that the more we try to get our minds around the dramatic unfolding of events, the more they seem to get themselves around us. We wake up in the morning to Colonel Gaddafi promising no mercy for Libyans defying his tyranny, and by the time we go to bed he is running for his life. We watch Ali Abdullah Saleh of Yemen on the BBC News website being fearsome and defiant, then access Al Jazeera in time to see him sent to a hospital in Saudi Arabia. These events are uncanny. News has become palimpsestic, translucent – events overriding themselves.

This euphoria, in both prose and politics, does not mean that these revolutionary uprisings we call 'the Arab Spring' are at all surprising or that they were unanticipated. I recall participating in a panel discussion on Al Jazeera with Marwan Bishara, senior political analyst and host of the station's 'Empire' program, soon after the emergence of the Green Movement in Iran in June 2009. At one point I suggested that were I in a position of authority anywhere from Morocco to Syria I would watch the unfolding events in Iran very carefully, for it was not just the young Iranians who were globally wired and impatient with their retarded politics of despair: soon their counterparts around the region, including even Israel, would join them. Bishara, I recall, laughed and said, 'You mean Iran is going to export yet another revolution to the region?', to which I said, 'Yes these kids will.'[5] I also recall that

---

5. To view this program see: www.youtube.com/watch?v=ezDRFb8olAA&feature=relmfu.

in a piece published on CNN's website the following month, on 21 July 2009, I wrote: 'Tehran, I believe, is ground zero of a civil rights movement that will leave no Muslim or Arab country, or even Israel, untouched.'[6] These suggestions, made almost a year and a half before the events in Tunisia and then Egypt, were offered not by way of a premonition of the Arab Spring; they were merely logical estimations of the reality beyond the politics of despair that had defined the cultural climate of the region since the end of European colonialism, and left no room for hope except for and through desperate acts of violence.

This deeply traumatizing memory is now collectively deposited in the State of Israel. Israel today faces serious challenges to the very idea of a 'Jewish State,' not because any Arab army is heading towards it, but because millions of human beings with an interest in democratic rights are looking at it. As a garrison state Israel has painted itself into the corner of only dealing with Arab potentates, and thus it cannot tolerate such a gaze: for it cannot imagine itself existing in a democratic neighborhood.

The Blossoming of the Arab Spring

As in the case of other dramatic historical events, the Arab Spring was all but inevitable. But the how, when, and wherefore had been awaiting the ignition that the desperate suicide of a young Tunisian, Mohamed Bouazizi, occasioned on 17 December 2010.

Two years into the life of the Green Movement that began in June 2009 and a few dramatic months after the blossoming of the Arab Spring in January 2011, it became clear that what we were watching unfold was in fact a succession of vastly consequential and yet inconclusive social uprisings that required a reconsideration of the very notion of 'revolution' as we have inherited and understood it so far. The Green Movement had galvanized political discourse

---

6. See my essay 'Middle East is Changed Forever,' CNN, 20 July 2009, http://articles.cnn.com/2009-07-20/world/dabashi.iran.domino_1_geopolitics-iran-middle-east?_s=PM:WORLD. Some two years later, the eminent *New York Times* columnist Roger Cohen quoted these words and cited my CNN essay in his 'Iran Without Nukes,' *New York Times*, 13 June 2011, adding: 'Seldom were there more prescient words'; www.nytimes.com/2011/06/14/opinion/14iht-edcohen14.html.

and social action in Iran but left the belligerent theocracy in power;[7] the Tunisian and Egyptian revolutions toppled two tyrants but left the ruling regime intact; the Libyan uprising was bloodied by both Gaddafi and the US and NATO military intervention. Less than six months into the uprisings, the ruling regimes in Bahrain and Yemen were shaken but still remained in power, one aided and abetted by Saudi Arabia and the other by US disregard. The Syrian uprising was brutally checked by the Bashar al-Assad regime, but it had exposed the regime's illegitimacy for the whole world to see. These were not conclusive revolutions as we have understood them in the exemplary models of the French, Russian, Chinese, Cuban, or Iranian revolutions of the last three centuries. 'Revolution' in the sense of a radical and sudden shift of political power with an accompanying social and economic restructuring of society – one defiant class violently and conclusively overcoming another – is not what we are witnessing here, or not quite yet. There is a deep-rooted economic malaise in all of these societies, underscored by widespread social anomie and cultural alienation, all within a politically dysfunctional and corrupt context. No single and sudden revolution could address all of these issues simultane-ously. No single angle of vision – economic, social, political, or cultural – would reveal the totality (and yet inconclusive disposi-tion) of these massive social uprisings. Instead of denying these insurgences the term 'revolution,' we are now forced to reconsider the concept and understand it anew.

The paramount metaphor to describe the successive unfolding of these transnational uprisings, one that captures the inconclusive yet purposeful nature of the developing revolution, is that they proceed more like a novel than an epic – so it is not a Mohammad Mosaddegh, a Gamal Abd al-Nasser, or an Ayatollah Khomeini that we must look for here, but rather the dialogical develop-ment of a narrative in which, in the terms of Mikhail Bakhtin, characters have the mind of their own and thus events transpire

---

7. For a collection of my essays on the Green Movement, see Hamid Dabashi, *The Green Movement in Iran*, ed. with an Introduction by Navid Nikzadfar (New Brunswick NJ: Transaction, 2011). For a wider selection of essays on the Green Movement, see Nader Hashemi and Danny Postel, eds, *The People Reloaded: The Green Movement and the Struggle for Iran's Future* (New York: Melville House, 2011).

in an open-ended manner. These uprisings, in the long run, will leave not a stone unturned in the economic, social, political, and above all cultural disposition of these societies, and by extension the geopolitics of their region and thus beyond into the global configuration of power. The longer these revolutions take to unfold the more enduring, grassroots-based, and definitive will be their emotive, symbolic, and institutional consequences.[8]

By virtue of these transnational revolutionary uprisings, and despite the fact that multiple counter-revolutionary forces[9] are hard at work to thwart them, the old geopolitics of the region is effectively overcome; hence we must begin re-imagining the moral map of 'the Middle East,' first by discarding that very nasty colonial concoction that has cast the fate of millions to the middle of some colonial officer's imagined East. These revolutions are happening in countries both friendly and hostile to that supreme chimera of all ages, 'the West' – thereby once again dismantling the fictive centrality of that decentering centre of the world. The events unfolding from Morocco to Syria, and from Iran to Yemen, are effectively altering the very geography of how we think and fathom the world. This is no longer the middle of anybody's East, or the north of any colonial divide in Africa. Much of course remains to be done; precarious and uncertain is the path, powerful and resilient the counter-revolutionary forces – from the US and Israel to Saudi Arabia and the Islamic Republic, along with their allies embedded within these countries' ruling regimes – albeit that the floodgates of some subterranean reservoir of democratic will and defiant determination have now been let loose and only the future will tell what measures of success chart the way.

The counter-revolutionary forces now fully geared to oppose and reshape these uprisings are not limited to the US and NATO military intervention in Libya (an attempt to secure a military

---

8. For an excellent critique of the early takes on Egyptian revolution, see Jillian Schwedler, Joshua Stacher, and Stacey Philbrick Yadav, 'Three Powerfully Wrong – and Wrongly Powerful – American Narratives about the Arab Spring,' *Jadaliyyah*, 10 June 2011, www.jadaliyya.com/pages/index/1826/three-powerfully-wrong_and-wrongly-powerful_americ.

9. For an early assessment of counter-revolutionary forces in Egypt, see Goha, 'Counter-Revolution,' *Jadaliyyah*, 28 February 2011, www.jadaliyya.com/pages/index/759/the-counter-revolution.

foothold in the uprisings to control their outcome), or to the murderous Saudi occupation of Bahrain, or to the hiring of Blackwater mercenaries to quell potential uprisings in Abu Dhabi. Attempts to distort the reality and the factual evidence of these uprisings and reassimilate them into tired old (persistently Orientalist) clichés are equally being made by observers entirely alien to the region. US commentators such as Thomas Friedman struggle to present a clear picture to readers of the *New York Times*: 'this uprising, at root, is not political. It's existential. It is much more Albert Camus than Che Guevara.'[10] He cannot imagine Arabs as inherently dignified, and these revolts as an expression of that dignity in manifestly and decidedly *political* terms. On the contrary, for Friedman and others who possess a racialized imagination, this quality is precisely what the Arabs lack. He must have them always on a wild goose chase to find it: 'All these Arab regimes to one degree or another stripped their people of their basic dignity. They deprived them of freedom and never allowed them to develop anywhere near their full potential.' Friedman is also far from alone in his desperate act of wishing the Arab Spring Israel-friendly, being closely followed, for example, by his French counterpart Bernard-Henri Lévy, who went so far as to engineer a French military strike in support of the rebels to ensure that post-Gaddafi Libya would be pro-Israel. But all of these counter-revolutionary forces, frightened by the prospect of a free and democratic world outside their military power and impoverished vocabulary, are doomed to fail when vast waves of humanity have arisen to reclaim their history. Israeli people do not need these false friends; they should (and will soon) themselves join the democratic uprisings. For what would their hawkish warlords do if millions of people just walked from Tahrir Square to the Rafah border in Gaza – not with tanks or guns, but with bread and potable water and food for the 1.3 million human beings incarcerated in the largest prison camp on planet earth? Use their nuclear warheads?

---

10. See Thomas Friedman, 'I Am a Man,' *New York Times*, 14 May 2011, www.nytimes.com/2011/05/15/opinion/15friedman.html?_r=3.

Overcoming the Politics of Despair

I concluded my last book by arguing that the US and its allies faced a dilemma vis-à-vis the Islamic Republic: they will strengthen it no matter what course of action they take with the belligerent theocracy, hostile or conciliatory. At the same time the Islamic Republic itself faced an identical paradox vis-à-vis the massive civil rights movement that has shaken it to its foundation. By reference to this double paradox my aim was to draw closer attention to the fate of nations that are often overshadowed by the transnational geopolitics of the region. Now I believe that with the commencement of the Arab Spring that paradox is in fact resolved, and the geopolitics of the region is being altered so radically that the Islamic Republic no longer enjoys that advantage, being deeply and widely exposed and vulnerable. By joining Iranians in overcoming their politics of despair, Arab nations have in effect strengthened the Green Movement by weakening the Islamic Republic and curtailing its strategic power in the region.[11]

The Green Movement, I believe, was the historic moment when national politics erupted into and ignited regional politics; then, in the course of the Arab Spring, regional geopolitics in turn engulfed the national scene from Morocco to Afghanistan and from Bahrain to Yemen. This criss-crossing between the *national* and the *transnational* will have two simultaneous consequences: (1) it will confuse and confound the counter-revolutionary forces, which include the US, Israel, Saudi Arabia, and the Islamic Republic, and make control or diversion of the revolutions difficult; and (2) it will ultimately contribute to the remapping of the region, and with it the global configuration of power, in open-ended and unanticipated ways. The counter-revolutionaries and their actions – such as the US/NATO military operation in Libya; the Israeli killing of Palestinians on the anniversary of Nakba on 15 May 2011; the Saudi and Gulf Cooperation Council invasion and occupation of Bahrain, and the al-Khalifa regime's brutal crackdown of the

---

11. For an assessment of the Arab world in general in the wake of the 'Arab Spring,' see Rashid Khalidi, *Sowing Crisis: The Cold War and American Dominance in the Middle East* (Boston MA: Beacon Press, 2010).

revolutionary uprising in that country – rely on deadly military power, while the opposition by and large expresses itself in peaceful uprisings. While on occasion, and within specific national contexts, the situation may seem hopeless and debilitating, the transnational synergy is beyond anyone's control. There is no doubt that the US and its European and regional allies will do everything in their power to prevent the success of these democratic uprisings. But they will fail.

The ebb and flow, the progress and regress, of these specific cases notwithstanding, I believe we are moving – almost imperceptibly perhaps but nevertheless consistently – towards the discovery of a new world. The road is bumpy and fraught with degenerate potentates and their US and European supporters trying to hold on to power, but these dramatic events will unfold like an open-ended novel rather than as a monological epic. In this unfolding we will witness a shift towards the restoration of a repressed and denied cosmopolitan culture rather than a blind revolution with a limited and cliché-ridden political agenda.[12] There has always been a cosmopolitan worldliness about these cultures, which are otherwise hidden beneath the forced categories of 'Religious' versus 'Secular,' 'Traditional' versus 'Modern,' 'Eastern' versus 'Western.' Such time-worn clichés have performed their service and done their damage in terms of representing and distorting the world they defined and have now categorically exhausted their possibilities. I believe the period of ideological contestations that produced such false binaries – all manufactured under colonial duress – is over; and over also is the period we have known as 'postcolonial.'

The End of the 'Postcolonial'

We are, in my view, finally overcoming the condition we have termed 'coloniality' and, *a fortiori*, 'postcoloniality.' Coloniality is finally overcome, not prolonged in the protracted ideological

---

12. I have argued this notion of 'restoration' of Islamic cosmopolitan culture in some detail in my *Islamic Liberation Theology: Resisting the Empire* (London: Routledge, 2008).

procrastination called 'postcolonial.'[13] What, over the past decade
in Iranian and Islamic contexts, I have called 'post-ideological' is
precisely the result of this overcoming of that condition in which
many ideologies – from Third World Socialism to anticolonial
nationalism to militant Islamism (vintage postcolonial ideologies)
– were manufactured and put into practice. The epistemic condition of that state of coloniality has finally exhausted itself. The
emergence of the condition of knowledge production is signalled
by perhaps the most emblematic Egyptian slogan in Tahrir Square:
Huriyyah, Adalah Ijtima'iyah, Karamah, 'Freedom, Social Justice,
Dignity.' This overcoming of the condition of coloniality, which
had effectively faded into what we have known as postcoloniality,
signals the retrieval of some quintessential cornerstone of civic
life that was lost in the aftermath of European colonialism in Asia
and Africa and that had crafted grandiloquent (but false) claims
of ideological passage to liberation. These revolutionary uprisings
are postideological, meaning they are no longer fighting according
to terms dictated by their condition of coloniality, codenamed
'postcolonial.'

We are thus witnessing more a restoration of what was politically possible but overshadowed rather than a clichéd conception
of revolution – of one dictatorship succeeding another. Here by
'restoration' I mean recovering precisely the cosmopolitan worldliness in which alternative notions and practices of civil liberties
and economic justice can and ought to be produced. Thus this
cosmopolitanism is precisely the opposite of 'Westernism'; it is in
fact the end of 'Westernism' as an exhausted and depleted mode of
bipolar knowledge production. Not only has 'the West' imploded
as the constant producer of, or catalyst for, binary oppositions,
but the European Union is in reality retreating back to national
borders and national identities due to fear of labor immigrants
coming north from Asia and Africa (and Latin America in the
case of the US). The Arab Spring, then, signifies the discovery of
a new worldliness, the restoration of a confidence in being-in-the-
world, that is made conscious of itself by virtue and force of these

---

13. I have argued the details of this 'overcoming' in my *Post-Orientalism: Knowledge
and Power in Time of Terror* (New Brunswick, NJ: Transaction, 2008).

revolutions. The revolts, in consequence, are not a return to any absolutist ideology but a *retrieval* of a cosmopolitan worldliness that was always already there but repressed under the duress of a dialectic sustained between domestic tyranny and globalized imperialism.

The rise of this cosmopolitan worldliness announces the end not only of militant Islamism but of all absolutist ideologies and the false divisions and choices they have imposed on the world. In *Brown Skin, White Masks* I tried to get to grips with the singular role of comprador (expatriate) intellectuals in manufacturing consent for imperial projects by way of exacerbating their self-raising and other-lowering proclivities.[14] In the aftermath of the Green Movement and the Arab Spring, all such ideological lies are evident, I believe; thus these 'native disinformers' have been exposed for what they are and rendered entirely obsolete. They were particularly useful in a bipolar world, where initially the Soviet Union and the US had divided the world the better to rule it, and then later when the Soviet Union collapsed and the frightful prospect of a unipolar world was fast upon us. A 'new world order' is what President George H.W. Bush (1989–93) called that world; and 'the Project for a New American Century' was the nightmare that American neoconservatives had envisioned for how to rule it. Allan Bloom, Francis Fukuyama, Samuel Huntington, and Niall Ferguson were the leading preachers of the new order – before Antonio Negri and Michael Hardt put forward an alternative vision. Then 9/11 happened and we entered the post-ideological age of not just post-Islamism, but in fact post-Americanism, post-Westernism, underlining the implosion of 'the West' as a catalyst of knowledge and power production.[15] The rampant Islamophobia that soon engulfed Europe and North America was just a manifestation of the xenophobia triggered by the fear of foreigners as 'guest workers.' The Arab Spring has put an end to that politics of despair. We are, in this spring season, moving on; indeed we are on the cusp of discovering emerging new worlds, a liberation geography

14. See Hamid Dabashi, *Brown Skin, White Masks* (London: Pluto, 2011).
15. As I have demonstrated in my *Islamic Liberation Theology: Resisting the Empire* (2008).

that will require and produce a new organicity for the intellectual – this time involving the citizenry and civil liberties.

Delayed Defiance

My principal argument in this book – which I write in the midst of the Arab Spring, at once bloody and blooming, exhilarating and frightful – dwells on the central idea of a delayed defiance as the modus operandi of these revolutionary uprisings that has engulfed multiple countries and political climes from Morocco to Iran, from Syria to Yemen. I propose this idea by way of a specific reading of the end of coloniality in terms that I will make very clear. I see these revolutions as inconclusive and open-ended, wherein national politics will have consequences transnationally, and vice versa. The Tunisian revolt triggered the Arab Spring transnationally, and the transnational revolt across the region has had specific national consequences, such as the rapprochement between Hamas and Fatah in Palestine, which in turn has triggered a response from the Palestinians in Lebanon, Syria, and Jordan, who have goaded Israeli forces and stormed into their occupied homeland. These dynamics spell the end of the politics of despair and business-as-usual, in which the US and its European and regional allies on one side and the Islamic Republic and its subnational allies – Hamas, Hezbollah, and the Mahdi Army – on the other held hostage the democratic aspirations of masses of millions of human beings. Pathological entities like al-Qaeda and Osama bin Laden are now entirely dead and discarded figments of imagination that the US had manufactured and in the end destroyed. It was not only Osama bin Laden who was buried in Tahrir Square; so was the military might of Israel, with its wanton disregard for human decency. What triumphed at Tahrir Square was the power of non-violent civil disobedience, the categorical denunciation of violence – the only language Israel speaks and the means by which it has sustained its colonial occupation of Palestine. The same holds true for the Islamic Republic of Iran, for Syria, and for Hezbollah. Hamas has already decoupled itself from the Islamic Republic and joined Fatah. We are, in short, at the point of experiencing a new world, a new geography of liberation, beyond the limited imaginations of terrorists and imperialists alike.

The rise of the Green Movement in Iran was a clear indication of the constellation of what I have called *societal modernity* supplanting the failed attempts at *political modernity*. Political modernity, I have argued, was ultimately a defeated project because it was predicated on the grand narrative of absolutist ideological metanarrative constructed against initially European colonialism and subsequently American imperialism. These direct contestations had produced three distinct (prototypical) ideological grand narratives: anticolonial nationalism, Third Word socialism, and militant Islamism.[16] In Iran, militant Islamism has outmaneuvered the other two ideologies, cannibalized and consumed their energies, destroyed their organizations, murdered their leaderships, and succeeded in forming an Islamic Republic – a brutal theocracy that has perfected tyranny into an art form. This was a paradoxical success, for the Islamic Republic both perfected the ideological narrative of militant Islamism and, through the innate paradox of Shi'ism, at the same time exhausted it and brought it to an ignominious end. In the Islamic Republic, then, militant Islamism both triumphed over all its ideological rivals and epistemically depleted itself – its ideological prowess was overtaken by historical events and became outdated. The result is not just the end of Islamism, or the beginning of post-Islamism, as scholars such as Asef Bayat have argued, but the end of colonially conditioned ideologies as such and the commencement of a far more cataclysmic closure to all absolutist ideologies manufactured in dialogical contestation with European and American imperialisms. By post-ideological in this context I mean overcoming the post/colonial – for all ideological productions over the last two hundred years in much of Asia, Africa and Latin America have been in response to colonial domination and corresponding postcolonial state formations.

The exhaustion of Islamic ideology also means the end of political Islamism as we have known it. This does not mean that Islam

---

16. I provide a detailed unfolding of these three ideological formations in the Iranian context over the last two hundred years in my *Iran: A People Interrupted* (New York: New Press, 2007).

will no longer play a role in the emerging politics; it will, because Muslims (qua Muslims) will be part and parcel of that politics. What it does mean is that the ideological parallax between 'Islam and the West' has epistemically exhausted itself, and that Islam as a world religion is retrieving its innate cosmopolitan context, which in its new manifestation will have to accommodate non-Islamic thinking.[17] The emerging world I identify as being characterized by *cosmopolitan worldliness* – which, I will argue, has always been innate to these societies and is now being retrieved with a purposeful intent toward the future. This purposeful retrieval I call *liberation geography*.

There is a direct link between the Green Movement and the Arab Spring, not in terms of one having caused or even triggered the other – although there can be no doubt that Tunisian and Egyptian youth were influenced by their witnessing the actions of Iranian youth in the Islamic Republic in 2009 and those of Kashmiri youth in the summer of 2010 against the Indian occupation of their homeland – but more in the sense that the events in the Arab and Iranian worlds and beyond are both signs and symbols of a brand new form of revolutionary dispensation. Entrenched as the Islamic Republic and Saudi Arabia may be, and determined as the US and Israel may be to keep the Saudis in power and dismantle the Islamic Republic in their own terms, these two theocratic and tribal banalities have been deeply affected, troubled, and traumatized by the democratic uprisings. The two equally belligerent yet mutually hostile regimes may resort to all manner of devious devices and distractions to stay in power, but they will fall – hard and heavy – one way or another. The delayed defiance that has befallen them will bring them down. They are old, they are decrepit, they are remnants of a dreadful political imagination that is already dead. Brute, banal force and cliché-ridden manipulation of people's religious sentiments are the only means left to them. Opposing them are revolutions without end. Their measured successes are not a sign of defeat but in fact a perfect indication of their health.

---

17. An argument I discuss in some detail in my *Islamic Liberation Theology*.

They will patiently advance as they persist in dismantling the regime – for *al-Shab Yurid Isqat al-Nizam.*

Back into the Force Field of History

It seems like an eternity ago when we were told that History had ended. The Arab Spring has propelled us back into the force field of history. These revolutionary uprisings prove every theory of modernization, Westernization, Eurocentricity, the West as the measure of the Rest, the End of History, the Clash of Civilizations, ad absurdum, wrong. Furthermore, they pull the rug from under an entire regime of knowledge production that has kept departments and libraries of political science and area studies in business for too long. The entire combined machinery of North American, Western European, and Israeli propaganda, predicated on a depleted paradigm of conjugated terms iterated to no end, had for over half a century worked to manufacture the Arab world as constitutionally backward, congenitally vile, violent, and incompetent. Commentators who support such devastating clichés, writing for their sophomorically arrested readership, cannot imagine a world in which these very same Arabs are not just the agents of their own history, but in fact the discoverers of a whole new world. This is the moment of a Copernican heliocentricity pulling the earth from under our feet. This emerging world is not just beyond the retarded growth of the myopic provincialism that calls itself 'the West,' but in fact beyond the reach of the coloniality that had falsely bestowed upon the Mubaraks, Ben Alis, and Gaddafis of the world the presumption that they were 'postcolonial leaders' of nations they had wrongly claimed as theirs. In the blossoming of the Arab Spring we are all liberated from that trapping map of our universe and reaching far beyond the very presumption of that coloniality. In place of that presumption, and the ideological formations of subservient knowledge that sustained the falsifying phantom of 'the West' in order to subjugate the liberating imagination of 'the Rest,' we are finally witnessing the epistemic end of that violent autonormativity whereby 'the West' kept reinventing itself and all its inferior others. In these open-ended revolts, staging a delayed defiance long in the making, we are in fact beyond the borders of democratic cliché, remapping the imaginative geography of a liberation that has finally moved beyond and been liberated from any *ethnos*, and that reaches deep and far into the configuration of a new planetary *ethos*.

ONE

Decentering the World:
How the Arab Spring Unfolded

The Arab Spring began in the dead of winter, on 17 December 2010, when Mohamed Bouazizi, a 26-year-old vendor from Sidi Bouzid in Tunisia, set himself on fire in protest against the confiscation of his produce cart. At the time it was an inconspicuous act – no one, not even the US Department of State, had heard of the incident. It was off the world's radar, but not for long. Protests began the very same day, locally, in Sidi Bouzid, but then spread across the country; the scale was so massive and surprising that it forced President Zine El Abidin Ben Ali, in office since 1987, to issue a warning on 28 December that dissent would be severely punished. The Arab Spring had marked up its first successful seesaw of popular protest and official denunciation, a pattern that would soon become a familiar trope throughout the Arab world. By 6 January 2011, widespread protest had started in Algeria, with rising prices the principal point of contention. Two Arab countries were now playing hide-and-seek with global media. By 9 January casualties among the unarmed protestors were reported in Tunisia, along with defections from the ranks of the police and military. Within a matter of days, on 13 January, Ben Ali made unprecedented public concessions and promised to investigate the killings. But by the following day he had packed and left Tunisia for Saudi Arabia, leaving prime minister Mohammed Ghannouchi in charge.

Following less than a month of demonstrations, Tunisia fell and Ben Ali had run away. The uprising had been successful. The Arab and Muslim world was watching with incredulity, wondering: was this really possible – is it that easy?

Three days after Ben Ali left Tunisia, on 17 January 2011, a 40-year old Egyptian restaurant owner, Abdou Abdel-Monaam Hamadah, set himself on fire near the Egyptian parliament in protest against the dire economic situation. This was a copycat action, but it attracted very little attention. It wasn't until 25 January, a national holiday dedicated to an appreciation of the police, that tens of thousands of Egyptians poured into their streets, for what they called a 'Day of Rage,' openly denouncing the Mubarak regime. Such protests were not unusual in Egypt, but this one was different inasmuch as it was in direct response to events in Tunisia. There was a synergy in the air. The international media were on alert. Al Jazeera had not blinked. Four days later, on 29 January, Egyptian troops were on the streets and President Mubarak, in power since 1981, had dismissed his government. But he refused the demand of protestors to step down. The following day US President Obama was asking for a smooth transition of power in Egypt. On 31 January hundreds of thousands of Egyptians had swarmed into their Tahrir Square – in festive spirit, determined, with an air of carnival, the protest gaining momentum with every passing hour. The cat-and-mouse game had started. Mubarak promised democratic reform and pledged he would not run again for office, but it was not enough. On 1 February, an estimated 1 million Egyptians were in Tahrir Square demanding he step down. The following day the regime staged a pro-Mubarak rally, sending in armed gangs on camels to attack the demonstrators. This made for quite a media spectacle, but it backfired. The protesters became more determined and the World was watching. On the following day, 4 February, hundreds of thousands of Egyptians staged a 'Day of Departure,' demanding that Mubarak leave. On 5 February, the newly appointed prime minster Omar Suleiman said he would talk with opposition parties, including the Muslim Brotherhood; he also announced a 15 per cent pay raise for government employees. But it was too little, too late: by 9 February labor unions had joined the protest. Mubarak gave yet another address on 10 February, this one 'from the heart,' promising further reform, pledging not to stand for re-election, but still refusing to go. Those present at Tahrir Square persisted in their demand that he go. The following day, on 11 February, Omar Suleiman, the newly appointed vice president, announced that Hosni Mubarak had stepped down, and that the army was now in charge. In just over two weeks, following the fall of Ben Ali, the regime of Hosni Mubarak too had fallen: the Arab world was watching, and learning. The Obama administration was caught off guard, Europeans were baffled, Israel was scared. The Islamic Republic rushed to call the Egyptian Revolution an Islamic Revolution, but an immediate communiqué from the Muslim Brotherhood declined the offer: this was not an Islamic revolution; it was an Egyptian revolution. The Arab Spring now had its biggest apple, and events was in full swing. What country would be next?

On 16 February, protests erupted in Benghazi, Libya; further clashes with the police and security forces were reported the following day. The immediate cause was the arrest of a human rights activist, Fethi Tarbel, known for his tireless work with families of the victims of a notorious 1996 massacre at the Abu Salim prison, where it is believed over a thousand prisoners were executed. By 21 February, hundreds of protestors were reported killed in clashes with police and security. Yet not all members of these forces supported the crackdown; early in the uprising, two air force pilots, refusing to bomb civilians, defected to Malta, while diplomatic defections were reported at the UN in New York. On 22 February, Gaddafi, in power since 1969, delivered a belligerent speech threatening protestors with a swift crackdown. Protests now spread to Tripoli, where many were shot. By 3 March, President Barack Obama was asking for Gaddafi to leave. Meanwhile the International Criminal Court (ICC) announced that it would be investigating Gaddafi for crimes against humanity. Heavy fighting was reported in Zwiyah, 30 miles from Tripoli. By 9 March the UK prime minister David Cameron and Obama announced they were preparing military options should Gaddafi not step down. On 18 March, the UN Security Council passed a resolution approving a no-fly zone over Libya and authorized NATO to take 'all necessary measures' to protect civilians, short of putting troops on the ground. On 19 March the first air strikes were launched by the US and its European allies against Libyan targets. By 4 May, the ICC announced that Gaddafi had committed war crimes, and issued an arrest warrant. By late June, the African Union was meeting in Pretoria to find a peaceful resolution to the evident stalemate in Libya, while Lt Gen Charlie Bouchard, the Canadian military commander in charge of NATO operations in Libya, was confident that they would force Gaddafi to surrender. France was instrumental in launching a military strike against Gaddafi. The US and its allies were now officially at war with yet another Muslim country. The US soon handed operational authority to NATO, as Obama was beginning to concentrate on his re-election and wished to avoid the perception that the country was involved in yet another war, and Congress was adding to the pressure by indicating that it would oppose military involvement in Libya. By now, Israel was very nervous and wanted to make sure that any post-Gaddafi regime was friendly toward the Jewish state. But against the odds Gaddafi stood firm; he had become a finger against the wind of the Arab Spring.

Protests in Yemen began as early as 23 January. In response, on 2 February, President Ali Abdullah Saleh, in power since 1990, told the Yemeni parliament that he would not be seeking re-election when his term expired in 2013. On 3 February, the Yemenis planned a 'Day of Rage' to express their opposition to the ruling regime and some 20,000 took to the streets in Sana'a. A young Yemeni human rights activist and journalist, Tawakkol Karman, became world famous as she led thousands of her compatriots in demonstrations. On 12 February thousands more demonstrated, calling for political reforms. President Saleh – baffled by the speed of events, as was his patron, the US – held an emergency meeting. On 10 March, in response to the continued protests, Saleh announced he would draw up a new constitution. Later in the month, pro-reform demonstrations resumed, after police snipers opened fire on peaceful demonstrators in Sana'a, killing scores. Senior military figures, including a key general, Ali Mohsen al-Ahmar, now declared their backing for the protest movement.

Several ministers and other senior regime figures also defected. In April, the pattern of unrest and violent government response continued; President Saleh vowed to remain in office. In May, dozens more died in clashes between troops and tribal fighters in Sana'a. Alarmed by the uprising, the US feared an al-Qaeda resurgence in Yemen. Soon airports were shut down while thousands fled the city. In June, President Saleh was injured in a rocket attack on his presidential palace and was flown to Saudi Arabia. Saudi Arabia had now become the main haven for runaway dictators fleeing the Arab Spring, its own ruling regime becoming ever more heavily involved in suppressing the movement. Meanwhile, the US too had much to fear, for Yemen was a major US ally, being a vital military base for operations in the Indian Ocean and Africa.

On 14 February Bahrain launched its own 'Day of Rage,' organized through social media. Demonstrators were mostly Shi'a. The ruling Sunni regime soon denounced the uprising, arguing that it was different from the Arab Spring, and in fact instigated by the Islamic Republic of Iran. The Shi'i–Sunni divide, however, was a ruse. The more fundamental matter of political corruption lay at the root of the action. Two demonstrators were killed in Manama. To commemorate their death, on 15 February, thousands of demonstrators gathered at Pearl Square, and the main opposition party withdrew from parliament in protest. On 17 February, an early morning raid cleared Pearl Square of the thousands of protestors who had camped there; four people were reported killed. The king, Hamad bin Isa Al Khalifa, his family ruling Bahrain since 1942, released a number of political prisoners as a conciliatory gesture, while ordering an even more severe crackdown on the protests. Meanwhile prominent Shi'a opposition figure Hassan Mushaima, the secretary general of the Haq Movement, returned from exile. On 14 March, Saudi Arabia and other Gulf Cooperation Council (GCC) states sent troops to assist Bahraini security forces in suppressing the uprising. The following day martial law was declared by the ruler, but the protests continued. Soon after, due to the fear of a repetition of Egypt's Tahrir Square, the focal point of demonstrations, the Pearl Square, was demolished. In April, the government banned the two main political parties representing the

Shi'a majority. Four protesters were sentenced to death. By June, the heavy security remained in place, while scores of activists were sentenced to imprisonment, ranging from two years to life. As the home of the US Fifth Fleet, Bahrain is of vital strategic significance to the US, whose naval forces in the Persian Gulf, Red Sea, Arabian Sea, and coasts of East Africa are heavily invested in the stability of the tiny island.

On 5 February 2011, Syrians, following Egyptians, declared a 'Day of Rage,' using Twitter and Facebook. However, only a few hundred participants dared to attend and many who did were arrested. By now the 'Day of Rage' had become a leitmotif in the Arab Spring, whereby people declared and demonstated their angry defiance of the status quo. By March, massive protests were being held in Damascus demanding the release of political prisoners; many more were arrested. On a similar rally in the southern city of Deraa, security forces killed demonstrators, triggering further rallies. The government announced a few conciliatory measures and released some prisoners, but to no avail. President Assad accused the protesters of being Israeli agents. On 12 April, a number of soldiers were reportedly shot for refusing to fire on protestors. The crackdown intensified. On 16 April, Assad promised to lift the Emergency Law. But more arrests, more crackdowns, and more casualties followed. The US announced that it was considering imposing sanctions on Syrian officials; by early May the EU had done so for human rights violations. On 21 April, the state of emergency was lifted – but mounting casualties were now numbering in the hundreds. In May, Syrian army tanks entered Deraa, Banyas, Homs, and suburbs of Damascus to try to crush anti-regime protests. By mid-June thousands of Syrians had fled their country to Turkey for fear of persecution, and a humanitarian crisis was mounting on the Syria–Turkey border. Turkey was incensed and condemned the Syrian crackdown. But President Bashar al-Assad was adamant, and his army lethal.

Thus, between January and June 2011, a period of only six months, the map of the Middle East and North Africa changed radically. From Morocco to Iran, from Syria to Yemen – from one end of the Arab and Muslim world to the other – demonstrations spread in a relentless wave, and they were producing results. Major oppositional rallies in Morocco in February forced King Hassan II, in June, to promise constitutional reform. In Algeria similar demonstrations broke out in January over food prices and unemployment. In response, the government ordered cuts to the price of basic foodstuffs. In February in Oman, protesters demanded jobs and political reform. Sultan Qaboos immediately reacted by promising more jobs and benefits. In Saudi Arabia, in February, King Abdullah announced increased welfare spending; but by March protests had been banned, after small rallies were held, in mainly Shi'a areas of the east. Inspired by a wave of protests across the Arab world, Saudi women were now pushing for reform, defying official bans against their driving. In March, in Kuwait, hundreds of young people demonstrated for political reform, demanding more meaningful participation in the affairs of their homeland. In Morocco, by June people were voting in a referendum on a revised constitution designed to curb King Mohammed VI's absolutist rule.

Not a single Arab state was spared by the Arab Spring, though the momentum and the intensity of revolts varied. On 14 February, thousands of anti-government protesters demonstrated in Tehran, in solidarity with the Arab Spring, resuming and radicalizing their own Green Movement. By mid-June the tally of casualties was high, but varied from country to country. In Tunisia it was hundreds, in Yemen more, in Egypt many more; in Syria the number exceeded 1,000, and in Libya it was much higher.[1]

Every one of these postcolonial nation-states and political climes has a special significance in the blossoming of the Arab Spring. From the tiny Bahrain to the colossal Egypt, millions of people have revolted against domestic tyranny and foreign domination alike. The rise of each country has a significance of

1. The *Guardian* website has an excellent interactive timeline of events: www.guardian.co.uk/world/interactive/2011/mar/22/middle-east-protest-interactive-time-line. Specifically on the Egyptian revolution the Al Jazeera website has a detailed timeline: http://english.aljazeera.net/news/middleeast/2011/01/201112515334871490.html; for Tunisia's timeline, see http://english.aljazeera.net/indepth/spotlight/tunisia/2011/01/20111414222382736I.html; and for Libya, see http://english.aljazeera.net/news/africa/2011/04/20114191142177768868.html.

its own. The changes in Tunisia have challenged the European Union's attempt to dominate the Mediterranean basin; events in Egypt have radically compromised the influence of the United States in the region; violence in Libya has resulted in the country becoming a testing ground for NATO and the EU to flex their military and diplomatic muscles in the cause of complete control of the Mediterranean basin. Change of any magnitude in Syria will affect the geopolitics of the region the most because of its strategic alliance with Iran and Hezbollah; while Yemen will have defining consequences for the Saudi kingdom to the north and East Africa beyond the peninsula. The democratic uprising in Iran is the gateway to Central Asia. If the tyrannical regime in the Islamic Republic were to collapse, Afghanistan and Pakistan would immediately be affected, as would the Central Asian republics. The Pakistani military is now trying to find new markets for its military services; to them the tiny kingdoms in the Persian Gulf look quite suitable, despite the need to compete not only with US arm manufacturers but also with mercenary outfits like Blackwater Worldwide.[2]

The regional and global consequences of the Arab Spring are yet to be fathomed, let alone assayed. It would therefore be wrong to allow the notion of an 'Arab' or even 'Muslim' Spring to detract attention from larger frames of references. As is evident from Greece, Spain and the UK, the unrest is not limited to the Arab or to the Muslim world. The sense of dissatisfaction extends well into the Mediterranean, from labor migrations to a variety of economic woes demanding 'austerity measures.' From Senegal through to Zimbabwe and Djibouti, African courtiers are equally affected by these uprisings, but for now they are mostly below the radar, perceived as part of the map of the 'Arab world.' As the initial interaction between Tunisia and Egypt spread to Libya and on to Bahrain, Yemen and Syria, it became clear that this was a full-fledged dialectic between the national and the transnational. If the counter-revolutionary forces – ranging from the US, Israel, and Saudi Arabia to outdated outfits like the ruling regime in the

---

2. For more on Blackwater Worldwide, see Jeremy Scahill, *Blackwater: The Rise of the World's Most Powerful Mercenary Army* (New York: Nation Books, 2007).

Islamic Republic and Hezbollah (and including even the morally and intellectually bankrupt 'left,' which does not quite know what to say about the dramatic events) – wanted to contain any national scene, the transnational will to resist tyranny comes to the fore and prevails. Above all, on the emerging map of these adjacent regions, the old categories of the 'Islam and the West' have disappeared. The world is in effect decentering – albeit that in reality the center was never more than a powerful delusion.

Remapping the World

In one of the most beautiful visionary recitals of medieval mystic philosopher Shahab al-Din Yahya Suhrawardi (1155-1191), *Risalah al-Tayr*, 'Treatise of the Bird,' tells the story of a group of birds who are duped into a trap. Some of these birds manage to escape from the trap and are about to fly away when they notice that a few items from the old trap still cling to their wings, preventing them from flying.[3] The allegory is sublime in its power of implication and has one of the most powerful, surprising, and earthly endings in Suhrawardi's entire œuvre. But a vital paradox remains at the heart of the parable.

The expression that Suhrawardi uses for the trapping paraphernalia that remains with the birds and thus prevents them from flying away is very crucial. He uses the two words *dahul-ha va band-ha*. *Band-ha* is straightforward: it is the plural of 'band,' which here simply means 'strap.' But *dahul-ha* is a wholly different matter, involving a fantastically paradoxical double-bind. *Dahul-ha* is the plural of *dahul*, which means both 'scarecrow' – a crude image or effigy of a person, which is to say a fake human being, that farmers set up in a field to scare birds away from growing crops – and 'decoy,' namely a fake animal that hunters set up next to their trap to attract the birds they want to kill.

It is this word *dahul* (both 'scarecrow' and 'decoy'), which is deceptive in two contraposing senses – the one pretending to be

---

3. For an English translation of this and other treatises in this genre by Suhrawardi, see Sheikh Shihabuddin Yahya Suhrawardi, *The Mystical & Visionary Treatises of Suhrawardi*, trans. W.M. Thackston, Jr. (London: Octagon Press, 1982).

human to scare animals away, the other pretending to be an animal to attract real animals – that is most helpful for us in overcoming the major hurdles to understanding the unfolding revolutionary uprisings in Asia and Africa we indexically call the Arab Spring. *Dahuls* in this case are the spin doctors (on which I shall elaborate shortly), who don't pose as such to confuse the beholders, because they are themselves confused, pulling the wool over their own eyes so they won't see what is right in front of them. When Egyptians in Cairo or Syrians in Hama chant *al-Sha'b Yurid Isqat al-Nizam*, 'People Demand the Overthrow of the Regime,' the word *Nizam* means not just the ruling regime but also the *régime du savoir*, the regime of knowledge production that is, *ipso facto*, in the absence of conspiracy, in the business of distorting reality by way of making it understandable in the form of tired and old clichés – a mode of knowledge that is conducive to domination, namely 'the West over the East,' the ruling regime over the defiant population.

It is foolhardy to imagine any revolutionary uprising of the magnitude we are witnessing in Asia and Africa today, the pro-verbial parable of birds trying to fly away and alter their cir-cumstances, without a recognition of the forceful fury of the old regimes clinging to their wings and trying to hold on to their power and pre-empt or co-opt the uprising by any means pos-sible. Every revolutionary movement quite obviously generates and sustains its own kind of counter-revolutionary forces and alliances – *dahuls* clinging to brave birds trying to fly away. While the massive popular uprisings are yet to unfold their full revolutionary momentum, counter-revolutionary forces with their own vested interest in maintaining the status quo have created alliances to ensure business as usual.

There are two particularly disruptive sorts of spin-doctor *dahuls* at work to (mis)interpret the events to their, and their clients,' re-spective advantage: let's call one *analysts* and the others *annalists*. A representative example of the analyst who assimilates things to their habitual thinking is Bernard Lewis on the Arab Spring:

> The Arab masses certainly want change. And they want improvement.
> But when you say do they want democracy, that's ... a political concept

that has no history, no record whatever in the Arab, Islamic world. ... We, in the Western world particularly, tend to think of democracy in our own terms ... to mean periodic elections in our style. But I think it's a great mistake to try and think of the Middle East in those terms and that can only lead to disastrous results, as you've already seen in various places. They are simply not ready for free and fair elections. ... In genuinely fair and free elections, [the Muslim parties] are very likely to win and I think that would be a disaster.[4]

Here, at least, the Orientalism is explicit, and racism is not hidden behind spurious geopolitical rhetoric. But the common denominator between old-fashioned Orientalism and spin doctors is that neither has any hope, trust, or care for anything remotely democratic in this region.

Such blatant brokering of power for a corrupt and abusive state like the Islamic Republic, and the spinning of old-fashioned Orientalist clichés on behalf of Israel notwithstanding, what has happened in Iran since the contested June 2009 election now seems like a shot in the dark compared to the chorus of liberty echoing in the region. There is a much wider frame of reference, one that the old school of Orientalist analysts or the newly minted Area Studies specialists have no capacity to comprehend or imagination to fathom. But their combined effect is testimony to the modes and manners of mundane knowledge production that influence those American (and European) analysts trying to make sense of the Arab Spring. The Arab Spring itself – with its day-to-day cry of 'People Demand the Overthrow of the Regime,' has made such outdated chicanery obsolete.

The impediment to our understanding of the unfolding events, however, is not limited to corrupt and compromised analysts. The false anxiety of influence – in short, whose example did the Arabs follow in their Spring – is a relatively benign factor, but is nevertheless a distraction that has confounded the effort to begin to tell the narrative of these revolts more constructively. The prominent British journalist Robert Fisk, for example, suggests that,

---

4. See www.jpost.com/Opinion/Columnists/Article.aspx?id=209770.

in reality, the 'Arab awakening' began not in Tunisia this year [2011], but in Lebanon in 2005 when, appalled by the assassination of ex-prime minister Rafiq Hariri (Saad's father), hundreds of thousands of Lebanese of all faiths gathered in central Beirut to demand the withdrawal of Syria's 20,000 soldiers in the country.[5]

This is a deeply flawed argument. The March 14 ('Cedar Revolution') and March 8 (formed in opposition to March 14) alliances are unfortunate manifestations of the deeply rooted sectarian politics of Lebanon, and as such precisely symptomatic of the divisive politics of despair that the Arab Spring is now overcoming. It is factually and analytically wrong to reduce the Arab Spring to a development of the March 14 alliance, to disregard the March 8 alliance, and to drag these revolutions back to the pothole of sectarian politics in Lebanon (a gift of the French colonial legacy, which keeps giving). If anything, the Arab Spring will assimilate the sectarian politics of Lebanon to its emancipatory imagination, rather than the fractious politics of Lebanon dragging the Arab Spring down to its level.

But even beyond its analytical flaw, this sort of annalist reductionism is an entirely pointless wild goose chase offering no significant insight into what is unfolding before our eyes. It even inadvertently reignites the racialized binary of Muslim–Christian, Sunni–Shi'i, or Arab–Iranian seesaw, and indulges in the false anxiety of influence. To begin to make an assessment of these revolutionary uprisings, and put an end to the futile merry-go-round, we might in fact begin with 14 December 2008, when no major event took place but there was a fateful one-to-one encounter between an Iraqi citizen and an American president: on this day during a Baghdad press conference the Iraqi journalist Muntadhar al-Zaidi shouted 'This is a farewell kiss from the Iraqi people, you dog' and threw his shoes at US president George W. Bush. Predictable and time-worn Orientalist clichés were immediately deployed to interpret the meaning and significance of the shoe in Arab and Islamic culture – but, as usual, those wielding them

---

5. See www.belfasttelegraph.co.uk/opinion/columnists/robert-fisk/the-arab-awakening-began-not-in-tunisia-this-year-but-in-lebanon-in-2005-15142827.html.

were barking up the wrong tree: for sometimes a shoe is just a shoe, the only object you have to throw. I believe that the instance when Muntadhar al-Zaidi threw his shoe at President Bush was a cathartic moment, and the iconicity of the act was reinforced by the fact that the president dodged the shoe and therefore no harm was done to him – he even managed a nervous chuckle. The truly symbolic gesture is when precisely nothing happens, when the illuminative act has no instrumental function.

The catharsis of this moment was Aristotelian in its precision, iconically invoking the moment in the *Poetics* when Aristotle theorizes the literary effect of an action on either the characters of a tragedy or on the audience, or preferably both, thereby releasing pent-up energy and restoring the world to equilibrium. In precisely Aristotelian terms, the shoe-throwing Muntadhar al-Zaidi relied on the theatricality of the event to bring the emperor out of his sanitized environment to face his subjects. Ideas from Aristotle to Freudian cathartic aggression come together to give meaning to the momentous occasion when Muntadhar al-Zaidi publicly declared that the emperor's pants were down and thus symbolically paved the way and saw us off to Tahrir Square.

Uprisings versus Empire or versus Imperialism?

Neither pathology nor genealogy, neither the racist dismissal of the Iranian and Arab uprisings nor the wild goose chase after one commencement date or another, will damage the texture and fabric of what is unfolding. Genealogy is no explanation; nor will the anxiety of influence unveil the inner dynamics of these events. It was a gracious gesture on the part of those Egyptians in Tahrir Square who sported a sign bearing the Tunisian flag, declaring (with a pun on a Muslim prayer): *antum al-sabiqun, wa nahnu al-lahequn*, 'You are the first, and we follow you.' The jigsaw puzzle is coming together in and of itself.

Leaving aside both analysts and annalists, those who would reduce the Arab Spring to psychopathological traits and those who insist on assimilating it, retrogressively, to unending historical antecedents, the question remains: what is it we are witnessing taking shape before us? Within what frame of reference can we make sense of it? We seem to be caught in the dialogue between Hamlet and Polonius:

> *Hamlet*   Do you see yonder cloud that's almost in shape of a camel?
> *Polonius*   By th' Mass, and 'tis like a camel, indeed.
> *Hamlet*   Methinks it is like a weasel.
> *Polonius*   It is backed like a weasel.
> *Hamle*   Or like a whale.
> *Polonius*   Very like a whale.[6]

So is it a camel or a whale – or perhaps a weasel? How we read the events unfolding in 'the Arab and Muslim world' is precisely contingent on how able we are both to see and to place these events within that unraveling concept, and yet allow them to transcend the world that thus seeks to contain and codify them and point to another, more expansive, more liberating, more open-ended, and yet-to-be-named world. To see that world emerging, the one these events announce and promise, we must begin with our current understanding of the world beyond the falsifying binary of 'Islam and the West.' That binary – a particularly potent version of 'the West and the Rest' – is the most powerful disfiguration of multiple world maps over the last two hundred years; it is precisely that imperial map (code-named 'the West') that the Arab Spring is now altering, reconfiguring, recasting.

If we leave the propaganda officers of US imperialism, such as Francis Fukuyama ('the End of History') and Samuel Huntington ('Clash of Civilizations'), out of the picture – for by now the banality of their propositions has become self-evident[7] – by far the most valiant effort to make sense of our world over the last decade has been the collective insights of Michael Hardt and Antonio Negri's *Empire* (2000), later extended into their *Multitude* (2004) and *Commonwealth* (2009). They argue that the nature of globalized capital and the massive network of information technologies and monetary and political bureaucracies it has engendered have preempted the

---

6. William Shakespeare, *Hamlet* 3.2.

7. I, among many others, have discussed the shallowness of such analyses and their function within the propaganda machinery of American imperialism in my *Brown Skin, White Masks* (London: Pluto, 2011).

possibility of singular imperial control from any metropolitan center. We have exited, they propose, the age of imperialism and entered the era of Empire, predicated on a pervasive network, not hierarchy, of domination. What defines our world today is not pyramidal relations of power but an amorphous network of domination, benefiting the ruling regimes and disenfranchising the rest of the globe. Hence Empire is a web, not a pyramid, of domination. Empire is 'a *decentered* and *deterritorializing* apparatus of rule that progressively incorporates the entire global realm within its open, expanding frontiers.'[8] The age of the nation-state has ended, they assert, and no nation, even the United States, can act as the center of an imperialist project. The very concept of nation-state is now a nostalgic notion, entirely useless.[9]

This appears to be an exciting and clear-headed way of looking at our world, except that when we consider it more closely it seems that Hardt and Negri have simply imagined the rampant globalization of the 'Western world,' *ipso facto* rendering obsolete both the postcolonial nation-states and the European models on which they were predicated. They do not offer a radically different view of the world, just a perspective that projects a radical exacerbation of the existing state of affairs: to them 'the Western world' and all its peripheral boundaries have been erased in a gridlock of domination. 'The construction of *Empire* is a step forward in order to do away with any nostalgia for the power structures that preceded it and refuse any political strategy that involves returning to that old arrangement, such as trying to resurrect the nation-state to protect against global capital.'[10] Though politically quite distinct from Fukuyama and Huntington, Hardt and Negri nevertheless effectively take the triumph of 'the West' for granted, even though they believe it has now succeeded and exhausted itself, and entered a more abstract phase of domination – the globalization of its own innate logic. While their Eurocentricism remains intact, they judge

---

8. Michael Hardt and Antonio Negri, *Empire* (Cambridge MA: Harvard University Press, 2000): xii.

9. There have been many cogent critics of Hardt and Negri's thesis – among them Partha Chatterjee's 'Empire after Globalization' (*Economic and Political Weekly*, 11 September 2004): 4155-64.

10. Hardt and Negri, *Empire*: 43.

that the mode of domination that 'the West' exerts has entered a new phase of governmentality.

It is not just the nation-state but also localism that is outdated in Hardt and Negri's account of Empire. Localism is not external to globalization but integral to it, they maintain. We need counter-globalization, whilst accepting the universalization of 'the Western world' and seeking a manner of resisting it in terms that are domestic and familiar to that dominant world. Empire is now the economic logic of domination at large – it does not have specific agency. The nation-state, Hardt and Negri emphatically insist, is disappearing, and abstracted modes of domination have emerged. But they seem to have disregarded the fundamental fact that the nation-state was never the modus operandi of capital. If for European national economies, from the time of Adam Smith's *The Wealth of Nations* (1776) onwards, the assumption of 'the nation' was a mere bookkeeping mechanism, in the colonial world it was a method of mobilization and resistance against an already globalized capital. That is, what Hardt and Negri believe to be a new development – a network of domination rather than a one-to-one imperial relation of power – has been the modus operandi of capital since the day one. However, Hardt and Negri fail to acknowledge that, while capitalism's logic of global domination has always been transnational, the mode of resistance to it has been – and must remain – national and regional. You don't fight an amorphous domination with an amorphous resistance, but at concrete sites of resistance. But there is a need to cease universalizing 'the West' (as if God Almighty from the Heavens had mapped the world with it) and stop confusing it with the world that resists imperial domination.

In contrast to imperialism, Hardt and Negri propose, Empire establishes no territorial center of power and does not rely on fixed boundaries or barriers; it is a decentered apparatus of rule that progressively incorporates the entire globe within 'open, expanding frontiers.' But in fact that has always been the way both capitalism and imperialism have operated. The assumption of a centered metropole for the operation of capitalism or imperialism (coded 'the West') was always an illusion. It is good to be cured of that illusion; but that is not synonymous with an entry into a new phase of either capitalism or imperialism. Any unwanted (illegal/'guest') laborer from Asia, Africa, or Latin America will testify that national boundaries mean nothing when they are chasing after their daily bread. Capital has never had a center. Imperialism, as thinkers such as Max Weber and Schumpeter realized, is predatory capitalism – the abuse of labour by capital multiplied by the global map. This operation of capital has manufactured the illusion of a center, to assure itself of civilizational superiority, the Eurocentric conception of which seems finally to have been identified – which is a positive development. But viewed from the colonial angles of its operation, capitalism was global from the start – and thus the question of why it developed 'here' and not 'there' is really an exercise in futility, for from the very beginning capitalism was a global and globalizing *event* and it did not matter if it happened as a consequence of Protestant ethics or the Industrial Revolution in Europe; or in Africa, Asia, or Latin America; and with a Buddhist, Hindu, or Islamic world-view. Europe, as Fanon noted, is and remains an invention of the Third World – by which he meant the colonized world – at a certain moment of the operation of capital, which in and of itself has always been transversal in its inner logic and operation. Capitalism has never had a center, and thus no periphery. Imperialism has never operated without a network of material and normative institutions that facilitate and hide its naked brutality, for as capital has violently crossed national borders in pursuit of raw material, cheap labor, and markets, so has cheap labor smuggled itself into the presumed centers of capital. What Hardt and Negri have discovered in the academy – the brute force of capital and the abused reality of labor – have in fact long been known and experienced.

> Our basic hypothesis, however, that a new imperial form of sovereignty has emerged, contradicts both these views [of those who endorse or oppose the assumption that the US rules the world]. *The United States does not, and indeed no nation-state can today, form the center of an imperialist project.* Imperialism is over. No nation will be world leader in the way modern European nations were.[11]

---

11. Hardt and Negri, *Empire*: xiii–xiv.

It is precisely the assumption of that imperial centrality, of it ever having existed, that is at issue. Neither the United States nor any other nation has ever held that position. And it is precisely for that reason that there always been a relentless crescendo of uprisings against imperialism. The assumption that world capitalism has a center and a periphery has always been a powerful illusion that has helped the hegemony of that figment of imagination code-named 'the West,' casting 'the Rest' of the world to the presumed margins – the ideological manufacturing of a white supremacist *mission civilisatrice*. This chimera was believed in for some time, and now in the works of Hardt and Negri it seems finally to have been challenged. But this belated recognition makes little difference to the way in which the material operation of capital has been wrapped around the globe (transgressing national boundaries violently to steal raw materials, secure cheap labor, and expand markets), nor to the fact that peripheralized worlds around this delusional center have always imagined themselves and thrived at the heart of their own different universes.

Hardt and Negri's conception of 'Empire' remains constitutionally Eurocentric, even Eurotriumphalist, in effect declaring the triumph of 'the West' over 'the Rest' as accomplished, with no option but to acknowledge that triumph, and seeking modes of resistance domestic to it. Underlying this Eurocentricism, furthermore, is a profoundly Christian theology that informs their politics of resistance. As early as *Empire* (2000), the immanence–transcendence binary that Hardt and Negri suggest by way of the distinction they detect between Empire and imperialism was already the indication of an evident Christianization of the imperial imagining – for the terms are primarily Christological in the postmodern theology they entail. Hardt and Negri's differentiation of *Empire*, which for them is aterritorial, immanent and hybrid, from *imperialism*, which is aterritorial, transcendent, and with fixed boundaries, exposes a transparent Christology. But it is not until the appearance of *Commonwealth* (2009) that the two contingent concepts of *love* and *poverty* make it quite clear that we are indeed in the presence of two deeply Christian thinkers. The fungible disposition of these sorts of ideas – immanence-transcendence – which we have learned how to detect in disguise at least since Max Weber's sociology of religion, here becomes the framework for two Christian thinkers yet again trying to Christianize the world in secular (Marxist) disguise – a Christian colonization of our critical faculties. There is, of course, nothing wrong with two Christian Marxists seeing the world through their Christological bifocals. But the issue is how valid would that vision be for the non-Christian world at the mercy of Christian colonial missionaries since the debates between Bartolomé de las Casas (1484-1566) and Juan Ginés de Sepúlveda (1489-1573), one opposing, the other endorsing, Spanish colonialism – both in Christian terms.

The events of 9/11 in the US and the two major US-led imperialist invasions of sovereign Muslim nation-states, predicated on the premeditated designs of the neoconservative manifesto the Project for the New American Century, challenge the theory of the end of imperialism and the commencement of Empire. The US-led invasions of Afghanistan and Iraq were territorial and transcendent – very old-fashioned imperialism. Soon we were to witness the Israeli invasion of Lebanon in 2006 and the re-conquest of Gaza in 2008-09 – two mini-imperialist follies by the Israeli settler colony acting in conjunction with US imperialism. These backfired and made Hezbollah and Hamas, now joining forces with the Mahdi Army, even more powerful than they were before – with Syria and the Islamic Republic coming together in a battle formation effectively outmaneuvering the US/Israel and their European and regional allies. All these maneuvers were still very much territorial and transcendent, with national and subnational configurations facing up to the imperial formation of the US and its European and regional allies.

We must recognize and retrieve the multiple worlds that 'the West' has concealed. Imperialism has always been an Empire, and Empire imperialist, if we simply recognize that capitalism never had a center, and the civilizational manufacturing of boundaries was a heuristic mechanism to sustain the autonormativity of instrumental reason as the heteronormativity of benevolent progress. The rise of the Arab Spring has occasioned the possibility of altogether abandoning the further theorization of the West into a globalized Empire, and considering the possibility that all such grand illusions are in fact trapped inside a world they are trying to reform.

Hardt and Negri are of course fully aware of, and indeed concede, the Eurocentricity of their vision of the world, but the explanation they offer for it reveals even more.

> The genealogy we follow in our analysis of the passage from imperialism to Empire will be first European and then Euro-American, not because we believe that these regions are the exclusive or privileged source of new ideas and historical innovation, but simply because this was the dominant geographical path along which the concepts and practices that animate today's Empire developed in step, as we will argue, with the development of the capitalist mode of production. Whereas the genealogy of Empire is in this sense Eurocentric, however, its present powers are not limited to any region. Logics of rule that in some sense originated in Europe and the United States now invest practices of domination throughout the globe. More important, the forces that contest Empire and effectively prefigure an alternative global society are themselves not limited to any geographical region. The geography of these alternative powers, the new cartography, is still waiting to be written – or really, it is being written today through the resistances, struggles, and desires of the multitude.[12]

This vision of the global geography continues to separate the site of the colonial from the assumed centrality of the capital and mars the perspective from which they view the world. The condition of coloniality, as integral to the operation of capital, has no place either in the formation of the capital or in the transition to Empire. Because the 'non-West' is not on their radar, they categorically state: 'In our much celebrated age of communication, *struggles have become all but incommunicable.*' Tiananmen Square, Chiapas, Los Angeles, France, the Intifada and South Korea seem struggles which not only have no connection or communication with one another, but which are actually incommensurable. 'The proletariat is not what it used to be, but that does not mean it has vanished.' The assumption that these struggles are 'blocked from travelling

---

12. Hardt and Negri, *Empire*: xv–xvi.

horizontally in the form of a cycle, [and thus] are forced instead to leap vertically and touch immediately on the global level'[13] seems, alas, embarrassingly flawed given the events of 2011 and the resonance of the singular chant *al-Sha'b Yurid Isqat al-Nizam.*

The problem with works such as those of Hardt and Negri is that they continue to spin grand theories predicated entirely on a Eurocentric assumption of a globality that cannot see any other world – one still operating very much within a singular 'Western' imaginary that they see globalized, and that in a progressive politics they seek to overcome in its own terms. They remain indifferent to or unaware of other worlds – not only worlds past, but worlds emerging in spite of the 'Western world' that has colonized and captivated their imagination. The alternative site of resistance to imperialist globalization involves first and foremost the retrieval and recognition of multiple worlds that have existed prior to and alongside, and are now superseding, the imperial manufacturing of 'the West,' which the imperial hubris of Francis Fukuyama and Samuel Huntington, and the colonized minds of those around the globe who are still talking to the West, have successfully camouflaged. What Hardt and Negri are doing in effect is not overcoming capitalist globalization but yielding to the power and authority of the world that it has generated. Appealing to the amorphous multitude is not where resistance to 'the West' (that is to say globalized capitalism) lies, but in specific worlds and national and transnational alliances that this very multitude can and will generate and sustain.

The Arab Spring is revealing another world, one long in the making, which the postcolonial world had promised but failed to deliver and thus concealed, and the world that the imperial mapping of 'the West' had made invisible. Noble and pathbreaking as their visions are, Hardt and Negri are not transcending 'the West,' or even decentering it. By way of making it immanent, they are making its transcendence even more metaphysical, precisely at the moment that it is imploding.

---

13. Ibid.: 54, 53, 55.

Ethnos *sous rature*

If we are to de-Christianize the transcendence–immanence binary and use it to help our understanding of these dramatic events, then we need to abandon the teleological temptation of memorial transcendence, which is an open-ended recollection of history, and opt for the more palpable *moment of immanence* in which we live and witness these democratic uprisings. The vastness of the developments taking place in multiple countries requires a hermeneutic matrix that is at once immanent in its recognition of the worldly transformations we see and yet historically transcendent in recognition of every individual nation-state in which the democratic uprisings are being launched. In other words, in understanding each one of these events – in Tunisia, Egypt, Syria, Iran, Bahrain, Yemen, or Afghanistan – we need to be at one and the same time historically transcendent and geographically imminent. Each of these countries requires a vertical, historically transcendent axis in terms of the particular colonial and postcolonial experiences it has generated and shared, and yet simultaneously a horizontally immanent axis through which it is giving birth to a new geography of liberation. History will remain transcendent for individual countries on this matrix, while allowing geography to exude its worldly immanence. Neither historically determinist nor geographically presentist but, rather, at once historically transcendent and geographically immanent seems to be the matrix on which these events can begin to make sense.

The worldly immanence of a new emerging geography, not the historical transcendence of the colonially manufactured 'Middle East,' is the basis for understanding these uprisings – a worldly immanence in which the history of specific colonial experiences, rather than the divinity of any given ideology, is embedded – what Hans-Georg Gadamer would consider their *effective history*.

At this point we are in a position to mark the fact that the events in Africa and Asia are only strategically coded as 'the Arab and Muslim world,' which must be used *sous rature* (under erasure), no longer valid but still useful. Why is the term still necessary and even productive, and at once no longer valid and arguably

counterproductive? It is strategically productive, perhaps necessary, because the synergy that has been generated in the countries
facing insurgences dwells on the moment of the Arab Spring;
that dwelling is procreative and regenerative, and makes it very
difficult for the US and its European and regional allies, or the
Islamic Republic and its retinue, to micro-manage or derail the
succession of uprisings. But it is also counterproductive because
the more we consolidate and exacerbate such inherited branding
of the liberated world the more we obfuscate the picture emerging before our eyes beyond this naming; for the unfolding events
are in fact geared towards an open-ended dialectic committed
to the recovery or discovery of new worlds that can no longer be
defined as Arab or Muslim. The losers in these unfolding events
are not just US allies such as Tunisia, Egypt, or Saudi Arabia, but
also the Islamic Republic and its regional satellites – Hezbollah,
Hamas, and the Mahdi Army, unless they decouple themselves
(as Hamas has quickly done) from the fate of falling tyrannies.
What the appellation 'Arab and Islamic world' thus conceals is
by virtue of its ethnicizing in 'Arab' and ideologizing in 'Islamic'
what in effect has already transcended both the *ethnos* and the
logos of the Arab and the Islamic world and reached for the *ethos*
of a renewed retrieval of the cosmopolitan facts of these societies. What we are witnessing unfold is the transformation of the
ethnos of the presumed 'Arab and Muslim world' into the *ethos*
of a moral and imaginative uprising, the contours of which are
yet to be determined.

The last grand revolution to take place in the region was the
Islamic Revolution of 1977-79, which was predicated on grand
illusions of freedom and liberty that were brutally brushed aside
when a tyrannical theocracy took over. Today thirty years of repressive theocracy is in the deep background of all the revolutionary
uprisings we know as the Arab Spring. What the world around the
Islamic Republic is exposing is the historic lie that the theocracy
has tried to hide for three decades – for the cosmopolitan fact
of these societies, which the ruling regime (and the *régime du
savoir* that it violently manufactured) viciously repressed, has now
returned for the whole world to see. That is to say, these revolutions

are the return of the Islamic Republic's repressed: what it had to
deny and suppress to manufacture itself as an 'Islamic Revolution,'
to posit itself as an 'Islamic Republic.' The region is 'outing' the
Islamic Republic, exposing the skeletons in its closet, revealing the
euphoric uprising that shaped the revolutionary hopes of 1977-79,
before it was ferociously suppressed, its victims mutilated, murdered, and buried in mass graves. The site of Khavaran cemetery,
where the regime buried the thousands it cold-bloodedly killed in
the 1980s, is now haunting the belligerent clergy.

The neocons in the United States are afraid that the Arab Spring
might be the harbinger of yet another 'Islamic uprising,' while
the custodians of fear and intimidation in the Islamic Republic
are quick to declare the events the manifestation of yet another
'Islamic revolution.' But what occurred in Iran three decades ago
was not an 'Islamic revolution,' and what people fought for was
not 'an Islamic Republic.' Rather, a multifaceted cosmopolitan
revolution was violently Islamicized by a succession of cultural
revolutions, university purges, mass executions, forced exiles, and
the conniving abuse of a regional crisis. The Islamic Republic has
spent thirty years repressing its own people and manufacturing
an image of legitimacy and even a revolutionary disposition for
itself, and now these magnificent revolutions around it are putting
on stage precisely the initial euphoria that the theocracy killed.
Thus the custodians of the Islamic Republic are as uneasy about
the revolutions as are the US, Israel, and Saudi Arabia, and like
them endeavors to put its own spin on them.

But all that is water under the bridge. The Arab Spring is
blossoming, like a beautiful constellation of waterlilies, from the
muddy and murky waters of once cruel and fertile grounds.

TWO

Towards a Liberation Geography

In an essay for Al Jazeera, 'Are Palestinian Children Less Worthy?' (2011), Joseph Massad, the distinguished scholar of modern Arab politics and intellectual history, asks perhaps the salient (though scarcely raised) question at the heart of the Arab-Israeli conflict:

> What is it about Jewish and Arab children that privileges the first and spurns the second in the speeches of President Barack Obama, let alone in the Western media more generally? Are Jewish children smarter, prettier, whiter? Are they deserving of sympathy and solidarity, denied to Arab children, because they are innocent and unsullied by the guilt of their parents, themselves often referred to as 'the children of Israel'? Or, is it that Arab children are dangerous, threatening, guilty, even dark and ugly, a situation that can only lead to Arabopaedophobia – the Western fear of Arab children?[1]

Massad spends the rest of the essay dissecting with meticulous precision the historical dimensions of what he aptly terms Arabopaedophobia.

Whence comes this 'Arabopaedophobia'? Or, to ask the same question in reverse, this unabashed privileging of Israeli over Arab

---

1. See Joseph Massad, 'Are Palestinian Children Less Worthy?' Al Jazeera, 30 May 2011, http://english.aljazeera.net/indepth/opinion/2011/05/201152911579533291.html.

children? On more than one occasion, President Barack Obama has compared and identified Israeli children with his own children, but never has he dared to imagine Palestinian children as his own Malia and Sasha. Why? Massad remarks on one such occasion:

> It is important to note that Obama might have met these same blond girls [who were pictured writing messages of death on bombs being dropped on Lebanon in July 2006] when he visited Kiryat Shmona a few months earlier, in January 2006. He recalled later that the town resembled an ordinary suburb in the US, where he could imagine the sounds of Israeli children 'at joyful play just like my own daughters.'

There are other – even more pointed – occasions when Obama has assimilated Israeli children to his own children. Defending what Israelis called their operation 'Cast Lead,' launched on 27 December 2008, the newly elected president declared: 'If somebody was sending rockets into my house where my two daughters sleep at night, I'm going to do everything in my power to stop that. And I would expect Israelis to do the same thing.'[2] This is the same operation in which Palestinian children were deliberately targeted by the Israeli army and at times used as human shields or murdered at point-blank range – a fact noted even by the timid and self-doubting Goldstone Report.[3] Children are children: what difference does it make if they are killed by one side or another? Both should be condemned. Why is it that Barack Obama, the president of the United States, turns a blind eye to or ignores Palestinian children, but is instantly reminded of his own children when it comes to Israeli children? He is not Israeli; he is American – an African American. What accounts for the connection?

---

2. See Michael Abramowitz, 'Israeli Airstrikes on Gaza Strip Imperil Obama's Peace Chances,' *Washington Post*, 28 December 2008, www.washingtonpost.com/wp-dyn/content/article/2008/12/27/AR2008122700962.html.

3. For the details of Justice Richard Goldstone's report, see UN Human Rights Council, 'United Nations Fact Finding Mission on the Gaza Conflict,' www2.ohchr.org/english/bodies/hrcouncil/specialsession/9/factfindingmission.htm. Judge Goldstone later partially retracted his findings in an op-ed published in *Washington Post*; see: http://israelstreams.com/i.html?http://wpost.com/opinions/reconsidering-the-goldstone-report-on-israel-and-war-crimes/2011/04/01/AFg111JC_story.html. The pressure Judge Goldstone had to endure in the aftermath of issuing his report included being barred from attending his own grandson's bar mitzvah; see the report in *Haaretz*, www.haaretz.com/news/report-zionist-group-bans-goldstone-from-grandson-s-bar-mitzvah-1.284324.

Massad twice pointedly notes Obama's identification of his own children with 'blonde' Israeli children, raising the question even more clearly as to how exactly it is that two African-American girls, born to African-American parents, can be so easily assimilated to and identified with blonde children – at the expense of ignoring the plight of Palestinian children? Why is it that as a Christian, for example, the president does not identify with Christian Palestinian children, or, as the son of a Muslim, with Muslim Palestinian children, or, as the descendent of an African, with *Arab* children? The racialized politics of both the assimilation and the comparison marks the overriding incorporation of Israeli and American children into a singular category that sidesteps a bloody history of African slavery. That category, paramount in the geopolitics of global domination, is coded 'the West.' Israeli and American children are 'Western,' the code commands; Palestinian children, as Arabs, are not 'Western,' they are 'Eastern.' As the supreme poet of British imperialism Rudyard Kipling (1865-1936) decreed:

Oh, East is East and West is West, and never the twain shall meet,
Till Earth and Sky stand presently at God's great Judgment Seat.

Obama sees his own daughters as 'Western' and thus instantly identifies with Israeli children but not with Palestinian children, for they belong to a different tribe – they are 'Eastern,' and as such are excluded from full 'Western' auto-normativity, because they are not worlded; they are othered, atomized, cast upon the winds, delegated to a hinterland as the others of civilized humanity, a humanity that is thus exclusively coded as 'Western.' Palestinians – all of them, along with all the other Arabs, other Muslims, the rest of Asia, Africa, Latin America, the entire world outside the exclusive category of 'the West' – are not worlded. Rather, they are other-worlded – the geography of their hinterland the subterranean fear of 'the Western world.' If these children were allowed to come up to breathe, to be counted as human, something terrible would happen: 'the West' would disappear. It would no longer be. Such children and their parents must remain subhuman in order that humanity (which is always 'Western,' particularly when it goes 'universal') survive. These children – their being, breathing, demanding, and exacting their liberties – are the undoing of 'the West.'

The Arab Spring is confusing (turning upside down) the global map of imperial domination. The Arab and Muslim world, and precisely as 'the Arab and Muslim' world, has been termed – over a long and protracted history of colonial domination, Orientalist learning and imagination, and Area Studies expertise (a *régime du savoir* that extends in its longevity from the British colonization of India in the eighteenth century to the US-led invasion of Iraq in the twenty-first) – into the most potent component of 'the West versus the Rest' bipolarity of global domination.[4] Orientalists in their very person and by the protracted durability of their services, link British and American imperialism together via a singularly successful Orientalist career: manufacturing an Orient that must, by virtue of its flawed DNA, serve 'The West' for its own good. Libraries and museums of scholarship, journalism, visual and performing arts, imaginative landscapes, and so forth, have been produced to manufacture the figure of the Arab and the Muslim as the absolute, and absolutely horrid, reversal of the white man – the white man with whom even a black man like Barack Obama identifies. It is that regime of knowledge, that massive topography of emotive imagination, convincing itself that Arabs and Muslims are constitutionally incapable of even imagining democracy let alone being the principal site for inaugurating an event of world historical magnitude, that is now being powerfully challenged, that is troubled by the prospect of losing the ground on which it stands. The destabilization of that regime of knowledge is the first and foremost fact about these uprisings.

Against a vast imaginative landscape of domination, the Arab Spring is both inaugurating and being unfolded upon a liberation geography.

---

4. See Edward Said's *Orientalism* (New York: Vintage, 1979) for the groundbreaking critique of Orientalism. For further reflections on the current condition of knowledge production, see also Hamid Dabashi, *Post-Orientalism: Knowledge and Power in Time of Terror* (New Brunswick NJ: Transaction, 2008).

De-ethnicizing the Worlds

In mid-April 2011, I was invited by Museo de América in Madrid to deliver a keynote speech at a conference of European ethnographic museums, at which leading curators and museum directors discussed the moral conundrum they face in staging exhibits on non-European peoples and their cultures and heritage for the viewing pleasure, amusement, and education of their European visitors. Ethnographic museums and the entire project of ethnography on which they are predicated and built are the remnants of an age in which the European project of colonial modernity repressed the constitutional coloniality of its origin and *telos* by way of feigning a universality that necessitated the primacy of *ethnos* in defining its relation to the world. The condition we call postcoloniality is the historical moment of the critical exposure of that relation of power in which Europe erased the question of its own ethnicity by way of a universality that required the denominational attribution of ethnicities to the worlds it conquered, ethnicized, and museumized at one and the same time. Today that outdated *ethnos* is overcome by the necessity and primacy of an *ethos* that must overcome the pathos of the domination of man over man and over nature and yield to *an ethic of responsibility* (Max Weber) of people for people as they all brace for the planetary fragility of the world. This overcoming of the *ethnos* by *ethos* is possible via the recognition of worlds that have always existed but that have been repressed under the overpowering fallacy of 'the West,' but only by way of recognizing the multiple worlds that are emerging. The resurrection of the category 'the Arab and Muslim world' in these democratic uprisings is one such occasion.

More broadly – and before and beyond the Arab Spring – what and where are the worlds (plural) that are emerging to overcome the talisman of 'the West'? That factual and imaginative geography is the key conceptual category that needs rethinking. This becomes more evident the instant we designate a geographical span where these worlds are emerging through massive revolutionary uprisings. The assumption that these revolts are occurring in 'the Arab and Muslim world' is of course at once imaginatively productive while factually flawed. African nations from Senegal to Djibouti, the non-Arab nations of Afghanistan, Pakistan, and Iran, and non-Muslim countries ranging from Spain to Greece, and even non-Mediterranean sites, best exemplified in the Occupy Wall Street movements, are in one way or another replicating the phenomenon of Tahrir Square. This very transnational fact is an indication of the transformative geography we are facing. Under the general condition of that global reconfiguration of our received geographies, 'the Arab and Muslim world' is one such potent topography that is proverbial for many more.

Decolonizing Theory

In *Feminism without Borders*, the distinguished transnational feminist scholar Chandra Talpade Mohanty looks for ways of 'decolonizing theory and practicing solidarity.' She proposes that

> any discussion of the intellectual and political construction of 'Third World feminism' must address itself to two simultaneous projects: the internal critique of hegemonic 'Western' feminism and the formulation of autonomous feminist concerns and strategies that are geographically, historically, and culturally grounded. The first project is one of deconstructing and dismantling; the second one of building and constructing. While these projects appear to be contradictory ... unless these two tasks are addressed simultaneously, Third World feminism runs the risk of marginalization or ghettoization from both mainstream (right and left) and Western feminist discourses.[5]

This is a perfect example of trying to decolonize theory by simply submitting the term 'the West' to a couple of compromising quotation marks, while resigning oneself to the alternative of the 'Third World' as a legitimate geographical allocation. But 'the Third World' is itself the creation of 'the First World,' of 'the West.' Why should we yield and accept where the 'First World' has placed us? It is precisely the site of that allocation, the thirdness of that world

---

5. Chandra Talpade Mohanty, *Feminism without Borders: Decolonizing Theory, Practicing Solidarity* (Durham NC: Duke University Press, 2003): 17.

to the presumed firstness of 'the West,' which as a category remains unquestioned, which is, as it has long been, the question. Where is the first, what happened to the second, and by what authority is the greater part of humanity subjected to the outlandish designation 'the Third World'? As long as 'the West' and 'the Third World' remain categorically viable – even if incarcerated within quotation marks – those borders have not been crossed. They have in fact been thickened and barbed-wired.

Geography is the hidden map of racially profiling and ideologically foregrounding a fictive white supremacy, on the basis of which ethnographic discourses narrate a pre-historic origin for the white man's destiny as the master of the universe. In this process cultures beyond and beneath (the white man's?) lived experiences are 'museumized,' and a regime of knowledge production that cannot but assimilate world-historic events like the Arab Spring retrogressively into what we know, what we have been taught, is supported. The task is to dismantle that regime of knowledge, as the Egyptians, Tunisians, and others are dismantling the regimes of tyranny that had ruled them. The *isqat*, dismantling, of a political regime and the regime of knowledge must go hand in hand.

The autonormative primacy of 'the West' in the imaginative geography we have inherited from the sustained legacy of European colonialism and American imperialism is the very condition of the manufacturing of *ethnos* that is at the root of ethnography as a discipline, and the very foundation of ethnography museums, which by their existence institutionalize the racialized subdivisions of the world into conquerable units. With the implosion of 'the West' as a normative category in the aftermath of the collapse of the Soviet Union, and with the unification of Europe, the rift between the US and the EU since the commencement of the Iraq War, and now with the massive uprisings in Asia and Africa, these ethnographic museums have themselves become museumized. We enter their halls and wonder what made some people put other people inside glass boxes and stare at them – be it for entertainment, amusement, education, or domination.

In the American Museum of Natural History in New York, people walk with their children through the exhibition corridors looking at Native Americans, Africans, Eskimos, Indians, Arabs, Iranians, and so on, intermixed with the remnants and replicas of strange animals ranging from extinct dinosaurs to buffaloes, yaks, elephants, giraffes, lions, chimpanzees, and forth. I once approached an African-American museum guard and asked, only half in jest, what about white folks, did they not have a civilization worth encasing behind one of these glass windows? He laughed gently as he said 'Please do not touch' to a child who was leaning on the glass case of eagles next to a case of figurines representing Zoroastrians and Jews. In the Museum of Natural History, which combines ethnography and zoology, animals and human beings are gathered together. Here, the past of 'the West' is equated with the present of 'others,' and both with the bestial existence of animals – thus vertical with Europe, horizontal with the world, and diagonal or transversal with the animal kingdom.[6]

The institutional function of the ethnography museum has been to order and name the heteronormative alterities of European modernity by way of authorizing its own auto-normativity. These museums collect, organize, conserve, and interpret vertically 'the West' and horizontally the world, equating its own history with world geography. Museums have been instrumental, indeed definitive, in facilitating a reading of European modernity that posits them as a site of auto-normative superiority, of its own divinity secularized. Can museums indeed work towards an inclusive and non-hierarchic 'We' without coming to terms with the fact that European modernity made itself universal by virtue of suppressing the marker of its coloniality? Can postcolonial modernity – namely, a democratic distribution of reason and progress – be posited as the modus operandi of our renewed being in the world? If the last two hundred years are any indication, the fact is that the very presumption of postcoloniality has extended the colonial domination of the world into the normative domination of knowledge production against which people revolt not only to topple their

---

6. The immensely popular movies *Night at the Museum* (2006) and *Night at the Museum: Battle of the Smithsonian* (2009), directed by Shawn Levy, are both set in New York City's American Museum of Natural History, where we can see all these ethnicities and animals – extinct or still up and about – come alive for the further amusement of their 'white' museum guard, a night watchman, and his desire to impress his son.

ruling regimes but also the *régime du savoir* that entraps their struggles in the dominant terms.

Nationalizing Geography

In the United States, *National Geographic* magazine, the imaginative heart of 'the Empire,' has been the principal culprit in this ethnographic othering of cultures and climes. When Americans or even Europeans hear the word 'Arab' or watch or read on their televisions or computers something about 'the Arab Spring,' it is fair to say that their accumulated volumes of *National Geographic* represent at least one crucial lens in the visual and emotive apparatus through which they see, hear, or read. Two critical examinations of *National Geographic* magazine, a veritable institution in the United States and Europe that reaches far and wide into schools, public libraries, and households, have already mapped out the details of this ethnographic alienation of cultures from themselves in order to make them familiar (by way of making them foreign) to their fictive white readers' sense of identity and superiority in a universal history of themselves. In 1993, Catherine A. Lutz and Jane L. Collins, in their pioneering study *Reading National Geographic*, demonstrated how this magazine had posited itself as 'a window to the world' from which people perfectly familiar to themselves had become foreign to North American audiences in search of 'exotic peoples and places' to alleviate their boredom. The magazine taught very little about the cultures and climes it examined, but a lot about the systematic ethnographic alienation of the world. Almost a decade later, in 2000, Linda Steet, in *Veils and Daggers: A Century of National Geographic's Representation of the Arab World*, showed how the very same magazine had consistently portrayed Arab and Muslim people as the dangerous alterity of North American people.[7]

---

7. See Catherine A. Lutz and Jane L. Collins, *Reading National Geographic* (Chicago: University of Chicago Press, 1993) and Linda Steet, *Veils and Daggers: A Century of National Geographic's Representation of the Arab World* (Philadelphia, PA: Temple University Press, 2000).

What *National Geographic* has in effect done is not 'represent' these cultures but in fact manufacture them. In a mere critique of representation, there are representations and misrepresentations; all representations are misrepresentations and likewise all misrepresentations are representations. What magazines like *National Geographic* and the entire spectrum of public media that it represents in North America and Western Europe do is not represent but *present* – that is, constitute, manufacture, engineer – reality. Through such narratives and visual registers as framing, point of view, color, pose, and so on, they picture a space that is 'non-Western' in order to posit a centrality that is 'the West.' The ethnographic manufacturing of the 'non-West' is central to the conceptual engineering of 'the West.' *National Geographic* is the mirror of the Other, so that by staring at it 'the West' will believe in its Self. If you deny 'the West' its ethnographic lens, it will cease to exist, for it has nothing to look at as its own mirror image, its reversed angle. The Arab Spring is the removal of that mirror – the end of *National Geographic* magazine.

Anthropology and Colonialism

What we observe in the case of *National Geographic* is only the more popular version of the more disciplined project of anthropology as a discipline – the link between colonial power and the colonized spectacle, as Talal Asad's edited volume, *Anthropology and the Colonial Encounter* (1973), had demonstrated in the early 1970s.[8] This seminal work is so crucial that we should consider it carefully:

> The story of anthropology and colonialism is part of a larger narrative which has a rich array of characters and situations but a simple plot. When Europe conquered and ruled the world, its inhabitants went out to engage with innumerable peoples and places. European merchants, soldiers, missionaries, settlers, and administrators – together with men of power who stayed at home – they helped transform their non-European subjects, with varying degrees of violence, in a 'modern'

8. See Talal Asad, *Anthropology and the Colonial Encounter* (New York: Prometheus Books, 1995) for the earliest critic of anthropology in this respect.

direction. ... [The story] tells of European imperial dominance not as a temporary repression of subject populations but as an irrevocable process of transmutation, in which old desires and ways of life were destroyed and new ones took their place. ... It was in this world that anthropology emerged and developed as an academic discipline. Concerned at first to help classify non-European humanity in ways that would be consistent with Europe's story of triumph as 'progress', anthropologists then went out from Europe to the colonies in order to observe and describe the particularity of non-European communities, attending to their 'traditional' cultural forms or their subjection to 'modern' social change. There is nothing startling today in the suggestion that anthropological knowledge was part of the expansion of Europe's power, although there is a general consensus that the detailed implications of this bald statement need to be spelled out. ... If the role of anthropology for colonialism was relatively unimportant, the reverse proposition does not hold. The process of European global power has been central to the anthropological task of recording and analyzing the ways of life of subject populations, even when a serious consideration of that power was theoretically excluded. It is not merely that anthropological fieldwork was facilitated by European colonial power (although this well-known point deserves to be thought about in other than moralistic terms); it is that the fact of European power, as discourse and practice, was always part of the reality anthropologists sought to understand, and of the way they sought to understand it.[9]

The 'transformation' of which Talal Asad speaks is the fundamental act of subjection by which non-Europeans were made into the simulacra of 'human beings.' In other words, they were made 'human' as, and only as, objects of anthropological investigation and subjects of colonial domination at one and the same time. It is thus not just 'old desires and ways of life [that] were destroyed and new ones took their place.' The whole 'world,' and consciousness of that 'world,' in which these desires and ways of life were located, was erased from the map of the earth. Whether or not this process is 'irreversible' remains to be seen – it is a point of contention whether this colonial erasure of history, identity,

---

9. Talal Asad, 'Afterword: From the History of Colonial Anthropology to the Anthropology of Western Hegemony,' in George Stocking (ed.), *Colonial Situations: Essays on the Contextualization of Ethnographic Knowledge* (Wisconsin MN: University of Wisconsin Press, 1993).

and above all worldliness can undergo reversal, the retrieval of lost worlds. 'It was in this world,' Asad rightly observes (and by which he means the colonial world, the world that had written itself over and against other worlds that it had conquered), 'that anthropology emerged and developed as an academic discipline.' Anthropology's 'classification' of the non-European world was the invention of the non-European world – which was both pre-modern Europe and the entirety of the colonized planet. The world that anthropology invented, and continues to invent around the globe, not least by the endeavors of a new generation of native anthropologists, it invented by way of the world of the white an-thropologist's domination of it. It is crucial to keep in mind that it was not the case that anthropology just 'classified' an existing world. Anthropologists invented a world, by way of eradicating all that resisted the colonial map, that would, by virtue of that invention, yield and submit to that map. In a moment of generosity Asad suggests that, 'if the role of anthropology for colonialism was relatively unimportant, the reverse proposition does not hold.' The point, however, is not just the symbiotic relationship between anthropology and colonialism. Crucial for us today, as we leave behind the phenomenon of 'postcoloniality,' is the central role of anthropology in wiping out the existing, resisting, non-European worlds precisely at the time that it moves to 'study' them. An-thropology, in other words, was as instrumental in the European colonial conquest of multiple worlds as the soldier who carried the gun. The anthropologist's pen was, and remains, mightier than the colonial officer's sword.

It was soon after Talal Asad's anthropological investigation into the manufacturing of the ethnographic others of the colonial project that Edward Said in *Orientalism* (1978) investigated the mimetic manner of representation of the Orient in literary and po-litical terms. 'The Orient' – from Talal Asad to Edward Said – was and remains, above all, a geographical designation, posited against the Occident, from its ancient, through medieval, and down to its modern usages. The geographical designation was then imbued with an imaginative universe that juxtaposed it against its alterity in the form that now called itself 'the West.' From geographical designations, 'the East and the West' conceptually transmuted to opposing moral universes – a development that reveals the strange fact that 'the Orient' was a non-space, the absence of a space, the vacated space, like a phantom fissure, something that seems to have a reality but does not: an irreality.

Edward Said later supported Talal Asad's critique of anthropology even more directly in his seminal essay 'Representing the Colonized: Anthropology's Interlocutors (1989).[10] By the late 1990s it was quite evident that as a colonially mitigated discipline of anthropology was always the anthropology of other people, which fact eventually resulted in a magnificent essay, 'The Stakes of an Anthropology of the United States' (2007), by Nicholas de Genova, a renegade anthropologist, who observed:

> At the outset, in the face of this astounding and glaring (yet seemingly taken-for-granted) absence, we must frankly recognize that there is plainly no guarantee that such an endeavor – an anthropology of the United States (even a 'critical' one, as I have suggested) – may be presumed to be a viable proposition.[11]

The principal function of this discipline was now revealed to be not just the manufacturing of a world for the anthropologist to know and make known to the unfolding colonial projects, but the preempting of the possibility of turning the anthropological gaze towards the home front. What anthropology prevented, *ipso facto*, was the watching of the watchers;[12] for if that gaze were to be cast, the whole *raison d'être* of anthropology, just like the pointed gun of the colonialists, would have been turned around, and the anthropologist-cum-colonialist would have been shot – just as if the very first anthropologist to 'study' cannibalism were to be properly seasoned, marinated, and consumed.

---

10. See Edward Said 'Representing the Colonized: Anthropology's Interlocutors,' *Critical Inquiry* 15, no. 2 (Winter 1989): 205-25.

11. See Nicholas De Genova, 'The Stakes of an Anthropology of the United States,' *CR: The New Centennial Review* 7, no. 2 (Fall 2007): 231-77.

12. I examine the impossibility of this reversed gaze, particularly in the case of 'Third World Art,' in Hamid Dabashi, 'Quis custodiet ipsos custodes: Who Watches the Watchers?' *Middle East Journal of Culture and Communication* 1 (2008): 24-9.

What we are witnessing unfold in the Arab Spring is an epistemic emancipation from an old, domineering, dehumanizing, and subjugating geography – the geography that anthropologists have mapped out for colonialists to rule. By reclaiming a global public sphere and restoring historical agency, the world is finally discovered to be a planet, not a metaphysical bipolarity along an East-West axis. But that discovery is always delayed by the power of the old geography that refuses to let go of its habits.

From the founding moment of anthropology as a discipline to the appearance of Thomas Friedman, we have witnessed the disciplinary constitution of savagery and primitivism, all in search of some *tabula rasa* of humanity with a fictive Modern White European Man as its teleological destiny. The project is ultimately Hegelian, with Hegel and Napoleon as the foretold destiny of history. This Hegelian conception of history casts pre-modern world history and non-European world geography as the two simultaneous antecedents of the Reason and Progress that have come together to manufacture the idea of 'Europe' as the final destination of History: the same History that Hegel inaugurated in Europe in 1806 (when Napoleon won the Battle of Jena–Auerstedt and Hegel thought he saw 'World-Spirit on horseback') and Fukuyama declared ended in Washington in 1989 (when George H.W. Bush declared a New World Order). The phenomenon of colonialism and, indeed, the condition of coloniality are both the blind spot and the Achilles heel of this conception of history, on the basis of which not only the discipline of history but also the entire gamut of social sciences and humanities is predicated. On this spectrum anthropology is something you do to others and sociology something that you do for yourself. The discipline of sociology, from Auguste Comte (1798–1857) onward, doesn't just study European society; it invents it, by way of distancing its *Geselleschaft* (society) from the *Gemeinschaft* (community) of both the pre-modern world and the non-European universe. That universe is not granted the status of a society. It is either the mechanical solidarity of *Gemeinschaft* in anticipation of the organic solidarity of European *Geselleschaft*, or else the primitive *anthropos* of 'Western' anthropology.

Europe might indeed be, as Fanon famously said, the creation of the Third World. But this was after Europe had already invented the Third World: and never were the twain to meet.

Alternative Maps of the World

My proposition that the commencement of the Arab Spring is the inaugural moment of not just a new historical but, more importantly, a new emancipatory geographical imagination doesn't come out of nowhere. There have always been multiple worlds. Contrary to the world-destructive projects of anthropology and Orientalism, there have always existed alternative modes of rethinking the world in differential geographies. José Martí (1853-1895), for example, in his essay 'Our America' (1892), posited the existence of a world entirely different from 'the Western hemisphere' under the imperial hegemony of the United States, and by extension 'the West.' Fighting against Spanish imperialism, Martí knew very well that the next imperial force would be American hegemony and thus the positing of a different conception of 'our America.' Another example is the distinguished Spanish historian Américo Castro (1885-1972), who in *The Spaniards: An Introduction to Their History* (*España en su Historia*) (1948) took his homeland outside the framework of 'Europe' and argued for an entirely different worldly context in which Islam and Judaism would be as critical as Christianity. He sought to demonstrate that the history and culture of the Iberian peninsula are not entirely assimilable to the idea of 'Europe.' The formation of three commingling traditions – Islamic, Christian, and Jewish – had from the ninth century on given Spain a unique character. The formation of the idea of the Spaniard was achieved at the cost of great epistemic violence to those three formative forces. Castro sought to replace the myth of European Spain with a more faithful and nuanced conception of Spain in and of itself. There are numerous instances further back in time. For example, Ibn Khaldun (1332-1406), who in his *Prolegomena* (*Muqaddimah*) posited the Mediterranean basin as a universal basin of civilization. Another is Alberuni (973-1048), who in his *India* developed a vision of a world in which Islam, the

Greek heritage, and Hindu culture had posited a world-historic context of the Ghaznavid Empire. Contemporary instances include Étienne Balibar's *We, the People of Europe? Reflections on Transnational Citizenship* (2003), and Seyla Benhabib's *Another Cosmopolitanism* (2008), both of which conceive of alternative ways of mapping the world.

The urgency of the need to see these and other alternative maps can scarcely be exaggerated. The constitution of the *ethnos* as the defining moment of nations, climes, and cultures has hitherto cast the world into opposing ideologies, the most catastrophic European expression of which was the Jewish Holocaust, the most recent translation into terror in the colonial context the Rwandan genocide of 1994. In the emerging worldliness of the world, stripped of its inherited illusions, the primacy of *ethnos* in defining ethnic nationalism and thus dividing the world will be replaced by the *ethos* of a collective awareness of the fragility of the globe.

Extensive labor migrations around the globe will be the defining moment of this new geography – for all geographical boundaries are forced open by economic necessity. The prospect of a black Europe is what in part kept tyrants like Muammar Gaddafi in power (his son Saif al-Islam warned Europe that Africans would be in Lampedusa if he and his father were to leave office). These continental shifts have been in the making, at an accelerating rate, for over half a century, conditioned by the circularity of labor and capital chasing after each other. And this mass migration has further consequences. In Europe Islamophobia is the most immediate manifestation of the xenophobia that accompanies any period of mass labor migration.

The pressing need for *ethos* to overcome *ethnos* is underlined by recent and pending environmental catastrophes from the Gulf of Mexico to the Sea of Japan, involving incalculable global consequences. Highly radioactive water from earthquake-damaged nuclear reactors has been draining into the Pacific Ocean; contaminated clouds have been detected from China to the West Coast of the United States. The nuclear chain reaction and terrifying environmental consequences know no ethnic boundaries, and thinking through critically how to counter this catastrophic course of events is an ethical not an ethnic problem. Hence the migration of labor and environmental catastrophe are the two dominant factors that will alter the current geography of despair (the West pitted against the Rest) we inhabit and shape the moral map we will face. The very idea of an 'Arab' Spring will have to be thought through as the conduit for the underlying forces facing humanity at large.

A geography of liberation begins with people's struggles for bread and dignity and builds from there the moral map of their worldly whereabouts to wrap around a fragile planet. On this map there is no East or West, South or North, invested with ideological racialization, one against the other. When a word/world ('the West') is exclusively invested with Reason and Progress, intermittent moments of its madness and banality shatter it to nullity and divest it of any hope of salvation. Both ethnography and ethnography museums exist within a structure whereby the European observes and non-Europeans are observed. This posits the idea of Europe as not just outside history but, even more pointedly, outside geography. On this ethnographic map of the world Europe is the *terra incognita*, the transparent appearance – an illusion that neither sees itself nor can be seen, observed, subjected to ethnography, archived or catalogued in any museum. By denying 'non-Europe' to Europe, by stealing from 'the Western' 'the Eastern' mirror in which it has seen itself, the emerging worlds in fact restore Europe to itself, to its own materiality, so that it too can escape from the museum, as curator if not as curated – hence both curator and curated are released to return to the world, or rather to embrace the emerging worlds.

The East and the West, the Orient and the Occident, have been each other's doppelgänger for over two centuries now, since the invention of 'the West' – short for 'Western civilization' – in the aftermath of the French Revolution of 1789, which would gradually replace 'Christendom,' the categorical context of European dynasties since the Fall of Rome in 476 CE. The invention of 'the West' and all its civilizational others (Indian, Islamic, Chinese, etc.) by platoons of Orientalists dispatched around the globe was so categorically successful that they were projected back into history, into pre-eternity, to make 'the West' the measure of truth and the moral center of the universe. 'The West' in fact cast itself as the geographical simulacrum of a hidden Christianity that (in disguise) wanted to bless the world and save it for Jesus Christ's Second Coming. The invention of 'the West' as the normative simulacrum of Christianity was coterminous with the colonial conquest of the world. From the Portuguese conquest of Ceuta in 1415 to Napoleon's conquest of Egypt in 1798, to the French invasion of Algeria in 1830, to the British takeover of the East India Company in 1858, the European colonization of the Americas, Asia, and subsequently Africa is coterminous with the systematic and eventual manufacturing of 'the West' as the *locus classicus* of a self-asserting world that has eclipsed all others that it has conquered. Today, the release of those worlds from the bonds of a closed-circuit history doesn't just liberate them from the last dinosaur regimes that are ruling them, but, more importantly, will liberate them from a trapped geography of despair, permanently cast on the Eastern shadows of a sun that had oddly decided to rise from the West. The new sun will rise neither from the East nor from the West, neither from the South nor from the North – nor, *a fortiori*, will it opt to go morally and imaginatively bankrupt and see the world as flat. The new sun, seeing the magnificent globality of planet earth, will stand still as it really is, hovering by the magnetic force field of the universe. It neither rises nor sets. It just stays there, watching and marveling at a fragile but regenerative earth that keeps spinning around itself, as its inhabitants imagine their own otherwise than being coming out of its mountains and valleys, rivers and oceans, lakes and ever more promising landscapes. On that new landscape, having now dawned, Barack Obama cannot but see the fate of impoverished and tyrannized children around the globe to be identical with that of his own.

THREE

A New Language of Revolt

To what extent is the notion of 'revolution' appropriate in reading the current uprisings in the Arab world – and do these revolutions perhaps posit and purpose a new language for reading them that accords to them the primacy of authoring their own meaning?

Hannah Arendt's *On Revolution* (1963) – a comparative study of the American (1776) and the French (1789) revolutions – is usually read and interpreted as a critical rebuttal of Marxist thinking on revolution by way of pitting what she believed to be the success of the American Revolution against the failure of the French Revolution. Arendt's criticism of the French Revolution is that the economic plight of the French masses distracted the revolutionaries from the more pertinent (to Arendt) legal stability and political purpose of the revolution. Those economic needs, she thought, were in fact regenerative and insatiable and thus derailed the revolutionary course from its political purpose, the opening of the public space for a wider, more effective, more inclusive, participation of citizens. Arendt (1906-1975) was not that sanguine about American Revolution either. She thought that it had stayed the course of constitutional guarantees of political rights but that it had become so ossified that the majority of Americans did not in fact participate in the political process.

Arendt's primary concern was to posit the political possibility of maximum public participation, minus the chaotic anarchy that she associated with socialist revolutions – revolutions that thought of themselves as recommencing the advent of history. Arendt argued that the modern conception of revolution as 'the course of history suddenly begins anew' was entirely unknown before the French and American revolutions. Instead, she made a crucial distinction, in her reading of revolution, between liberty and freedom. *Liberty* she defined as freedom from unjustified restraint, *freedom* as the ability to participate in public affairs, a purposeful expansion of the public space for political participation. Using the French and the American revolutions as her model, she proposed that initially revolutions had a restorative force to them but that in the course of events something of an epistemic violence occurs in the revolutionary uprising.[1] It was in the aftermath of the French Revolution in particular, she thought, that the very idea of 'revolution' assumed its radical, contemporary, and enduring, disposition. It was wrong for the French revolutionaries to forget, she thought, that their task was merely to liberate people from oppression so that they could find freedom, and not to address the unending (as she saw it) economic scarcity and poverty. It was futile and even dangerous for the revolutionaries to imagine they could find a political solution to economic deprivation. The advantage of the American Revolution, she believed, was that it left the economic issues at the door of the constitutional assembly. In a chapter titled 'Constitution Libertatis' she praises American revolutionaries for their consensus view that the principal aim of the revolution was the constitution of freedom and the foundation of a republic.

In what is a determined rush to offer an anti-Marxist reading of revolution, much of what Arendt says remains valid, even salient, as we look at the unfolding of the Arab Spring. The binary that she posits – on the one side, constitutional guarantees of civil liberties, liberation from tyranny, freedom to participate in the political practices of the nation; on the other side, endemic, enduring, even regenerative economic factors – does not preclude

---

1. Hannah Arendt, *On Revolution* (London: Penguin, 1990): 28-9, 29-30, 43.

one side from the other, if we historicize the two revolutions that Arendt compared. The French Revolution took a turn towards 'the social question' not because the revolutionaries so willed it, but because the congested class conflict was quite intense and organic to the revolutionary uprisings, and the working class had a say in the matter. In the American Revolution that 'social question' was not yet organic to the revolutionary uprisings; the vast spatial expanse, the absence of a self-conscious laboring class, and the disenfranchisement of slaves from the public domain prevented full participation in the revolution. Thus it was basically a fraternity of learned men who met and drafted a legal document to define their independence from a colonial power and govern their common destiny from that moment on. These were two entirely different contexts: the one old European, the other new American. The French Revolution had no option but to address the class ('social') issue; while the American Revolution had the luxury of sidestepping it. The post-Holocaust, post-Hiroshima context of 'revolution' is equally crucial, and anxiety is written all over Arendt's seminal study. Today, as we witness the unfolding of the Arab Spring, an entirely different economic situation pertains, one in which the ravages of neoliberal economics, unfettered greed, and an irresponsible orgy of deregulation have suddenly made Keynesian economics a plausible strategy for survival, albeit only in the short term.

Today, with the class struggle seen in the French Revolution a global phenomenon, the masses involved in the Arab revolts are right to demand that their economic plight be addressed, being as they are at the receiving end of the ravages of a militantly globalizing neoliberalism. Leading Arab intellectuals are warning that US imperial domination will either help beleaguered Arab leaders suppress the uprisings or else will 'support' the Arab Spring in order to keep Arab nations in line with the priorities of neoliberal economics. 'There is an increasing understanding among US policy makers,' Joseph Massad has warned, 'that the US should ride the democratic wave in the region in those countries where it cannot crush it, and that in doing so, it should create political conditions that would maintain the continued imperial pillage of their

economies at the same rate as before and not threaten them.' He
further elaborates:

> Saudi money followed by American money and IMF and World Bank
> plans and funds are all geared to supporting the business elites and
> the foreign-funded NGOs to bring down the newly mobilized civil
> society by using the same neoliberal language of structural adjustment
> pushed by the IMF since the late 1970s. Indeed, Obama and his business
> associates are now claiming that it is the imposition of more neoliberal
> economic policies that is the main revolutionary demand of the people
> in Egypt and Tunisia, if not the entire Arab world, and which the West
> is lovingly heeding. That it is these same imperial policies, which were
> imposed on Poland by the IMF (and produced Solidarnosc in 1980), and
> ultimately led to the fall of the Soviet Union, as they marched onwards
> to impoverish the entire globe, with special attention to Africa, the
> Arab World, and Latin America, is glossed over as socialist whining.
> In this sense, the US will ensure that the same imperial economic
> policies imposed by international capital and adopted by Mubarak and
> Ben Ali will not only be maintained, but will be intensified under the
> cover of democracy.[2]

Whether or not globalized neoliberalism will actually be able
to implement these policies very much depends on the revolutionary vigilance of the Arab Spring. Economic and political matters go hand in hand, and without civil liberties there cannot
be independent labor unions, women's rights organizations, or
student assemblies. These in turn require – and will have to
demand and exact – freedom of expression, freedom of the press,
and freedom of peaceful assembly, all of which are needed not
just to guarantee civil liberties but, through those liberties, to
form voluntary associations to protect the otherwise atomized
individual from totalitarianism, as well as the most vulnerable,
namely the working class, against the wanton disregard practised
by neoliberal predatory capitalism. All such considerations can be
assembled within the expansion of the public space, systematic
and regular political participation, as proposed by Arendt, as
indeed we witnessed in Egypt when Egyptians returned to Tahrir

---

2. Joseph Massad, 'Under the Cover of Democracy,' Al Jazeera, 8 June 2011, http://
english.aljazeera.net/indepth/opinion/2011/06/2011689456174295.html.

Square in their millions in mid-July 2011 after the success of their revolution in mid-February. So we can transcend Arendt's binary by advancing her still perfectly pertinent insights not by pitting the French against the American revolution, but in fact by combining them.

An Open-ended Revolt

My reading of the Arab Spring offers the idea of an 'open-ended' revolt as a way of coming to terms with the dynamics of these unfolding dramatic events – reading them more as a novel than an epic. No national hero such as Jawaharlal Nehru, Gamal Abd al-Nasser, or Mohammad Mosaddegh will emerge from these revolutions – and how fortunate that is, for it was precisely in the shadow of those heroes that tyrants like Muammar Gaddafi, Hafiz al-Assad, and Ayatollah Khomeini grew. To see the events as an open-ended course of revolutionary uprisings, we need to decipher the new revolutionary language – concepts, ideas, aspirations, imagination – with which people talk about their revolutions, so that events are not assimilated retrogressively to the false assumptions of Islamism, nationalism, or socialism, or even, conversely, translated into the tired old clichés of Orientalism, as we have understood these to date. The task we face is to recognize the inaugural moment of these revolutionary uprisings and thus be able to read them in the language that they exude and not in the vocabularies we have inherited. Even the sacrosanct idea of 'democracy' now needs to be rethought, and if need be reinvented. No justification is required for such reconsideration. The world has many democracies, but both within and outside those de-mocracies misery abounds – and the fragile peace and prosperity enjoyed by some living within these democracies is very much contingent on conditions that entail and indeed sustain others' misery. So, suppose what follows in Tunisia or Egypt is indeed 'democracy' as we know it in North America or Western Europe, and yet unfathomable poverty and destitution prevail, what use is that 'democracy' to the massed millions of impoverished people? Consider India: what does the word 'democracy' mean in a country where 800 million human beings live on less than 30 cents a day?[3] As a term or even an ideal, 'democracy' should not be fetishized. It is a political medium for instituting a larger public good, which cannot, by definition, exclude economic justice. Even Adam Smith, the grandfather of capitalism, asked poignantly in his *Wealth of Nations* (1776):

> Is this improvement in the circumstances of the lower ranks of the people to be regarded as an advantage or as an inconvenience to the society? The answer seems at first sight abundantly plain. Servants, laborers, and workmen of different kinds, make up the far greater part of every great political society. But what improves the circumstances of the greater part can never be regarded as an inconvenience to the whole. No society can surely be flourishing and happy, of which the far greater part of the members are poor and miserable. It is but equity, besides, that they who feed, clothe, and lodge the whole body of the people, should have such a share of the produce of their own labor as to be themselves tolerably well fed, clothed, and lodged.[4]

Democracy can only be meaningful in these open-ended revolts if *the political* is used and expanded as the bedrock of people's *public good*, which must include their economic well-being.[5] That requires the discovery and cultivation of a new language, a language that is already spoken at Tahrir Square for the Arab Spring, a language that transcends our inherited anxieties, fears and furies. In learning how to hear and speak that language we need to learn how to change our interlocutor too. The open-ended disposition of these revolutionary uprisings amounts to laying claim to the emerging public space in a language that both speaks to it and at once abandons dead interlocutors.

---

3. For more details, see Arundhati Roy on this conference panel: www.youtube.com/watch?v=XFlQpNRmjEU&feature=share.

4. Adam Smith, *The Wealth of Nations* (1776): Book I, ch. 8, 'Of the Wages of Labor'; available at: www.fordham.edu/halsall/mod/adamsmith-summary.html.

5. For a brief critique of unregulated capitalism as the Arab Spring was unfolding, see Joseph Stiglitz, 'The Evils of Unregulated Capitalism,' Al Jazeera, 10 July 2011, http://english.aljazeera.net/indepth/opinion/2011/07/20117714241429793.html.

Neo-Orientalism?

In 'Orientalizing Egyptian Uprising' (2011), an essay written for the online magazine *Jadaliyya* (which is run collectively by leading Arab academics and intellectuals), Rabab El-Mahdi, a political scientist at the American University in Cairo, provided a sustained critique of the way the Egyptian revolution was being depicted in the media, both 'international and local.'[6] El-Mahdi's contention is that the old-fashioned Orientalist trope of 'Arab exceptionalism' (Arabs are not capable of democracy) has been replaced by the equally Orientalist trope of 'Arab Awakening.' This trope, she suggests, is marked by '(1) "othering" – "they" (Arabs or Muslims) are different from "us" (Western, specifically European) who are the normative standard; and (2) romanticization and exoticization – this oriental "other" is mystical and mythical.' She does not spare leading Arab and Muslim intellectuals from criticism: 'as Edward Said explained years ago, Orientalism is not only confined to "Western" depictions of the Middle East ... but it is also internalized and propagated by "local" elites.' El-Mahdi's critique, which received a wide range of reactions from other commentators on *Jadaliyya*,[7] was essentially targeted at the erasure of the class factor in readings of the Egyptian uprising:

> In the case of Egypt, the recent uprising is constructed as a youth, non-violent revolution in which social media (especially facebook and twitter) are champions. The underlying message here is that it these 'middle-class' educated youth (read: modern) are not 'terrorists,' they hold the same values as 'us' (the democratic West), and finally use the same tools (facebook and twitter) that 'we' invented and use in our daily-lives. They are just like 'us' and hence they deserve celebration.[8]

This assessment is flawed, El-Mahdi believes, because,

---

6. See Rabab El-Mahdi, 'Orientalizing Egyptian Uprising,' *Jadaliyya*, 11 April 2011, www.jadaliyya.com/pages/index/1214/orientalising-the-egyptian-uprising.

7. See, for example, Agnes Czajka, 'Orientalizing the Egyptian Uprising, Take Two: A Response to Rabab el-Mahdi and Her Interlocutors,' *Jadaliyya*, 1 July 2011, www.jadaliyya.com/pages/index/2016/orientalising-the-egyptian-uprising-take-two_a-res.

8. El-Mahdi, 'Orientalizing Egyptian Uprising.'

while many of these individuals did take part in the uprising – in different capacities – their status icons of the 'revolution' in when the majority of the Egyptian population and those who participated in the uprising are of the subaltern classes is both disturbing and telling. This majority of people have never heard of Dr. Sharp or Freedom House,⁹ have never studied at AUC, or worked for Google. More profoundly, they are antagonistic about 'Western' influence and presence in Egypt. Thus the class composition of dissent has been cloaked by a new imaginary homogenous construct called 'youth.'

It is in this context that the non-violent aspect of the uprising and its use of social media are being underlined. But, she points out:

There is no doubt that the anti-regime demonstrations were non-violent compared to the state-security use of ammunition. However, by the 28th of January all NDP (National Democratic Party) headquarters and most police stations were set on fire. This was a clear reaction to the state's systematic violence against subaltern classes, those who bore the brunt of the regime's daily torture and humiliation precisely because of their position within the neoliberal class matrix in Egypt. Unlike, the middle-class 'facebook' youth, they were not immune to state violence outside the realm of political activism. The exclusion of this part of the story further benefits the narrations of this uprising as a 'facebook' middle-class 'revolution.'

El-Mahdi's indictment is categorical:

The active agents of this narration are not only the media and politi-cians, but academics and international donors' funding agencies. ... Unfortunately, these different parties have the financial, moral, and political power for such narration to prevail. Once again we are witness-ing the 'empire' painting the picture of the 'fringe' and within this fringe the subaltern – 'the fringe of the fringe' – are being outcast.[10]

El-Mahdi's essay and the range of responses that it gener-ated point to, among other things, the issue of language and

---

9. Gene Sharp is an American political scientist specializing in non-violent move-ments. Freedom House is a Washington-based think-tank advocating freedom and democracy around the world as a tool of American neoconservative ideology.

10. Between July 2010 and January 2011, Rabab el-Mahdi was a fellow of the Open Society Foundation in New York. See: www.soros.org/initiatives/fellowship/fellows/rabab-elmahdi-2010.

representation in our reading of the Tunisian, Egyptian and, by extension, other sites of Arab uprising. Are we really still at the mercy of Orientalists and the Orientalist tropes that distort the reality of our lived experience? Are we crippled, we Arabs, Iranians, Turks, South Asians, Africans, Latin Americans – we 'Orientals,' as it were? Can we not talk, write, act, play, dance, sing, revolt – can we not, do we not, represent ourselves? Whence comes this unexamined power attributed to this fictive 'West' that can still misrepresent us and distort our realities? Orientalist tropes may indeed underline the racialized categories that mark 'the Arab Spring' or the 'Arab Awakening' – and Rabab El-Mahdi certainly has a legitimate point to make about the under-representation, misrepresentation, or indeed non-representation of what she calls 'the subaltern' in the way the Egyptian uprising is globally conceived. But, at the same time, the generic reaction to 'Orientalism,' especially Edward Said's critique of it, has now become a cliché in itself.[11] If we are to decipher the new revolutionary aspirations that inform the way people (Egyptians and others) talk about their uprising, we must abandon thinking and writing in terms that are the reactive to the clichés of Orientalism, as we have understood them over the last half a century and more. With 'the West' – as an idea, a colonial construct coterminous with 'the Orient' – having now imploded, there is no 'Occident' left to 'Orientalize' anything, no 'West' to manufacture any 'East'; though it seems to persist in the critical imagination of those still rightly worried about possible imperial intervention of one sort or another. The current condition of amorphous capital and the more amorphous imperialism contingent upon it (even if we remain within Hardt and Negri's parameters) no longer works with or reproduces nineteenth- or even twentieth-century modes of Orientalist knowledge. There is no 'West' (there never really was, of course) to Orientalize anything or anybody. That binary, false and falsifying from its very inception, has epistemically

---

11. For an articulation of the stages of Orientalism before and after Edward Said's seminal text, and the evolving modes of knowledge production in the aftermath of the 'War on Terror,' see my *Post-Orientalism: Knowledge and Power in Time of Terror* (New Brunswick NJ: Transaction, 2008).

exhausted itself – its phantom fear cannot continue distorting and deferring the reading of the event of our world with reference to non-existent ghosts.

Who cares what 'the media' say – what does the term mean today? Globalized media must now compete with Egyptian bloggers, Syrian tweeters, Tunisians on Facebook, Yemenis on YouTube, Bahrainis writing opinion pieces for Al Jazeera. And now Arab scholars and activists have come together to create *Jadaliyya*, by far the most progressive site for information and analysis on the Arab and Muslim world. 'The mainstream media' (the figment of a tormented imagination) have no power or authority to misrepresent anything. Do Bernard Lewis or Thomas Friedman have more power to misrepresent Egyptian realities than the millions of Egyptians and other Arabs in their streets and squares, and the thousands of highly educated, bilingual, eloquent Arab intellectuals, journalists, and scholars with access to the gamut of global media. The very notion of 'Western media' is a sham. Aren't Al Jazeera and *Jadaliyya* also 'media' – are they not also 'Western media' if they are read in 'the West'? 'Western' representation no longer has the authorial power to misrepresent anything. We who are resisting power and tyranny have, by virtue of the new media and by virtue of our numbers, more agility to represent than those in power do. If phantom fears of an all-powerful Western media are not abandoned, these fears will themselves manufacture non-existent enemies. Instead of imagining such alien forces at work distorting or misrepresenting Egyptian and Arab events, we must place such events within the hermeneutics of public space that forms part of their moral and imaginative landscape – a space that in fact preceded, and indeed anticipated, the Arab Spring.[12] To come to terms with the open-ended disposition of the Arab Spring requires abandoning these unfounded anxieties and commitment to listening carefully to the new language that people are singing

---

12. Read, for example, the exquisite work of Mara Naaman, *Urban Space in Contemporary Egyptian Literature: Portraits of Cairo* (New York: Palgrave Macmillan, 2011). This urbanity will, of course, have to be read in juxtaposition with the rural landscape; for which see the excellent work of Samah Selim, *The Novel and the Rural Imaginary in Egypt, 1880–1985* (London: Routledge, 2004).

from Tahrir Square and around 'the Arab and Muslim World' – for if we listen carefully, we will soon discard that term.

Towards a Hermeneutics of Public Space

Where and when to begin? Certainly before *Thawret 25 yanayir*, Revolution of 25 January, and on the periphery of Tahrir Square.

The sudden passing of Nasr Hamid Abu Zayd reminded me, as one of his long-time admirers, of not just one but two particularly towering Egyptian paragons under whose extended shadow that part of the world was blessed and made more meaningful. In the span of two years, we had lost filmmaker Youssef Chahine (on 27 July 2008) and hermeneutician and semiotician Nasr Hamid Abu Zayd (on 5 July 2010) – as if witnessing the sequential fall of twin towers that had graced the landscape of our moral and aesthetic imagination for more than half a century, and just before the blooming of the Arab Spring.

In the Arab and the Muslim world, and globally, those who knew Youssef Chahine rarely had reason to know Nasr Hamid Abu Zayd, and many of those who had read and admired Abu Zayd's extraordinary achievements would have been hard pressed to name two of Chahine's films, or claim to have seen his *Bab al-Hadid* (1958) when they were still teenagers.

We need to see and read one with and through the lens of the other. The society that has produced Nasr Hamid Abu Zayd and Youssef Chahine at the balanced center of its judicious self-awareness ought also to be aware of how precious that balance is, where the horizon of our moral and aesthetic imagination meets the earth and rests its case. There is an Egyptian balance of hope and despair, promise and paralysis, that seems to define all of us who were born and raised in the age of Mohammad Mosaddegh, Gamal Abd al-Nasser, and Jawaharlal Nehru – the anticolonial heroes who made us 'postcolonial.' The globality of vision that made them, and that in the same vein produced Youssef Chahine and Nasr Hamid Abu Zayd, has always been at the mercy of the fanaticism and brutality that have paradoxically emerged from the very same fountainhead that gives rise to our innermost hopes and aspirations. Sayyid Qutb and Ayatollah Khomeini misinterpreted our dreams and thoughts and delivered them as nightmares. Much is said, and rightly so, of the 'youthful disposition' of the Arab Spring; nevertheless the enduring wisdoms dwelling in the eye and the mind of Chahine and of Abu Zayd will demand fresh readings for a long time to come.

I first met Nasr Hamid Abu Zayd at a reception held for him by Edward and Mariam Said in New York; I had read him much earlier, in my graduate student years at Penn, having been introduced to his groundbreaking work on Qur'anic hermeneutics in the mid 1980s by my teacher George Makdisi (1920–2002). At the time very few people knew of Nasr Hamid's *Al-Ittijah Al-'Aqli fi al-Tafsir: Dirasa fi Qadiyat al-Majaz fi 'l-Qur'an ind al-Mu'tazila* (1982) or even his *Falsafat al-Ta'wil: Dirasa fi Ta'wil al-Qur'an ind Muhi al-Din ibn 'Arabi* (1983). Years later, when working on my book on Ayn al-Qudat, I discovered his *Mafhum al-Nass: Dirasa fi 'Ulum al-Qur'an* (1991) and *Naqd al-Khitab al-Dini* (1998). My late colleague Magda al-Nowaihi later introduced me to Nasr Hamid's *Al-Mar'a fi Khitba al-Azma* (1995) and *Dawa'ir al-Khawf: Qira'a fi Khitab al-Mar'a* (1999). Evident in all these texts was Nasr Hamid's relentless quest for a hermeneutics of the sacred embedded in the human language of the mundane. He never lost sight of their invisible interrelations. My favorite among Nasr Hamid's work, however, has remained his *al-Tafkir fi Zaman al-Takfir* (1998), a reflection on his condition of exile and apostasy written in the aftermath of the infamous incident when, following his request for academic promotion in March 1993, an Egyptian sharia court declared him an apostate from Islam and annulled his marriage, forcing him and his wife, Ibtihal Younis (Professor of French Literature at Cairo University), into exile in the Netherlands, where an extremist Islamist group subsequently issued a death sentence on him. This was during one of the darkest chapters in modern Egyptian history, when the killing in 1992 of Farag Foda and the attempted murder in 1994 of the Nobel prizewinning author Naguib Mahfouz had created an exceedingly tense environment in Egypt. Despite the banal horror of the death sentence pronounced on Nasr Hamid, there was always a delightful sense of humor evident in his reflections on the whole atrocious incident. He loved to tell stories about the cartoons that appeared in Egyptian periodicals in which husbands used him as a metaphor, wondering how they could arrange for a similar annulment of their marriage! When an Egyptian columnist mocked the couple for 'carrying on like Romeo and Juliet' because they had held hands during an interview with CNN, Nasr Hamid had quipped 'and what is wrong with Romeo and Juliet?' Equally important is that Nasr Hamid never allowed the sentence issued against him by fellow Egyptians to be abused by the European or America media as a weapon in their Islamophobic arsenal, and thereby use it – as have others, such as Salman Rushdie and Ayaan Hirsi Ali – to promote his own career. He endured the hardship of exile and life under a death sentence with grace and humility, remaining to his dying day a principled and dignified Muslim.

If my introduction to Nasr Hamid Abu Zayd was academic and it took me a while to get to know the warm and joyous man behind the ideas, my introduction to Youssef Chahine was playful and sparkled with the joy of discovery, and culminated in my teaching the full range of his cinematic work to my students at Columbia, to which classes I invited the great maestro to give lectures every time he came to New York. He always joked that my interest in his films had to do with my juvenile infatuation with Hind Rustom (the Sophia Loren of Arab cinema), the lead actress of his *Bab al-Hadid*. I saw Chahine's *Bab al-Hadid* (1958) in my late teens, while his adaptation of Abdel Rahman Al-Sharqawi's *Al-Ard* (1969) was instrumental in the political education of many in my generation. With his initial trilogy and subsequent quartet, Chahine became globally celebrated as the flamboyant autobiographer of his nation. From *Al Nasser Salah Ad-Din* (1963) to *Al-Massir* (1997), Chahine steadfastly held a mirror to his people, from the trauma of the Arab–Israeli wars to the horrors of religious fanaticism in his homeland – the same fanaticism that had forced Abu Zayd into exile.

Youssef Chahine and Nasr Hamid Abu Zayd are two complementary components of twentieth-century Egyptian intellectual and artistic cosmopolitanism; to know one fully is to know the other, and through them one understands the creative effervescence they both heralded. Abu Zayd's hermeneutics is entirely predicated on a structural semiotics that reads the Qur'anic literary tropes as the semiosis of a narrative logic that must be interpreted via an engagement with and through the rhetoric of the Muslim reader's faith. He made of faith – and this is the singular sign of his interpretative genius – a hermeneutic proposition in his semiotic reading of the holy text. This is in fact how he accounts for the central signifier of *wahy*, 'revelation' (as the modus operandi of Qur'anic revelation), in any reading of the sacred text that renders it a literary master sign without robbing it of its metaphysical import. That very open-ended semiosis becomes, in turn, the texture of a flamboyant aesthetics, which Chahine, for his part, borrows from later Italian neorealism, and from Fellini in particular, to craft his own cinematic sense of probing frivolity. Abu Zayd teases out unsuspected meanings from the Qur'an, employing the same hermeneutic free play with which Chahine unwinds the serious knots of reality in his own version of neorealism.

The enduring significance of Nasr Hamid Abu Zayd's hermeneutics, in consequence, is his positing of the Qur'an as an infinite (implosive) play of self-sanctifying signs that internally order the sacred text as the *locus classicus* of an inner sanctum that gives its believing reader/interpreter a compelling sense of in/voluntary belief, which is at once illusory and revelatory. In other words, by seeing the sacred text as a system of signs, Abu Zayd places the location of its revelatory disposition (of the hermeneutic camera, as it were) not above but within, not in the author's intention (which in this case is beyond human reach) but in the reader's hope (which is always already historical and worldly). To be able to do that and remain a believer – as he did – is a singular sign of hermeneutic genius. Abu Zayd reads the Qur'an in a manner that is comparable to the experience of watching a Youssef Chahine film: the text as a hall of mirrors full of sacred signs waiting to reveal themselves anew – not just the unseen through the seen, but the seer through the sign. He hermeneutically, in effect, re-enacts the moment of divine revelation – from the man-prophet Muhammad to the wo/man-believer Muslim. Nasr Hamid Abu Zayd planted, as it were, a Youssef Chahine camera inside the head of every Muslim who goes to see/read the Qur'an. The brain-dead and soulless 'Muslims' in his orbit instinctively saw the magnificent danger in that vision of the Qur'an and were frightened out of their wits – hence their sentence against perhaps the greatest Muslim hermeneutician of our time.

Nasr Hamid's concerns remained steadfastly hermeneutic. He was not primarily interested in desanctifying or resanctifying the Qur'an. For him the Qur'an was a sacred text whose hermeneutic circle and the idiomatic systematicity of whose signs were both mediated through an act of blind faith on the part of the reader in it revelatory sanctity. His genius was to treat the fact of that mediation as a hermeneutic trope, rather than keep it as an article of faith. As a result, he remained consistently concerned about how meaning is generated in that hermeneutic circle, mediated as it is through faith in a revelatory text.

Youssef Chahine and Nasr Hamid Abu Zayd are the two sides of Egypt as a sign, as a symbol of intellectual effervescence, and today as a model of open-ended revolutionary uprising – its worldliness, as Edward Said would say, the commanding disposition of its claim on our moral imagination. The prismatic lens of Chahine is needed to see through and make sense of Abu Zayd's daring hermeneutic imagination, to look at the Qur'an and perceive a system of signs gathered in a text waiting to mean anew, in the compelling semiotics of his worldliness. The reverse is also true: Abu Zayd's joyous and emancipatory hermeneutic frivolity – the pleasure of his literary waltzing with the sacred text – enable us to see what lurks behind the Felliniesque playfulness of Chahine's *Alexandria Quartet*.

Abu Zayd's hermeneutics is charged with the same literary and aesthetic sensitivities that are evident in Chahine's cinema – the life-affirming recognition of translucent signs that have defied the received and repressed semiotics of power and domination that experts in Islamic law have termed 'Religion/Din.' If Chahine's exuberant light-heartedness has an occasional tendency to transmute into kitsch, indicating a blind spot in his visionary carnivalesque festivities, as in his *Al-Massir*, in Abu Zayd a similar blind spot has shaped his reception by his Iranian disciples, reducing his liberating hermeneutics to an arrested fixation on making their 'Islam' still meaningful in the bloody aftermath of an Islamic Republic. At his best in the *Alexandria Quartet*, particularly *Alexandria... Why*, Chahine, like Abu Zayd in his *Mafhum al-Nass* (1991), reaches for a pure literary hermeneutics of the Qur'an and breathes new – and, for those arrested in the infancy of their reading of the text, frightful – life into it. In his hermeneutics, Abu Zayd is ultimately a semiotician who sees the vision of a magnificent constellation in the sacred text that is otherwise hidden to 'religious intellectuals' and their fanatical Muslim counterparts in Egypt, who have pulled and pushed the Qur'an in one distorting direction or another.

There is a semiotic correspondence between the literary dis-position of Nasr Hamid Abu Zayd's hermeneutics and the vibrant levity of Youssef Chahine's cinema that is categorically lacking in the period between the violent and bloody birth of 'religious intellectuals' on the Iranian scene and the self-alienating cinema of Abbas Kiarostami or the self-destructive cinema of Mohsen Makhmalbaf. These 'religious intellectuals' were the finest product of the theocratic killing of joy in Iran; their philosophizing was correspondingly somber, deadly serious, and entirely boring and banal. So, for precisely that reason, and despite the fact that Abu Zayd was 'excommunicated' and placed under a death sentence, he was able to return to his homeland and die in dignity, loved and admired by his fellow Egyptians. Whereas his Iranian followers are now mostly in exile; if they ever dared go back to their country they would either be forced to appear on television and confess that all they have thought and written was a mistake, and then to seek a pardon from the Supreme Leader, or else they would suffer the indignity of a long prison sentence or worse – all of which would be penance for the terror they had visited upon those who thought differently to them.

The River Nile that gave birth to a nation that could produce Youssef Chahine and Nasr Hamid Abu Zayd and others who share their daring imagination is the same River Nile on whose east bank stands Tahrir Square. Chahine and Abu Zayd are no longer with us to see the dawn of a new beginning in Iran, Egypt, and the rest of the Arab and Muslim world, where one hopes to see the reflection of their compound brilliance in the fully restored cosmopolitan consciousness of a people. But in their deaths, as in their lives, Youssef Chahine and Nasr Hamid Abu Zayd continue to show us a world dancing like particles of dusty light (Rumi's metaphor) right before our eyes – signs of an infinity of possibilities to alter the metaphysics (and inform the politics) of despair that had laid a violent claim on our souls. Filmmakers like Chahine and thinkers like Abu Zayd have already visually and imaginatively expanded, in both aesthetic and hermeneutic terms, the narrative space in which we can hear these revolutions speak of their open-ended possibilities.

The World in Itself

The task at hand is to begin to produce a body of knowledge in a language worthy of those heroes chanting in Tahrir and other squares. When they were shouting 'People Demand the Overthrow of the Regime,' they did not mean just the political regime; they meant also the *régime du savoir* and the language with which we understand and criticize things. We must allow for facts and realities domestic to these rebellions to speak to a renewed set of meanings, and not assimilate things retrogressively to what we know, and what we fear, and waste time picking fights with ghosts of bygone times, with 'Orientalism.' We need to overcome the anxiety of Orientalism and shift our theorizing lens to our evolving history and stop trying to explain things to that fictive white man who sat in Edward Said's mind for a lifetime.[13] That fictive white man is dead – he was never alive. He was a chimera – manufactured by a postcolonial age that had prolonged the life of the grand illusion of 'the West' with its corresponding 'the Rest.' Instead of quoting what Edward Said said some thirty or forty

---

13. I have explained this shift in interlocutor in some detail in the last chapter of *Post-Orientalism: Knowledge and Power in Time of Terror* (New Brunswick NJ: Transaction, 2008).

years ago, in an effort to figure out what is happening now, we must instead start thinking like him: what would he have said and thought if he, and indeed other thinkers of note, were still with us. For one thing, instead of trying to explain the significance of what happened in Tahrir Square to some superior intelligence in 'the West,' whose imprimatur is necessary for events to be perceived as real or having import, we need to think horizontally: let us look to comparative works in and about Asia, Africa, and Latin America, across the Arab–Iranian divide, the Sunni-Shi'i divide, the Muslim–Christian divide, and indeed the religious–secular divide. For these are the urgent and consequential explanations and understandings that we need, being much closer to lived reality than those works committed to prolonging exhausted conceptions and parameters.

Nasr Hamid Abu Zayd and Youssef Chahine came together – two among many – to create the hermeneutics and aesthetics of a self-assertive universe, which embraced and defined Arab world realities – combining the sacred and the profane, the sublime and the frivolous. What import do outdated Orientalists and sophomoric columnists have, except to produce a chuckle, to provide entertainment? The *New York Times* is no longer the paper of record; nor can CNN or the other so-called 'Western media' pose as the voice of authority. For a long time now the fictive center of this delusional apparition has not been able to hold. What does it matter if millions of people cannot read Arabic, Persian, Turkish, or Urdu, have never heard of our hermeneuticians, semioticians, philosophers, novelists, poets, mystics or scientists? We do know them, and we have all the languages that we need to speak, and write, and sing, and cry, and argue, and demonstrate, and convince.

For some sixty years the Zionists abused the memory of the European Holocaust to steal Palestine, and they possessed a propaganda machinery unrivaled in world history – with an entire empire at their disposal. Then what? A single novel by Ghassan Kanafani, a poem by Mahmoud Darwish, a short film by Elia Suleiman, a documentary by May Masri, an essay by Edward Said, a book by Joseph Massad – and generations began to be raised armed with information, reasons, documents, proof; furthermore, the world's best, from every continent, sail freedom flotillas to Gaza, risking and losing their noble lives to expose the criminal atrocities of the Israeli apartheid state. We must stop this tiresome business of picking fights with figments of our own imagination. Arab and Muslim academics trained in North America and Western Europe are particularly susceptible to haunted memories. Our camaraderie is global (Jews, Christians, atheists, young, old, men, women, homosexuals, heterosexuals, rich, poor), and there are plenty of enemies in 'the East.' Are Ben Ali, Mubarak, and Khamenei from the West or from the East? The East is no longer the East; the West is no longer the West. They have met. The East is the West; the West is the East. We must also stop asking the outlandish question, 'Can the Subaltern Speak?' Of course s/he does; of course s/he has. The subaltern needs no representation, or theorization, or terrorization from any English and Comparative Literature department. This is the enduring lesson of Edward Said, who pushed his liberating language out of the English department, and who to his dying day remained critical of his colleagues who were mystifying people's struggles in a prose and politics that even their own colleagues could not understand, let alone those people risking their lives fighting for 'freedom, social justice, and dignity.' Take a look at the streets, alleys and squares of the Arab world, from one end to the other in 2011 and beyond: the subaltern is speaking; Arabs are speaking. They are in fact crying out loud: *al-Sha'b Yurid Isqat al-Nizam.* It is gloriously simple; let's not mystify it.

Knowledge of Unfolding Things

A paradox of reciprocity operates between unfolding events and the language we use to describe them. That paradox is hermeneutically productive in the following way. Thinking and writing about urgent contemporary issues with a view to their projected thrust requires a certain balance of precision and perspective. The balance must be judiciously predicated on some measured depth of field and yet look forward to a turning point in our vision of things – of the unseen. This is no easy task. The multivariate palimpsestic nature of the news is such that it preempts any meaningful measure of attention span. Consider the first four months of 2011, which began with a rapid succession of revolutionary uprisings in Tunisia and Egypt and then spread like wildfire to Morocco, Syria, Bahrain and Yemen. That historic unfolding was suddenly brought to a stop – the opposing forces battling in Libya, Syria, and Bahrain notwithstanding – by the British royal wedding of their majesties the Duke and Duchess of Cambridge in late April 2011. For days on end the BBC website, in particular, abandoned the Arab Spring for its celebratory attention to the royal wedding. That colorful occasion was barely over when the beatification of Pope John Paul II took the front pages, concentrating attention on the Vatican. Scarcely had attention been drawn to that momentous event when the announcement of the death of Osama bin Laden in the late hours of 1 May 2011 hit the news. By this time the unfolding revolutionary events in the Arab world had seemingly become somewhat passé.

This short attention span obviously raises the paramount question of how to speak to the urgency of the unfolding events – in what analytical syntax, in what theoretical morphology. The slackening of the newsworthiness of events for the front pages is oddly replicated by the weakening analytical frames people bring forth to read them. If we opt (as we do habitually) to provide 'historical background by area experts,' as many Middle East specialists were rushed in to do across the global media, they would inevitably assimilate these events to what they already know. 'The rule of the experts,' as Timothy Mitchell would say,[14] projects the novelty of what we see backwards into the familiarity of what we know. Here the issue is not just the way such disparate phenomena as malaria, sugar cane, war, or nationalism come together, as Mitchell shows, to produce the technopolitics of a modern state, but, even more crucially, the fact that they constitute the knowing subject that is posited by such a transversal (colonially mitigated) *regime du savoir*. Experts invest in their own familiar insights, at the cost of forfeiting, of unknowingly covering up, the oddity of the events

---

14. See Timothy Mitchell, *Rule of Experts: Egypt, Techno-Politics, Modernity* (Stanford CA: University of California Press, 2002.)

unfolding – I say *oddity* by way of noting that their thrust is yet to be theoretically assayed.

As we thus assimilate things we witness back into things we know, the unfolding events become signs without their inherent significance – their anxiety-provoking semiosis instantly alleviated and incorporated into the comfort zone of a self-assuring semiotics, so that the actual thinking we do to understand or explain events is in fact counter-thinking; it further conceals what we intend to reveal. It is a paradox in which we become agents of our own ignorance by way of appearing to produce and procure a false knowledge. This is not merely a hermeneutic paradox; it is in fact more an agential irony, for in writing backward we in effect reproduce through our own falsely knowing subject the subjects that we are, the subjects that we have been discursively (colonially) made out to be.

We may thus return to Marx's famous dictum that we need to change the world and not merely interpret it. But in this case it seems to me that changing the world that is unfolding in front of our eyes is in fact entirely contingent on counter-interpreting it, interpreting it against the grain of our own knowing subjectivity. I say 'counter-interpreting' for I believe the whole notion of *interpreting* now requires renewed consideration, not from an abstract hermeneutical perspective, but precisely from that of the coloniality in which we have been the subject of interpretation – our subjectivity constituted by our having been interpreted.

Without the active retrieval of that mood (Heidegger's *Stimmung*) of being clear of the condition of coloniality and beyond the reach of postcoloniality we will never achieve the agency of thought necessary to project what we read today towards its emancipatory trajectory tomorrow. On it also depends the realization, for example, that the US Army and its military fortress Israel remodulated themselves after (what they called) al-Qaeda, only to be outmaneuvered by the people – ordinary, unarmed, brave, defiant people – who have risen up without resort to arms and with laughter, joy, humour, and dance to make a mockery of not only the US and its allies but in fact the whole politics of despair that had engulfed them. There is a paradox of reciprocity between proactively reading reality and the factual evidence of that reality, predicated on a hermeneutics of *différance* that keeps the crescendo of an open-ended revolutionary uprising on the horizon of its linguisticality – the language that it reveals and at once speaks – so that every act of reading is an act of liberation from an entire history of post/colonial de/subjection.

The Revolting Orientals

Al-Sha'b Yurid Isqat al-Nizam, 'People Demand the Overthrow of the Regime.' Echoes of the chant, rhythmically recited by millions of people, reverberate through 'the Arab and Muslim world' – in a manner that may in fact dismantle the very regime of knowledge that calls them by that name. This is the language of revolt in the Arab world. In the making of that revolt, language is everything, for language is where worlds reside: the one in which we live, and the ones awaiting emergence that have already spoken. On language depends the fact that we have a world at all – not just any world, but the world we are trying to change. But the language of the world – and of the worlds enabled by the dominant languages such as English, French, Italian, Arabic, Chinese, or Persian, and their variants, and indeed the worlds they thus constitute and stage – does not entail the only world possible. It is only the world with a will to power, the will to dominate. The will to resist that power has many other languages, yet to be discovered, thus many other worlds to reveal. As we speak, our language is changing, against all odds. You might be distracted by a royal wedding today, by a papal beatification the next day, and by the murderous revenge of a forgotten figment of a terrorizing imagination the day after, but the language of revolt is reverberating apace – for *al-Sha'b Yurid Isqat al-Nizam*; and that *Nizam*, that regime, is not just Ben Ali's or Mubarak's or Gaddafi's or Bashar al-Assad's. It is also the language that made them familiar to us.

The language we are hearing in these revolts is neither Islamic nor anti-Islamic, neither Eastern nor Western, neither religious nor secular – it is a worldly language, emerging from the depth of people's historical experiences in the world, towards the world, a language irreducible to any familiar cliché. Having escaped from such clichés, this language is worldly-wise in its texture, which means it is other-worldly; it is imagined on a space of *différance*, of differing by deferring, and it always points to some other world, yet to come, discrediting the one we are fighting at the time. But that other world is not beyond death or disbelief; it is right here and now, staring this world in the eye, but at a spatial distance that keeps promising, keeps inviting.

How is that space evident? In a magnificent essay for *Jadaliyya*, 'The Arab Spring and Adunis's Autumn,' the Iraqi poet, novelist, filmmaker, and essayist Sinan Antoon criticizes with some passion the retrograde politics of perhaps the greatest living Arab poet, the octogenarian Syrian Adunis (b. 1930), and his failure to endorse the revolutionary uprising in the Arab world.

In this light we might consider the column Adunis has written for more than two decades for the Saudi-owned pan-Arab daily *al-Hayat*. He has never uttered a word about the horrendous practices and politics of the Saudi regime, but often rehashes the stale Orientalist notion of 'the Arab mind' and reduces the complex challenges facing the Arab world to the need for a reinterpretation of religion. Arabs, he insists, are still imprisoned in the past and the concept of the individual does not even exist in Arabo-Islamic culture, as Arabs have yet to rebel against the super tribe.[15]

Antoon's double bind is to acknowledge the great inspiration that Adunis once was for his generation of young Arab poets whilst challenging his commentary and criticism. 'When the revolution's winds uprooted dictators in Tunisia and Egypt,' Antoon points out painfully,

> the 'revolutionary' thinker found no satisfaction in what people had done. What had taken place in these places, he said, was a 'youth rebellion.' Soon after, his compatriots in Syria revolted against a ruthless dictatorial regime that had suffocated them for four decades. You might expect a poet to salute the courage of unarmed citizens standing up

---

15. See Sinan Antoon, 'The Arab Spring and Adunis's Autumn,' *Jadaliyya*, 11 July 2011, www.jadaliyya.com/pages/index/2047/the-arab-spring-and-adunis-autumn.

to the bullets of a vicious regime with nothing but their voices and consciences. But Adunis did nothing of the sort.[16]

Adunis, for Antoon, is caught in an old and tired language, the most terrible thing that can happen to (of all people) a poet. Antoon's conclusion is paradoxical but pointed:

> Perhaps there was a time when Adunis, the intellectual, represented the promise of radical and revolutionary culture, but that time has long passed. Adunis the poet, especially the early Adunis, will always be at the heart of modern Arabic poetry. His poems will be read with admiration and awe, but perhaps it's time to forget about Adunis, the cultural critic and radical intellectual. The Arab Spring has consigned Adunis, the self-proclaimed revolutionary, to irrelevance.[17]

The key factor here is timing. There was indeed a time when from the depth of a politics of despair Adunis was eloquent. But no longer – in this politics of hope. The final note struck by Antoon in this essay is even more precise: 'And that is the beauty and poetry of revolutions.'[18] Revolution, as Antoon – a poet – knows, has its own poetry. To hear the language of that poetry, to learn it, and to speak it, we will have to unlearn the language (yes, even the poetry) we speak, the subject that we are, and the agency that we have been denied in a global configuration of power in which we – as Arabs, Muslims, Orientals, Latinos, Africans – have been named and interpreted. How to think and to write about the events in a manner that transcends the very designation from which you speak is no easy task. The necessity of thinking of not just the mode but also the mood of knowledge production in what is now identified as the 'Arab and Islamic World' is the most urgent task that faces anyone who cares about the future of people who are rising unarmed against neo-imperial warmongering and postcolonial banality alike.

---

16. Ibid.
17. Ibid.
18. Ibid.

Variations on an Orientalist Theme

The colonial category 'the Arab and Muslim World' conceals much more than it reveals. The successive layers of knowledge production about these regions are embedded in the word 'Orientalism,' from the Orientalism of the fear and loathing of the Greeks against the Persians, to the Orientalism of the rivalry of the Austro-Hungarian Empire and the Ottomans, to the Orientalism of domination of the French and the British against Arabs and Indians. To come to terms with today's revolutionary uprisings, we must both historicize and transcend this history of Orientalism, not prolong it. It is within that history that we as 'Orientals' have been both posited and de/subjected as the passive objects of the Orientalists' narrating. It is the task of this generation of 'Orientals' to articulate the terms of its emancipation, this having already taken place in the streets and alleys of our homelands, and not to prolong the assumption of its endurance in the dead certainties of irrelevant and outdated narratives.

Orientalism was a particular mode of knowledge production that began long before the advent of European colonialism in it varied forms: from the Greek to the Roman era, in the medieval period, and then through a particularly dramatic growth during both the European Oriental Renaissance that Charles Schwab identified and celebrated[19] and the more recent colonial attitudes that Edward Said studied and criticized.[20] But those modes of European knowledge production ceased with the end of classical colonialism, yielding to Area Studies at the time of the Cold War and thereafter to what I have called 'disposable knowledge' and the emergence of the New World Order.[21] The Orientalist will to knowledge was a manifestation of the European colonial will to power. The will to resist that very colonial power leads to the will to counter-knowledge, which I have argued requires a narrative with a new interlocutor. Muslims, Arabs, and Iranians have created

---

19. See Raymond Schwab, *The Oriental Renaissance: Europe's Rediscovery of India and the East, 1680–1880* (New York: Columbia University Press, 1987).

20. See Edward W. Said, *Orientalism* (New York, Vintage, 1978).

21. For the details of this argument, see my *Post-Orientalism*, particularly chs 6 and 7.

as such – open-ended propositions made into colonial subjects – by virtue of the specific relations of power that thus willed them as subjects. In his classic studies of European disciplines of subjection, Michel Foucault identified the disciplinary knowledges of linguistics, economics, and biology as effective means by which 'man' as a knowing subject was made possible.[22] In the same vein, the character code-named 'the Oriental' was manufactured, as Edward Said's magisterial work demonstrates, as the object of Orientalism, as the paramount mode of knowledge production about the Oriental – a self-perpetuating tautology.

Orientalism, however, was not the only mode of knowledge production in which the Oriental was constituted. In archeology, Near East and Far East sites were excavated in search of earlier stages of human development in a linear anticipation of the European *Homo sapiens*. In history, following the Hegelian model, the ancient world – Indians, Egyptians, Persians in particular – were examined in anticipation of the European *Geist* reaching its full and final destination. In linguistics, anthropology, ethnography, and political science, 'non-Western' societies were thus cauterized and branded in anticipation of their being Westernized. In modernization theories, the Orientals were called *traditional* in need of *modernization*, aka *Westernization*. In economics, they were now placed in the 'Third World,' in the aftermath of their having been in effect abused like the raw material from which commodities were manufactured for the First World.

While Foucault only looked in the European asylums for the positing of the unreason of European reason, and thus the divisive act of positing the European subject,[23] the real site of unreason was the Orient and the Oriental – the embodiment of, not fragmented, unreason. While the European subject was posited by the polarity of reason/unreason and law-abiding/criminal, the Oriental subject was framed as the embodiment of the exotically other, the criminally insane, the sexually perverted. As for the matter of

---

22. See Michel Foucault, *The Order of Things: An Archaeology of the Human Sciences* (New York: Vintage, 1994).

23. See Michel Foucault, *Madness and Civilization: A History of Insanity in the Age of Reason* (New York: Vintage, 1994).

sexuality, the Oriental became the transgressive space of lascivious eroticism; hence 'the Oriental' space is the space of transgression, while the European (as categorically Christian) is made virtuous by inhibitions that control those transgressions, with a remissive space positing the possibilities of 'Western civilization.'

Thus, in the same vein, colonially mitigated, we have become Muslim subjects by the practice of dividing – mad and insane, sick and healthy, criminal and law-abiding, heterosexual and homosexual. This practice of dividing is performed by reason of colonial power and the audacity of its knowledge production: the colonizing power becomes civilized by virtue of the Oriental being barbarian – progressive versus backward, healthy versus sick, reasonable versus passionate, judicious and legitimate in its use of violence versus the criminally insane and terroristic. Consider George W. Bush, who in the name of saving humanity from catastrophe was forced to use violence against Afghanistan and Iraq, and compare him to Osama bin Laden, Mullah Omar, and Saddam Hussein, and now of course the proverbial 'mad mullahs,' all characterized as criminally insane and wanting to destroy the world. And whereas it is perfectly legitimate for Israel to have the A-bomb because it is civilized, white, and reasonable, Iranians cannot have it because they are barbaric, mad, and terroristic.

These divisions are not just externally imposed; they are internally assimilated and reiterated, particularly when subjected to criticism. The active and aggressive formulation of Islamic ideology – Islam as a militant creed opposed to and committed to ending European colonialism – was performed mostly by Muslim thinkers and activists themselves, rather than by Orientalists. So Orientalism and the architects of Islamist ideology (from Jamal al-Din al-Afghani to Sayyid Qutb to Ali Shari'ati) were two sides of the same coin, helping sustain and exacerbate these dividing practices defining 'Islam and the West.'[24] All the exercises in anti-colonial nation-building, resulting in Gaddafi, Mubarak, Bin Ali, Ali Khamenei, and their ilk, along with the aggressive formation

---

24. I have documented and extensively argued this argument in Hamid Dabashi *Theology of Discontent: The Ideological Foundations of the Islamic Revolution in Iran* (New Brunswick NJ: Transaction, 2005).

of pan-Arabism, pan-Iranism and pan-Turkism, are products of the divisive colonial practices whereby Muslims have sought to prove that they are actually better than 'the West.'

'The West' is the critical iconic yardstick of these practices of division. The autonormativity of 'the West,' stemming from its imperial will to power, has been instrumental even in positing reproductive heteronormativity as the modus operandi of being human. As Joseph Massad has demonstrated in his groundbreaking *Desiring Arabs* (2007), the internalization of colonial conceptions of human sexuality has been definitive of the discursive making of Arab modernity at the cost of glossing over the fluidity of sexuality in colonized societies.[25] Through the instrumentality of the touch-stone of 'the West,' governmentality is no longer a relation between the state and the individual but in fact one between the condition of coloniality and the dialogical assumption of postcoloniality. 'The West' is the mantra of coloniality as the modus operandi of de/subjection, which is both subjection and alienation at one and the same time. As people in the streets cry 'People Demand the Overthrow of the Regime,' the discursive anger against Orientalism keeps reproducing Orientalism, turning a deaf ear to the liberating thunder of that cry. Freed from that anger, the open-ended revolutions have liberated a language of emancipation.

Re/subjecting a Revolutionary Persona

The history of the formation of the modern Muslim subject is one of de/subjection, the very microcosm of the formation of the modern colonial subject, without the militant dismantling of which we as a people will never be free. The term 'modern' is critical here, for this formation is entirely the product of European colonial modernity, an event that occurred in the shadow of European Enlightenment (capitalist) modernity, or, in more accurate terms, in the aggressive transmutation of colonizing Christianity into secularism.[26]

---

25. See Joseph A. Massad, *Desiring Arabs* (Chicago: University of Chicago Press, 2007).
26. As argued persuasively by Gil Anidjar in 'Secularism,' *Critical Inquiry* 33, no. 1 (Fall 2006).

The historical process by which we have been systematically de/subjected – become Iranian, Arab, Muslim, Oriental, and so forth; all the mnemonic others of what has coded itself as 'the West' – is precisely the process that is now being reversed in the making of a transnational uprising that will leave no 'nation' unturned. The discursive, external, and internal modes of de/subjection have all happened within the world called 'the West,' the world as described by 'the West,' the world worlded and inhabited by 'the West.' It is that world that ought to be, that is, altered. These varied forms of subjection have been the modes of power relations between the colonial and the colonized, and thus *governmentality* is not something suggested between a single state and its citizens but between the colonial power as civilized and the colonized subject as barbarian. Any mode of liberation that sees that relation of power and wants to alter it from within the world in which it was posited is limited and flawed. The only way that this debilitating, self-raising, other-lowering world (called 'the West') can be overcome is by the recognition of other worlds – that is, by overcoming 'the West.'

Revolutionary re/subjection occurs on the field of *différance* where heteronormativity becomes not merely autonormative, but also assertive, agential, actively conscious of its own historicality. Larbi Sadiki, of the University of Exeter, speaks of the Arab Spring precisely in these defiant terms, though he sees it as 'sublimation *en masse*':

> The children of the revolution – from Cairo to Tunis, from Manama to Deraa – have cathected God and their new avatars of 'freedom' and 'dignity.' Note how they have rechanneled anger, humiliation, and indignation at political disenfranchisement, social exclusion and the absence of the proverbial loaf of bread into socially constructive and associative energy. As if through sublimation en masse, they staged protests to counter state violence with peaceful protest, sang the national anthem in an electrifying chorus amidst a sea of charged up human souls, recited verses of defiance (Abu al Qasim al Shabbi) embraced the national flag, danced to music, and vocalized suppressed feelings about injustice and dictatorship. The relics of Arab autocracy now fear the creative use of vocal chords to shout and sing. The late Ibrahim Qashoush, who sang 'irhal ya Bashar,' enthused Hama's protesters last week. His throat was slit on the 4th of July. Voice, music, debka

(folkloric dance in the Levant), the technology of culture, is deployed with potency – threatening regimes and often times prompting violent, suppressive reaction.[27]

The revolutionary reconstitution of a liberating subject has already occurred – on the social body itself, with *vox populi* having now become *vox dei*. From the liberating voice of Ibrahim Qashoush were singing birds of a new dawn; from his slit throat was gushing forth the flood of a fertile memory that will continue to remember itself for generations to come.

27. See Larbi Sadiki, 'Psychosis of the Arab Revolution,' Al Jazeera, 11 July 2011, http://english.aljazeera.net/indepth/opinion/2011/07/201171187166788870.html.

FOUR

Discovering a New World

Where and, more importantly, what exactly is 'the Arab World?' The 'Arab World' refers to countries stretching from the Atlantic Ocean to the Arabian Sea, and from the Mediterranean Sea to the Horn of Africa and the Indian Ocean. The Arab world consists of twenty-one countries, with a population of some 360 million people, which in varying degrees have a sense of collective consciousness that might be identified simply as Arab transnationalism, whose roots go back to the declining years of the Ottoman Empire and the renewed ascendency of European colonialism. To be sure, not everyone living in the Arab World is happy with the term, instances being the Kurds, Armenians, and Berbers. Historically, of course, Arabs hailed only from the Arabian peninsula; it wasn't until the aftermath of the Muslim conquests of the seventh century that Arab Muslim armies spread from the Atlantic to Transoxiana. Although the Arab League was established in 1945 to represent Arabs, the pan-Arabism project is formed more by common historical experience than by bureaucratic representation. Until the rise of the Arab Spring, not a single Arab country was ruled democratically – through a free and fair electoral process, predicated on freedom of the press and peaceful assemblies, and leading to a rule of the citizenship via their elected representatives. To this day, countries ranging from Saudi Arabia and Bahrain to Jordan, Syria to Libya and Morocco, are ruled by medieval and modern potentates with not a single enduring institution of democracy to their credit.

'The Arab World' is also a state of mind – a site of contestation, a dream, a belated promise, a benighted joy, a vision, a vista, a landscape of emancipation.[1] Today, more than anything else, 'the Arab World' is the result of a collective memory of fighting against European colonialism and American imperialism – now fully evident in the gushing wound of Palestinian dispossession and Israeli colonial settlement.[2] The distant memories of the Ottoman Empire have now by and large faded, and two hundred years of French and British colonialism are shading into American imperialism as the most prominent factor in the making of the emotive universe of 'the Arab World.' The renewed flexing of European colonialism during the final decades of the Ottoman Empire resulted in the drawing of a map of the modern Arab World on North Africa and Eastern Asia. Palestinians are the only Arab people whose territorial claim to nationhood was stolen from them – by the Zionist project that established a Jewish homeland on the bent but not broken back of another people. Predicated on the pre-Islamic heritage, the making of Islamic civilization and early empires, and a sustained history of anticolonial struggles, Arab nationalism became coterminous with a regional pan-Arabism that always dreamt of a common homeland stretching from the Atlantic across North Africa and into the Eastern coast of the Mediterranean Sea. The dream never came true. 'The Arab World' is a promissory note. It has never been cashed. But it is always there – written.

Things Fall Apart

Upon the division of Sudan into two states and the official UN recognition of South Sudan as its 193rd member state on 14 July 2011, Lamis Andoni, a leading political analyst and commentator

---

1. For two classic studies of the Arab World, see Philip Hitti, *History of the Arabs* (New York: Palgrave, 2002); and Albert Hourani *A History of the Arab Peoples* (Cambridge MA: Belknap Press of Harvard University Press, 2003).

2. Two seminal texts on the Palestinian question lead directly to the centrality of Palestine in the Arab World: Edward Said, *The Question of Palestine* (New York: Vintage, 1992); and Joseph Massad, *The Persistence of the Palestinian Question: Essays on Zionism and the Palestinians* (London: Routledge, 2006).

on Arab affairs, wrote a probing essay for Al Jazeera calling the event 'a dangerous precedent,' recommending that 'the Arab world has to draw the right lessons from it if wants to avoid the break-up of other Arab states into ethnic and sectarian enclaves.'[3]

Lamis Andoni's warning, predicated on a deeply rooted and legitimate anxiety, was timely and apt. As she rightly observes,

> The birth of South Sudan is first and foremost a testimony to the failure of the official Arab order, pan-Arabism, and especially the Islamic political projects to provide civic and equal rights to ethnic and religious minorities in the Arab world. The jubilation that swept the people of southern Sudan at their independence from the predominantly Arab and Muslim north attests to the long-standing feelings of repression and alienation by a people, the majority of whom were born into the post-independence Arab world.

What Andoni marks is the failure of the Arab World to be a world able to contain all its constituent elements.

The history of modern Sudan begins with the Mahdist revolt against the Ottomans (1885–99) and comes to a colonial closure with the British domination (1899–1956), until independence and national sovereignty (1956–89), which culminated in the 30 June 1989 coup by colonel Omar al-Bashir (1989–). A harrowing civil war from 1995 to 2011 ultimately resulted in the cessation and formation of South Sudan in 2011.[4] South Sudan, severed from Sudan on racialized and sectarian lines, is the testing ground for the fractious disposition of the Arab World.

With this history in mind, Andoni acknowledges the role of the British in both fomenting and benefiting from such racial, ethnic, and sectarian divisions – a history that extends from British imperialism to Israeli interventionism to preserve the Jewish state in the midst of what appears as muddy waters to them. She quotes Avi Dichter, Israel's former interior security minister, as having said: 'We had to weaken Sudan and deprive it of the initiative to

---

3. See Lamis Andoni, 'How the Arab World Lost Southern Sudan,' Al Jazeera, 14 July 2011, http://english.aljazeera.net/indepth/opinion/2011/07/2011713135442172603.html.

4. For more on the history of Sudan, see P.M. Holt and M.W. Daley, *A History of the Sudan: From the Coming of Islam to the Present Day* (New York: Longman, 2000).

build a strong and united state. That is necessary for bolstering and strengthening Israel's national security. We produced and escalated the Darfur crisis to prevent Sudan from developing its capabilities.' Yet Andoni still insists that 'the Arab world cannot simply explain secession as a product of a Western/Israeli conspiracy. If anything, it is the repressive regime in Sudan, combined with an incompetent and corrupt official Arab order, that drove legitimately disaffected people in southern Sudan into Western and even Israeli arms seeking independence from a failing Arab world.'[5] Her concern is for the rest of the Arab world, which she fears is endangered by similar separatist movements, predicated on existing tensions, which could be taken advantage of by the counterrevolutionary forces now watching the Arab Spring like hungry hawks.

Arabs should reflect on their serious blunders and moral failure by facing the fact that the South Sudanese are an oppressed people whose grievances were against Arab rule and not against Western domination. It is true that the people of South Sudan may yet find themselves prey to greedy Western governments interested in their rich natural resources, but that does not change the reality that people of the new state celebrated the end of what they viewed as oppression by an Arab and Muslim elite.[6]

Lamis Andoni narrows her diagnosis to the critical and sensitive issue of Arab nationalism and pan-Arabism. She observes:

> while pan-Arabism was initially an anti-colonial movement, some of its branches – especially the Ba'ath Arab parties that ruled Syria and Iraq – demonstrated and practiced destructive chauvinist policies and actions against other ethnic groups and nationalities. The case of the Kurds in both Syria and Iraq testify to different degrees of exclusivist, supremacist and racist policies by both Ba'thist political parties.

It is not just in Syria and Iraq that Arab chauvinism (identical in its intensity to Iranian and Turkish chauvinism) has precluded the possibility of a pluralistic world that transcends ethnic racism. Andoni rightly criticizes 'the influence of pan-Arab nationalism

---

5. Ibid.
6. Ibid.

on the political culture,' which, she observes 'has not always been positive. Instead, it has actually created racist and chauvinist attitudes that obstructed serious condemnation and criticism of the way the national Sudanese government in the North dealt with the people of the South.'[7] What Andoni is doing here in effect is dissecting the racialized and sectarian divisions and subdivisions that have animated postcolonial nation-states and yet kept them camouflaged under the tight control of authoritarian regimes that have wrapped themselves in nationalist and pan-Arabist flags.

Andoni does not spare the Islamist project either:

> Accordingly, Sudan has been an utter failure for the Islamic movement in the Arab world, for it was the only regime where an Islamic movement had historically partnered with or dominated the regime. It is true that the Islamic movement in the Arab world is not monolithic and differs from country to country; there are many Islamic movements, and not only one movement. However, the failure in Sudan should challenge Islamic thinkers and leaders to review the failed experience of an Islamic movement that had attained power and actually took part in leading a country.

Here the point of contention moves from Arab nationalism to militant Islamism – these having come together to alienate a significant portion of a postcolonial nation-state strongly enough for it to secede and go its separate way. Her concern is diversity:

> It is only legitimate for the people of the new state of South Sudan to celebrate their independence, but it is also a critical point, while Arab uprisings are demanding freedom and justice, to remember that we cannot establish a better Arab order without embracing diversity and pluralism, instead of narrow nationalist or religious ideologies that have only served as tools for dictators.[8]

Andoni's diagnosis points to something more definitive about the exacerbated dialectic between the colonial and postcolonial experiences. The colonially manufactured postcolonial states, as well as being immune to the colonial abuses that gave birth

---

7. Ibid.
8. Ibid.

to them in the first place, are in fact their rhetorical extensions. Evident in Andoni's concerns is the fact that postcolonial nation-states and the colonial conditions that occasioned them are in fact mirror images. Pan-Arabism is not just a reversal of and reaction to European colonialism, it is also its replica and reproduction. That is the inner tension and paradox of pan-Arabism. Pan-Arabism is the product of European colonialism. The imaginative geography we call 'the Arab World' will either reconfigure its worldliness as an emancipatory proposition or else collapse upon its own postcolonial paradoxes. Regional resistances to amorphous imperialism will continue to define our history for generations to come – but only those resistances that are predicated on an acknowledgement and celebration of the plurality that informs them. Opposing that resistance is nothing other than brute financial and military interests. Israel, Pakistan, and Saudi Arabia, for example, are identical in providing their services for their own interests, which are not ideological but entirely economic. In face of this brutal fact, South Sudan fractures the Arab World and exposes its weak borders; imaginative boundaries that do not and cannot hold it together. What is at stake here is the difference between a cosmopolitan culture that sees, celebrates, and thrives on diversity, and a fractious polity that allows for a racialized reading of pan-Arabism that alienates non-Arab, non-Muslim, and *a fortiori* economically disenfranchised classes that cannot be sanguine about bourgeois nationalism.

Tahrir Square

As the Arab Spring was unfolding, Azmi Bishara, arguably the most influential contemporary Arab intellectual, became a critical voice of insight, guidance, and warning for the millions participating in and looking for a critical understanding of their revolutionary uprising. Writing and appearing regularly on Arab television channels, the ex-Knesset member (he is a Palestinian living in Israel) Bishara had a catalytic effect on people's perception of the Arab revolutions. 'It was crucial for me [to be back in Egypt],' he told his audience at Cairo University's Faculty of Political Science in mid-June 2011 upon his return to Egypt after a long forced exile. 'He emerged,' wrote Amira Howeidy, following Bishara's appearance, 'as crucial for the revolution ... at least in the eyes of many Egyptians who found in Bishara, 54, an ideologue of sorts during the uprising.'[9] The very presence of Bishara at Cairo University, after his having been banned from entering the intellectual capital of the Arab World, combined with Howeidy's report for *Al-Ahram* expounding on the Palestinian intellectual's thoughts on the Arab Spring, together constituted a vital insight into the formation of the public space that the revolutions have created. The combined wisdom of the French and American revolutions for Hannah Arendt was that the first posited the power of the people as the source of all legitimacy, while the latter posited that power in the formation of voluntary associations.[10] If the gathering at Tahrir Square was the first manifestation of the former, the meeting at Cairo University at which Azmi Bishara spoke freely to academics and journalists was an example of the latter. The former enabled the latter.

Azmi Bishara's admiration for Egyptian revolutionaries focuses on the moment when they took over Tahrir Square and did not let go. 'Very few revolutions in history were more organized than the Egyptian revolution,' he told his audience in Cairo.

> The genius of the Egyptian revolution was that the people could have dispersed on 25 January, but they continued and realized that this is bigger than a "Day of Anger' ... that they have something in their hands they can't let go of. [They] held their destiny in their hands and they heard the wings of history flapping. There can be no turning back.

In other words, the logic of the crowd gathering at Tahrir had taken over the course of history and did not let go. Bishara also praised the magnitude of popular participation in the revolution. 'The Egyptian people's participation in the revolution ... exceeds any other revolution in history where participation is almost always only one per cent, with the exception of the 1979 Iranian Revolution

---

9. Amira Howeidy, 'Revolution in Their Eyes,' *Al-Ahram*, 16–22 June 2011, http://weekly.ahram.org.eg/2011/1052/eg3.htm.

10. See Hannah Arendt, *On Revolution* (L.ondon: Penguin, 1990 [1963]: ch. 5.

where seven per cent of the population took to the streets.'[11] The scale of the crowd and the fact that they occupied Tahrir Square were the quintessential elements of their victory. This mass participation is the assertion of a vox populi without which no political formation of voluntary association can claim legitimacy. We are, in other words, in an inaugural moment, when the public space is reasserting its political potency and the political culture follows suit. Bishara's excitement – as an Arab and as a Palestinian – is naturally and rightly directed at this inaugural moment.

The nature of these revolutions, as Bishara understands it, is open-ended, for 'the revolutionaries [he is speaking of Egyptians] didn't take over power; they "knocked on its door" but "didn't assume it." This ... will have massive consequences on Egypt's history in the future and on other Arab regimes.' This is not to forget the enormous difficulties ahead: 'But if the Egyptian revolution was spontaneous ... building a democracy can't be left to spontaneity too. The revolutionaries are the primary people entrusted with the revolution. And whether they like it or not, they have to articulate the objectives of the revolution.'[12] Here, then, is the double bind: knocking at the door of power but not storming it; not assuming power and yet being vigilant regarding its future. Bishara's warning will, of course, remain the most important challenge that Egyptian and other revolutionaries face – to posit the will of the people and yet systematically to translate that raw power into political forms. 'Theoretically,' Hannah Arendt observes, 'the deification of the people in the French Revolution was the inevitable consequence of the attempt to derive both law and power from the selfsame source.'[13] Azmi Bishara and other Arab thinkers have every reason to be euphoric in this inaugural moment of liberation. But, as he rightly warns, 'knocking at the door of power' is not enough; political institutions need to endure. The systematicity of that translation will remain definitive of the enduring success of the revolution on the ground zero of Tahrir Square and of what it will mean for the future of the Arab Spring.

---

11. Howeidy, 'Revolution in Their Eyes.'
12. Ibid.
13. Arendt, *On Revolution*: 183.

It is hard to imagine a better metaphor for the unfolding revolutions in the Arab world than people knocking at the door of power but not storming the gate of tyrants. A few days before Mubarak stepped down the Al Jazeera cameras zoomed in on Tahrir Square and reported a rumor that people were planning to move towards the presidential palace. It never happened. They stayed put. They declared Tahrir a liberated space, a free republic, and remained there. Perhaps this is one crucial difference between the storming of the Bastille as the supreme sign of revolt at the commencement of the French Revolution and the crowd just gathering at Tahrir and demanding that Hosni Mubarak leave, with just one word *Arhil*, 'Leave,' high on their banners.

Not storming the presidential palace, and instead staying put in Tahrir Square and demanding that the octogenarian tyrant just (please) leave, redefines the *vox populi* (voice of the people) as the engine of history such that, as Azmi Bishara rightly says, Arabs as a people become an open-ended metaphor of something entirely new.

In an article by Robert Fisk during the Rupert Murdoch scandal in the summer of 2011, he (out of the blue) begins by comparing the Australian businessman to a caliph: 'He is a caliph, I suppose, almost of the Middle Eastern variety.'[14] The words 'I suppose,' followed by 'almost,' are the give-away sign of the astounding racial stereotyping to which he is habitually prone, not just when reporting on 'the Middle East,' but also, as in this case, when writing on matters that have absolutely nothing to do with the term. What we are witnessing in the Arab and Muslim world, the off-the-cuff clichés of people like Robert Fisk notwithstanding, is not only the active revolt of people against tyrants whom elected officials have kept in power but also actions that change the course of their own history, which become an open-ended proposition regarding who and what they are, their own metaphors for recasting the world. They are reinventing themselves not on the basis of who they have been made out to be, 'the white man's burden,' but on the premiss

---

14. Robert Fisk, 'Why I Had to Leave The Times,' *Independent*, 11 July 2011, www.independent.co.uk/news/media/press/robert-fisk-why-i-had-to-leave-the-times-2311569.html.

of what they want to be, what they have become on the site and in the citations of Tahrir Square.

As the Arab Spring unfolds, we are for the foreseeable future in an inaugural moment. 'The Arab World' is no longer what it was – it has become a floating signifier. Places like South Sudan may break away from it. But the events at Tahrir Square are emblematic of a renewed conception of what it means to be an 'Arab,' and thereby where and what 'the Arab World' would be beyond the colonial metaphors of 'the Middle East' and 'caliphs.' Tahrir Square is now the epicenter of a new geography of liberation, a new world, yet to be named. Beyond the racist clichés that the colonial imaginary continues to use as metaphors of banality and tyranny, a new world is taking shape that will demand and produce new metaphors. The ground zero of that new world is the public space that is being redefined in and about Tahrir Square, by millions of young and old Egyptians, Arabs, women and men, who are perfectly capable of representing themselves.

The widely popular Al Jazeera journalist Ayman Mohyeldin asked young Egyptian revolutionaries gathered in a café in downtown Cairo in what way they thought their revolution had succeeded or changed their lives.[15] Their responses – at turns pointed, purposeful, critical, doubtful, and yet forward-looking – were entirely tangential to the fact that their very gathering in a café in downtown Cairo for the global audience of Al Jazeera was the most potent sign of the success of the revolution. Their Tahrir Square was right there and then, and it had gone global. The necessity of overcoming the old geography of 'the West and the Rest,' or 'the North and the South' for that matter, in order to have a better grasp of the unfolding events, had already taken place, in that formal space between Mohyeldin and his unassuming revolutionary interlocutors. The global consequences of these regional developments are embedded in the way they are revealing alternative political and emotional geographies that the world at large has hitherto ignored.

---

15. Watch the segment here: http://english.aljazeera.net/programmes/thecafe.

It is impossible to exaggerate the possible consequences of these inaugural changes – for example, for the cause of Palestinian national liberation, symbolically the most enduring trauma of modern Arab history, at a time when Israel faces the most serious challenge since its inception; for it stands as the last outpost of European colonialism in a region revolting against the remnants of the postcolonial world. Israel has so solidly staked its continuation as an apartheid Jewish state on either massively inflicting or receiving a suicidal dosage of violence, and is so heavily invested in 'not/negotiating' and 'not/dealing' with illegitimate Arab and Muslim potentates, be they friend (Egypt) or foe (the Islamic Republic), that it cannot imagine a place for itself amid the nonviolent democratic uprisings that have now engulfed it. What Israel needs to deal with is Tahrir Square – the fact and unfolding force of the democratic will of the people that is altering the imaginative geography upon which the Jewish state has forced itself.

As physical space, urban metaphor, and revolutionary allegory, Tahrir Square is central to the Egyptian – and by extension Arab – uprising. It was instrumental in the fall of Hosni Mubarak and continues to be a center of revolutionary agitation. Protesters periodically go back to it when demanding, for example, security forces be held accountable for their crimes, or to agitate for parliamentary elections or the specifics of drafting a new constitution, or to demand that the military step aside and allow civilian rule. Al Jazeera has effectively become an extension of Tahrir Square, of the public space in which Egyptians and other Arabs would discuss their collective future. If police officers allegedly involved in the killings of protesters were released without trial, or if no one from Mubarak's family had stood in a courtroom, or if Egyptians suspected their revolution was in danger, they would appear on Al Jazeera (with Tahrir Square in the background), discussing precisely these issues – to be viewed by millions of Arabs around the world.[16] The Egyptian revolution succeeded in that very space

---

16. I refer to the episode of Al Jazeera's *Inside Story* of 8 July 2011, where the presenter Sohail Rahman was in conversation with Wael Eskandar, a political activist and columnist for *Al-Ahram* online, Sharif Abdel Kouddous, a correspondent for *Democracy Now!*, and Rami Khouri, the director of ISSAM Fares Institute for Public Policy and International Affairs at the American University of Beirut; http://english.aljazeera.

between Ayman Mohyeldin and his young Egyptian revolutionaries – hopeful, determined, open-minded – giving form and frame to the memory of Tahrir Square in their minds.

The implications of this public space and what is to be examined there extends from the body politic to the body itself. As Lisa Hajjar, of the University of California in Santa Barbara and a pioneer in exposing the horrors of torture in the global context, asks pointedly: 'Are the revolutions sweeping through the Arab world, and being confronted with violent counter-revolutions, in part a battle over the use of torture?' Her response is exemplary:

> The brutal murder of Khaled Said by Egyptian police on June 6, 2010, was both a catalytic and a symbolic event for the Egyptian revolution. The facebook page We Are All Khaled Said was a requiem for the dead blogger, and it was instrumental in the events that would follow half a year later. Last week, on the one year anniversary of Khaled's murder, anti-torture revolutionary activists stenciled Khaled's image all over Cairo. Egyptian revolutionary and blogger Hossam El-Hamalawy has created a website, Piggipedia, to document a running list of torturers and their post-Mubarak fates – often promotions in the 'transitional' government of Egypt. If knowledge is power, as El-Hamalawy contends, then showing these men's pictures and current postings is a means of enabling the revolution to target them, with insistent demands for accountability. Piggipedia is an effort to give teeth to the political aspiration of nowhere to run, nowhere to hide. Or, as some South Africans once chanted, never forget, never forgive. As long as a torturer is alive, he is a legitimate target of prosecution, if the conditions are right. (Are you listening, still-alive Henry Kissinger and Dick Cheney?)[17]

Hence, for Hajjar, the tortured and murdered body of Khaled Said is a monument to the otherwise unknown citizen on the occasion of whose death Tahrir Square became a metaphor for the unfolding of the expansive public space reaching out from 'the Arab World,' perhaps even to hold even Henry Kissinger and Dick Cheney accountable.

---

net/programmes/insidestory/2011/07/2011798302761o792.html.

17. See Lisa Hajjar, 'Following the Torture Trail through the Arab Spring: First Speculations,' *Jadaliyya*, 8 June 2011, www.jadaliyya.com/pages/index/1792/following-the-torture-trail-through-the-arab-sprin.

Exposing Hypocrisies – Left and Right

Because the Arab Spring is robust, true and shining, rising from the innermost hopes and aspirations of many nations, predicated on historical and material forces long in the making, it remains the measure singularly able to expose the otherwise hidden hypocrisies of old forces – left or right, pro- or anti-American. The remaking of the Arab World in reality and as a metaphor predicated on the building block of Tahrir Square as the public space par excellence will leave no stone in the region unturned. This will not be an easy task; nor will it be accomplished by the hanging of a dictator or the falling of a statue, as staged by the Americans after the fall of Saddam Hussein in Iraq. Counter-revolutionary forces range from the United States to the Islamic Republic, from Israel to Hezbollah. The habitual enemies are now exposed as united in their opposition to the inner logic of the Arab Spring; they remain distant from the facts and significance of Tahrir Square, the site of an active remaking of the Arab World into a new world, the mapping of a new moral and imaginative geography.

It was weeks into the unfolding of the revolutionary uprising in Syria in late spring/early summer 2011 that a key force in the geopolitics of the region, the Lebanese Hezbollah, led by Sayyed Hassan Nasrallah, showed palpable signs of being in trouble. But this time the worries of the secretary general were not caused by Israel, or arising from the sectarian politics of Lebanon. Sayyed Hassan's troubles, which this time around were the harbinger of his undoing as an outdated fighter, were coming from, of all places, the Arab Spring; the dawning of a new liberation geography had left the guerrilla fighter behind. The Arab Spring was rendering the aging warrior redundant – his habitually eloquent tongue now struggling for words. Two years before the rise of the Arab Spring, he believed he had got away with rejecting the democratic uprising in Iran (whose brutal ruling regime is his principal patron) as a plot devised by the US, Israel, and Saudi Arabia.[18] And he did get

---

18. I have dealt in some detail with this and other regional consequences of the Green Movement in Hamid Dabashi, *Iran, the Green Movement, and the USA: The Fox and the Paradox* (London: Zed Books, 2010): ch. 3.

away with it – aided and abetted by the moral and intellectual sclerosis of a stratum of Arab intellectuals who thought Mahmoud Ahmadinejad and the Islamic theocracy were the vanguard of 'resistance' to US/Israeli imperialism in the region and thus should be spared from criticism. And then Tunisia happened, and Egypt, and Libya, and Bahrain, and Yemen; and then – Hassan Nasrallah's and Ali Khamenei's nightmare – Syria happened. It was a sad scene: a once mighty warrior being bypassed by the force of history, and all he could do was to fumble in futility.

When Hasan Nasrallah came to the defense of Bashar al-Assad's regime in Syria, as it was mowing down peaceful protestors, signs of frailty were all over the old fighter's countenance. He asked Syrians for patience. He conceded that mistakes had been made by Syrians in Lebanon. He promised that Assad would reform. He pleaded for time. Déjà vu: for an uncanny moment the Hezbollah leader even sounded like and had the air of the late Shah of Iran days before his demise early in 1979: desperate, confused, and baffled by the unfolding drama, worriedly out of touch with what was happening around him.

'Hassan Nasrallah,' according to an Al Jazeera report on 25 May 2011,[19] 'had called on Syrians to support president Bashar al-Assad and enter into dialogue with the government to end weeks of ongoing protests across Syria.' But this situation was a far cry from the democratic uprising in Iran that started in June 2009, which Nasrallah readily dismissed as an American plot. These were Arabs up against their corrupt and cruel leaders, not 'Persians' whose money was good but whose historic struggles for civil liberties questionable. 'Bashar is serious about carrying out reforms,' Nasrallah was now pleading with his audience, 'but he has to do them gradually and in a responsible way; he should be given the chance to implement those reforms.' By the time he made these remarks more than 1,000 Syrian civilians had been gunned down by Bashar al-Assad's army and security forces. More criminal atrocities were to follow, forcing Syrians to abandon their homeland and flee to Turkey. The cruel and gruesome torture and

---

19. See 'Nasrallah calls on Syrians to Support Assad,' Al Jazeera, 25 May 2011, http://english.aljazeera.net/news/middleeast/2011/05/2011525174748827942.html.

murder of Hamza al-Khateeb was still in the offing, where 'in the hands of President Bashar al-Assad's security forces,' as reported by Al Jazeera,[20] the 13-year old boy's 'humanity [was] degraded to nothing more than a lump of flesh to beat, burn, torture and defile, until the screaming stopped at last.' Nasrallah, who clearly could not care less about the revolting behavior of his patrons, was now for a second time siding with a brutal, vicious tyrant and his criminally insane security forces against the democratic aspirations of the people – first in Iran in 2009 and now in Syria in 2011. What kind of 'freedom fighter' is this? Never mind the Shah, Nasrallah now sounded more like President Franklin D. Roosevelt, who once famously said of the Nicaraguan dictator Anastasio Somoza (1896–1956) that he 'may be a son of a bitch, but he's our son of a bitch.' Nasrallah did not care if Khamenei and Assad tortured and murdered their own people, so long as they kept him in business.

'Peaceful Syrian citizens,' declared a statement by hundreds of Syrian filmmakers and their colleagues from around the globe, 'are being killed today for their demands of basic rights and liberties. It is the same oppression and corruption that kept Syrians prisoners and swallowed their freedom, properties and lives for decades, that is assassinating their bodies and dreams today.'[21] Hassan Nasrallah would have none of this, as he appeared to have no patience with or sympathy for the scores of young Iranians kidnapped, tortured, raped, and murdered during the civil rights uprising of 2009. A belligerent sector of Arab and American intellectuals – ignorant of or indifferent to the historic struggle of Iranians for their civil liberties – had sided with him in dismissing the Green Movement in Iran as a Saudi/CIA plot. But, regardless, Syrians and Iranians were busy mapping out a new destiny for themselves. Sayyed Hassan Nasrallah and his supporters were visibly out of step with history.

---

20. See 'Tortured and Killed: Hamza al-Khateeb, age 13,' Al Jazeera, 31 May 2011, http://english.aljazeera.net/indepth/features/2011/05/201153185927813389.html.

21. The original Arabic and the English translation of the statement are available, with the list of signatories at Facebook page: A Call from Syrian Filmmakers to Filmmakers Everywhere.

The only language that Hassan Nasrallah understood, as he watched history leaving him behind, was the language that had kept him in power; condemning the US, the EU, Israel, and the Saudis. When Tunisia happened he said: 'We must congratulate the Tunisian people on their historic revolution, their struggle, and their uprising.'[22] He thought this was happening only to European allies, and that this was good. When Egypt happened, he said: 'In Tunis and Egypt, tyrants have gone away ... we call on the people of Egypt and the people of Tunis to unite, because division could be a prelude to the resurrection of the ruling regimes.' This was when he thought this was happening only to US allies. But why did he not send an encouraging word to 'the people of Iran,' when they did precisely what the Tunisians and Egyptians had done, rise up against tyranny? He instead categorically denounced the Iranian uprising. He had sided with identical tyrants like Ben Ali and Hosni Mubarak. He stated on al-Manar television that Iran was in the capable hands of his friend 'Grand Ayatollah Khamenei.' He did not even blink. For him it was payback time.

When Libya happened, Hassan Nasrallah said:

> a group of young men and women rose and they were faced with bullets; war was imposed on the popular revolution. What is taking place in Libya is war imposed by the regime on a people that was peacefully demanding change; this people was forced to defend itself and war broke out in the east and the west, with warplanes, rocket launchers, and artillery and brought back to our memory the 1982 invasion of Lebanon and all of Israel's wars. Such serious crimes should be condemned and the revolutionary people of Libya should be helped so as to persevere.[23]

That is all well and good. But what was the difference between Iranian or Syrians and the Libyan people? In Iran and Syria too 'a group of young men and women rose and they were faced with bullets.' Were arbitrary arrest, torture, and even rape not 'imposed by the regime on a people that was peacefully demanding change'

---

22. Sayyed Hassan Nasrallah's zigzagging positions have been gathered under the rubric of 'Nasrallah on Syria: More Equal than Others?' http://qifanabki.com/2011/05/26/some-arab-revolutions-are-more-equal-than-others.

23. Ibid.

here also? Was Iranian or Syrian blood any thinner than Libyan blood in Nasrallah's estimation? What sort of 'resistance' was this blatant siding with tyranny – and resistance to what? Resistance to Israeli expansionism by a band of militant thugs maiming and murdering their own people in Syria and Iran? Is this the choice that people were to have? The warrior's time was passing. The ground was shifting under his feet.

Similar double standards and hypocrisy would abound in the unfolding cases of Yemen and Bahrain. The magnificent aspect of the Arab Spring at this crucial historic juncture was that it exposed the identical hypocrisy of both the US (on Bahrain, Saudi Arabia, and Yemen) and Hassan Nasrallah (on Iran and Syria). Nasrallah stated that 'we as Lebanese shouldn't interfere in what is going on in Syria, but let the Syrians themselves deal with the issue.' But after Lebanese 'interference' in Morocco, Iran, Bahrain and Yemen, why not Syria? 'We should reject any sanctions led by the US and the West asking Lebanon to abide by them against Syria,' he asserted.[24] But why are UN resolutions against Israel good, but UN resolutions against Syria not good?

That Hassan Nasrallah was not fully aware of what was happening around him was evident in the belatedness of his observation that the US was 'seeking to hijack the wave of pro-democracy popular uprisings sweeping the Arab world.'[25] Of course they were, and are – but what was Nasrallah doing to safeguard and promote the revolutions, siding with Bashar al-Assad and Ali Khamenei? Nasrallah was now outmaneuvered, checkmated, made redundant by history – by, of all things, a magnificent Arab Spring in which he had no role, no say, and no power to make decisions. He had failed the test of history – knowing when to abandon tyrants benevolent to him for their own reasons but abusive and criminal to their own people. He was not watching Tahrir Square carefully. He backed the wrong side of history.

---

24. Ibid.
25. See 'Nasrallah: U.S. Keen to Hijack Arab Revolts,' *Daily Star*, 7 June 2011, www.dailystar.com.lb/News/Politics/2011/Jun-07/Nasrallah-US-keen-to-hijack-Arab-revolts.ashx#axzz1OsFyC37F.

It was no accident that Mahmoud Ahmadinejad (soon followed by Ali Khamenei) was on the same page as Hassan Nasrallah in defending the Syrian regime – for they are all cut from the same cloth. What was happening in Syria, Ahmadinejad believed, was a plot by a number of countries in the region, 'because Syria is in the frontline of resistance and the Islamic Republic is standing shoulder to shoulder with the Syrian state and nation'[26] However, the Syrian state was now murdering the Syrian nation. One could not be on both sides. To side with the regime was to endorse its murderous record of killing its people, as indeed the Islamic Republic, on Ahmadinejad's watch, had done to its own – with Nasrallah's full knowledge.

Ahmadinejad's support for the Syrian regime, however, should not confuse the fact that the Islamic Republic directly supported Hamas and Hezbollah. In defending the allocation of funding to these two organizations, the military strategists of the Islamic Republic make no bones about why it is that they support the Palestinian and Lebanese causes. 'The Palestinians are not fighting for Palestine,' one leading Iranian military strategist is seen explaining recently to a captivated audience, 'they are fighting for Iran; the Lebanese are not fighting for Lebanon, they are fighting for Iran. To have the courage to say this and the courage to demonstrate this means to provide a strategic conception [of what we do].'[27] Did Hassan Nasrallah know this, or was he taking advantage of the Islamic Republic the way it was taking advantage of him?

What's Good for the Goose

As with the two households of fair Verona, where from ancient grudge breaks new mutiny, the fate of Hassan Nasrallah is tied to his *raison d'être*, the apartheid garrison state of Israel. Hezbollah emerged as a perfectly legitimate political project in the aftermath of the Israeli invasion of Lebanon in 1982, giving momentum and

---

26. This according to a report in the leading conservative daily in Iran, *Keyhan*; www.kayhannews.ir/900318/2.htm#other203.

27. For a video clip of this speech by a leading Iranian military analyst, see 'Why Does the Islamic Republic of Iran Give Aid to Hezbollah and Hamas?' www.youtube.com/watch?v=i7J4QW15Z1Q.

purpose to the cause of millions of Lebanese Shi'a categorically disenfranchised from the sectarian politics of Lebanon – a gift of French colonialism that keeps giving. For close to three decades Hezbollah has defended both the cause of the Lebanese Shi'a and the territorial integrity of Lebanon with steadfast determination – outmaneuvering the expansionist Jewish state and granting renewed significance to asymmetrical warfare, wherein it has indeed managed to defeat the mighty army at its own game.

But today, as we have discussed, the Arab Spring has altered the very DNA of the region's geopolitics. Nasrallah's enmity towards Israel is in fact more important to him than the client relationship he has with Syria and the Islamic Republic. But Israel's troubles today are such that a war with Hezbollah could do little for the cause of preserving its fragile future as a Jewish aparheid state. Following President Obama's mere mention of the '1967 borders,' Prime Minister Netanyahu felt it necessary to justify his policies in a full frontal AIPAC attack and then before the US Congress to assure himself that he still calls the shots. He does not. The Arab Spring does. The Hamas leadership, for its part, has been infinitely wiser than Nasrallah in immediately reading the Arab Spring correctly and rushing for a rapprochement with Fatah and the Palestinian Authority, much to the chagrin of not just the Israeli leadership, but also the Islamic Republic and its client project Hezbollah.

The predicament of Hassan Nasrallah in Lebanon cannot thus be any cause for celebration by Israel. Quite the contrary: 'The only democracy in the Middle East' is frightened out of its wits by the prospect of democracy in the Middle East. Israel and Hezbollah are the mirror image of each other: a sectarian militia on the troubled border of the Jewish state is the perfect justification for both. The two belligerents can only understand the language of sectarian violence, a language that is now exposed for the banality of the evil it espouses. Today that language no longer speaks (if it ever did) to the millions of human beings arisen (in the words of the Egyptians) for their *Huriyya*, *Adalah al-Ijtima'iyah*, and *Karamah*, 'Freedom,' 'Social Justice,' and 'Dignity.' Nasrallah's speeches in defense of Bashar al-Assad and Ayatollah Khamenei express a self-delusion similar to that of Benjamin Netanyahu before the US Congress in

May 2011: both are outmoded warriors, unable to think beyond the comfort of their respective power bases.[28]

That Israel was in trouble was also evident in the way pro-Israel Americans were busy dismissing, when not frightened by, the Arab Spring. Ted Koppel, a prominent American journalist, pleads on behalf of Israel for the US to come to Saudi Arabia's help should the need arise. American allies can no longer rely on America, Koppel complains (he leaves it to your imagination to conclude that all the 'Arab allies' were corrupt tyrannies). Figures like Ted Koppel expose the fact that most liberal Americans side unabashedly with their conservative counterparts in actively opposing the rise of any democracy in the region. 'The canary in the coal mine on such matters,' Koppel observes, 'is Israel. None of America's allies is more sensitive to even the most subtle changes in the international environment, or more conscious of the slightest hint of diminished support from Washington.'[29] He is of course absolutely right: that was and remains the price that a colonial settlement pays for making itself contingent on the combined calamity of globalized imperialism and localized tyranny. Israel never imagined, from the time of its racist origin in Zionism, that Arabs were capable of democracy. This is a rude awakening: both Israel and its American allies must now deal with (and assuredly they will try to subvert) the inevitable uncertainties of a wave of democratic uprisings. But the best piece of convoluted reasoning is here: 'Overshadowing all other concerns is the fear that Iran is poised to reap enormous benefits from the so-called Arab Spring. "Even without nukes," one top official told me, "Iran picks up the pieces. With nukes, it takes the house."'[30] Koppel and his Israeli friends are still beating on the dead horse of Iran's nuclear program, desperate to pull evolving events back to the status quo ante, away from 'the so-called Arab Spring.'

---

28. A video of Prime Minister Benjamin Netanyahu's address to a rapturous US Congress can be viewed on the *Huffington Post* website: www.huffingtonpost.com/2011/05/24/netanyahu-speaks-to-us-co_n_866165.html.

29. See Ted Koppel, 'The Arab Spring and U.S. Policy: The View From Jerusalem,' *Wall Street Journal*, 29 April 2011, http://online.wsj.com/article/SB10001424052748 704330404576291063679488964.html.

30. Ibid.

With friends like Ted Koppel and the AIPAC-padded US Congress, Israel needed no enemies. The geopolitics of the region was changing, and Koppel and company had no clue in which way. The Islamic Republic was losing both its allies and its nemeses, as was Israel, and likewise the United States. These revolutions were occurring across the board: in countries hostile to the United States and Israel and in climes friendly to them. The net result was not just that the Islamic Republic was losing the power it had inherited rather than gained, but that the United States was losing the power it had gained and not merited. Israel was now completely exposed, and no weapon that AIPAC could procure for the Jewish state from the United States could protect it from what was coming its way.

Nothing could defeat Zionism – the Zionist pact with US imperialism, turning the Jewish garrison state into the largest aircraft carrier in the Mediterranean – made sure of that. But what was coming Israel's way was not a military attack, or a 'terrorist strike' (to use the violent language that the apartheid Jewish state understands and speaks very eloquently); not even more flotillas of brave peace activists for its navy to murder with impunity and then blame the victims (another art that Israel has perfected). Instead, coming its way was something entirely different, for which Israel has never been prepared. Imagine millions of Egyptians just walking from Tahrir Square to Jerusalem, not with guns or other arms, but with bread and water, food and medicine, for the millions of Palestinians incarcerated in their own homeland! What would Israel do – drop its atom bomb on them?

This has never been a real threat – but it is a possible eventuality, if not by the action of Egyptians then of Palestinians themselves. Early in June, *Haaretz* reported, the Israel Defense Forces Northern Command was 'on high alert ... ahead of a possible attempt by thousands of Palestinian refugees from the Damascus area to storm the border of the Golan Heights as a way of marking Nakba Day, the anniversary of the beginning of the Six-Day War.'[31] The

---

31. See 'IDF on High Alert as Palestinians Prepare for Naksa Day,' *Haaretz*, 5 June 2011, www.haaretz.com/print-edition/news/idf-on-high-alert-as-palestinians-prepare-for-naksa-day-1.365945.

critical part of the story is that the march was cancelled following the intervention of Hezbollah! 'Pressure from Hezbollah,' *Haaretz* reported, 'which does not want escalation with Israel, apparently also played a part in the cancelation of marches, as did pressure on the Lebanese army by United Nations Interim Force in Lebanon.' *Haaretz* was wrong in its assessment that Hezbollah wanted to avoid confrontation with Israel. Why would it? It thrives on the prospect of such confrontations. Rather, the Hezbollah leadership was opposed to the Palestinian initiative because it had not initiated or sponsored it, for it was outside its dominion and, above all, beyond its militant imagination. The non-violent character of such proposed action, which would make Israel defenseless, would threaten to put Hezbollah out of business too. Both Israel and Hezbollah have historically been prepared only for violent encounters, and never for actions of non-violent emancipation from the politics of despair that they have so successfully fostered. This was, and remains, the logic of Tahrir Square: its non-violent, non-militant, joyous, jubilant disposition rendered the Egyptian army, along with its American sponsor and Israeli counterpart, entirely dysfunctional.

'The difference between the Arab uprisings and Syria,' Hassan Nasrallah surmised, 'is that President Assad is convinced that reforms are necessary, unlike Bahrain and other Arab countries.'[32] But by this point it no longer mattered what Assad was or was not convinced of. He gave up any moral right to be president of Syria when his security and military forces fired the first bullets at defenseless Syrians. There was not one iota of difference between what Syrian people wanted and what the rest of the Arabs wanted: the dignity of self-representation in a free and democratic republic. The troubles that overtook Sayyed Hassan Nasrallah and Benjamin Netanyahu were symptomatic of a more acute malady that had now afflicted even segments of the Arab and Muslim left, which could not quite bring themselves to denounce the criminal atrocities of Bashar al-Assad's regime, on the grounds, they said – in words of

---

32. See 'Hezbollah Urges Syrians to Back Assad Regime,' *Middle East Online*, 25 May 2011, www.middle-east-online.com/english/?id=46327.

astounding banality – that they should not denounce or weaken 'the resistance.'

As clichés abounded and politicians lagged behind events, Arabs and Muslims from one side of their world to the other led the way, and like a pure gem shone as the measure of the mixed metallurgy of their leaders and intellectuals. Hassan Nasrallah ceased being a revolutionary leader and joined the ranks of corrupt politicians like Mubarak, Ben Ali, Gaddafi and their ilk when he sided with the regime of Ali Khamenei, long before he came out in support of Assad's regime. Yet the hypocrisy of this support soon hit home, and hard, not just discrediting Nasrallah's revolutionary leadership, exposing it as mere opportunism, but also revealing the bankruptcy of intellectuals who lacked the moral imagination to match their people's courage. The blood of every innocent Syrian killed by the regime of Bashar al-Assad was now on the hands not just of Hassan Nasrallah but of every intellectual – Arab or non-Arab – who failed to reject these leaders and side unequivocally with the Syrian people in the liberating flowering of the Arab Spring.

Imagining a New World

Hassan Nasrallah and Benjamin Netanyahu alike, along with all those who failed to support the Arab Spring, citing one exception or another in terms of which Arab countries to support and which to turn a blind eye to, suffer from one fundamental ailment: the failure to imagine committedly, or to commit imaginatively. What was the basis for supporting the Tunisian and Egyptian revolutions but not the democratic uprisings in Iran and Syria – the position taken by elements of the Arab and Iranian 'left'; or for supporting the insurgences in Iran and Syria but turning a blind eye to those in Saudi Arabia and Bahrain – as did the United States and Israel? So it transpired that, in a bizarre twist, parts of the Arab and Iranian 'left' (but by no means all) were united in hypocrisy with their arch nemeses, the US and Israel, as there emerged a collusion of interests between left and right, between the Islamic Republic and the United States, between Hezbollah and Israel, to dismiss one aspect or another of the Arab Spring as flawed, because it was either outside the scope of their limited imagination (some on the left) or determined by unlimited greed (the US and Israel). Egypt and Tunisia, then, were perceived as good for the left, but not Syria and Iran. The reverse was true for the right: any trouble coming Syria or Iran's way was good, but God forbid if it came Bahrain's or Saudi Arabia's way. However, and here was the rub, the Arab Spring, picking up from the Green Movement, was consistent, unswerving, steady, flowering with a shared but distinct effusion everywhere.

The events in Iran and the Arab world from the summer of 2009 to the winter of 2011 made a number of critical demands of anyone who cared to understand them, most importantly an appreciation of the languages of revolt, and how they were co-terminous with a liberation geography, and how that geography represented the horizon of a new world. So what kind of language was it that these citizen-revolutionaries were speaking? Consider *Ra'i-ye man kojast*, 'Where is My Vote,' and *'al-Sha'b Yurid Isqat al-Nizam*, 'People Demand the Overthrow of the Regime.' This is not the habitual parlance of anticolonial nationalism, Third World Socialism, or militant Islamism, the means by which people in this region had habitually spoken their politics of defiance. It is, rather, a new, 'overcoming,' language. Intimately related to this emerging language, and to the way it has transcended its antecedents, is the geography that it is imagining, implicating, forecasting.

When we say 'Iran and the Arab world' or 'the Arab and Muslim world' we are opting for an imaginative geography that is in fact no longer viable, and indeed not factually accurate. Similar events to those in Tunisia, Egypt and Syria, for example, were happening in sub-Sahel Africa, as well as beyond the Arab world in Iran, Afghanistan, and Pakistan. Even the clichéd designation 'Muslim world' now lacked validity, not just on account of the non-Muslim populations of Lebanon, Palestine, and Egypt, who needed recognition beyond the status of 'minorities,' but because the extension of North African developments into the rest of Africa was opening up the vista of an entirely different world.

If we are to discover the new language that these revolts are speaking and read the new map of the imaginative geography before us, then we must study the interface between language and the world, where, as Gadamer has demonstrated in *Truth and Method*,

> Language is not just one of man's possessions in the world, but on it depends the fact that man has a world at all. For man the world exists as world in a way that no other being in the world experiences. But this world is linguistic in nature. ... Language has no independent life apart from the world that comes to language within it. Not only is the world 'world' only insofar as it comes into language, but language, too, has its real being only in the fact that the world is represented within it. Thus the original humanity of the language means at the same time the fundamental linguistics quality of man's being-in-the-world.[33]

I wish to extend this hermeneutic wisdom into the political language people speak, be it to confirm to themselves where they are or to imagine themselves where they want to be. Militant Islamism was a political language (an *utterance* in Bakhtin's terms), as were Third World Socialism and anticolonial nationalism: languages people spoke to project themselves into the horizon of the world they wished to inhabit. In short, the language we hear spoken in these revolutionary uprisings that we call the 'Arab Spring' and decipher is instrumental, organic, integral to the world we are discovering mapped before us. We will interpret that language and chart the contours of that new world at one and the same time. The problem with the designation 'Muslim world' is that it reduces a multifaceted political culture to its Islamic dimension.

The ideological marker that most immediately offers itself, so far as the language of the revolts is concerned, is 'Islamist' parlance. Many commentators, from Ayatollah Khamenei to Bernard Lewis, view the revolutionary uprisings as the most recent expression of Islamic revolution (though one of these celebrates and the other fears it). The fear or hope that the Islamists will take over, that these are Islamic societies and their political language is influenced by Islam, is balanced by the alternative perception that what we

---

33. Hans-Georg Gadamer, *Truth and Method* (New York: Continuum, 2004): 401.

are seeing are (or ought to be) secular uprisings, in search of secular governments – which proposition leads us directly back to the false binary of 'tradition versus modernity.' Hence, before we know it we will be told yet again that if the objective of the revolts is democracy, then we will be disappointed because democracy is 'a political concept that has no history, no record whatever in the Arab, Islamic world.' In other words, we first posit something called 'the Islamic world' and then we hear it speak Islamically. The world and the language, as Gadamer notes, are integral to each other. If these movements are Islamic, they cannot be democratic; if they must be secular to be democratic, then as Muslims we are contradicting ourselves even to think of democracy. It follows that the movements are in fact chasing their own tail.

What Language, What World?

My reading of the unfolding world through the Arab Spring pre-dates the events. Over the last decade or so I have been attentively cultivating the idea of *cosmopolitan worldliness* as an alternative way to think about what is habitually identified as 'the Arab and the Muslim world,' the Orient, or 'the Middle East and North Africa' – all colonially informed conceptions of a world habitually posited as 'the East' by 'the West' that had manufactured it. This worldli-ness is neither ontic nor ontological, but existential (Heidegger's designation): historical, lived, experienced, remembered, acted. I first argued for the existence of cosmopolitan worldliness in the Introduction to a new edition of my *Theology of Discontent* (1993/2005), articulating it more extensively in the Iranian context in later works. I did so mostly but not exclusively through multiple deconstructive strategies in the fields of *différance* (Derridian differing by deferring) operative in an Islamic context, precisely because that was the term in which such cosmopolitanism has been systematically distorted and overcome; I wanted to reverse that overcoming in a counter-reading that used 'the Islamic world' to force it open. In *Theology of Discontent* I retrieved that worldli-ness by situating the rise of political Islamism within the larger context of a multivalent political culture of Islamism, socialism and nationalism. In *Iran: A People Interrupted* I did so by placing Iranian political culture within the production of literary cosmopolitanism. In *Islamic Liberation Theology* I posited *theodicy* as a way of accounting for worldly others in a given theology of resistance; and in *Shi'ism* I did it by way of sublating the idea of *taqiyya* in Shi'ism. The point of all of this was to retrieve the multiple worlds that have existed prior to and coterminous with 'Islam and the West.' Through that binary, now updated to 'Islamism versus Secularism,' the two sides of the coin are systematically corroborated at the cost of preventing the cosmopolitan worldliness that overrides them showing itself. Cosmopolitan worldliness becomes evident in the literary, visual, and performing arts. Art makes it possible for us to see and to make visible the pre-ontological disposition of this worldliness, for here the fields of ideology semiotically self-destruct as soon as we start looking at them aesthetically.[34] The intent of this theoretical position is to expose and decipher the palimpsestic map and read what is behind the overwritten cartography of 'the West and the Rest,' where 'the Arab and Islamic World' is located.

What I believe is happening in countries from Iran to Egypt and Tunisia to Morocco, predicated on 'the end of Islamic ideology,' is the retrieval of their organic cosmopolitan cultures, at once local and global in terms specific to their historical experiences. The uprisings are geared towards the restitution of this cosmopolitan worldliness. What I mean by cosmopolitanism is not what Kant has argued (and others after him), namely a philosophical and ethical argument for the delineation of moral, political, and legal prerequisites of a global conception of justice,[35] but precisely the opposite: a historical coming to terms with the factual existence of, not an imaginative wishing for, a cosmopolitan worldliness embedded in a variety of imperial experiences, from the Abbasids in the eighth century to the Ottomans in the nineteenth. By cosmopolitan worldliness, then, I mean the actual worldly experiences that have historically existed but that have been overridden and camouflaged

---

34. A key text in this regard is Hamid Dabashi, *Makhmalbaf at Large: The Making of a Rebel Filmmaker* (London: I.B. Tauris, 2008).

35. See Immanuel Kant, 'Idea of a Universal History with a Cosmopolitan Purpose,' in Garrett Wallace Brown and David Held (eds), *The Cosmopolitanism Reader* (Cambridge: Polity Press, 2010): 17–26.

by the heavy ideological autonormativity of 'the West.' It is those worlds, I argue, that we must conceptually and categorically retrieve, as they become manifest in revolutionary praxis across the region. Rereading those palimpsestic maps, which are there but hidden, means retrieving the worlds that are otherwise buried under two hundred years of colonial and imperial domination by an entity that calls itself (a practice habitually echoed by us) 'the West,' along with all of the civilizational alterities invented by mercenary armies of Orientalist and nativist intellectuals alike.

To retrieve the cosmopolitan worldliness that now informs the Arab Spring is not to put it on a pedestal and fetishize it, but simply to cultivate its theoretical contours in geographical, historical, and political terms, particularly the multiplicities of its discourses of legitimacy. To retrieve and posit that cosmopolitanism is also to put it up against the essentialist reading of Islam itself as it has been manufactured by Orientalists and Islamists alike: as a site of ideological contestation with European colonialism or 'the West.' More importantly, we need this retrieval and restitution in order to place it next to the many other instances of cosmopolitan worldliness that have existed either concurrently or consecutively across regions and cultures. The point is to identify one specific and meaningful frame of worldly reference among others, and thus to move forward to comprehend the contemporary parameters of the emerging worlds beyond the collapse of 'the East-West' binary.

The end of *that* Islam is coterminous with the end of 'the West' that dialectically produced it, which has now exhausted itself within its own original European and transatlantic matrix. While Francis Fukuyama's 1989 essay on 'The End of History' coincided with – and celebrated – the demise of the Soviet Union and the Eastern bloc and promised the triumphant rise of a unipolar US (neoliberal) imperialism, Samuel Huntington's essay 'The Clash of Civilizations' coincided with the first attempt to bring down the World Trade Center, on 26 February 1993, carried out by a band of militant Muslims. Thus, between the collapse of the Berlin Wall and the first attack on the World Trade Center – that is, the period of George H.W. Bush's presidency and the rise of what he termed the 'New World Order' – Soviet communism yielded to

Islamism as 'the West's' nemesis. The essays of Fukuyama and his former teacher Huntington dovetailed, leaving 'the West' in a state of limbo for some four years, not quite knowing what to do with itself after Fukuyama (remembering Hegel and forgetting Carl Schmitt) declared it triumphant, until Huntington (forgetting Hegel and remembering Carl Schmitt) manufactured a new global enemy for it.[36]

With the dual implosion of these ideological constructions and the rise of the Arab Spring, the world is once again up for grabs. In 'The Democratic Emblem' (2009), the distinguished French philosopher Alain Badiou plays with the French expressions *tout le monde* ('everyone') and *le monde* ('the world') in order to reveal the word 'democracy' as the untouchable emblem in the symbolic system called 'the West,' masquerading as *the* (one and only) world. Badiou posits *le monde* as 'the world that evidently exists,' and distinguishes it from *tout le monde* that 'the West' fancies itself to be. He observes:

> Everyone else is from the other world – which, being other, is not a world properly speaking, just a remnant of life, a zone of war, hunger, walls, and delusions. In that 'world' or zone, they spend their time packing their bags to get away from the horror or to leave altogether and be with – whom? With the democrats of course, who claim to run the world and have jobs that need doing.[37]

Badiou is exceptionally insightful in his demarcation between *the world* at large and *the* world in which democracy is the emblem, 'the West':

---

36. Entirely oblivious to this ideological manufacturing of 'Islam' as the trope of enemy, and equally to the lived experience of Muslims, Eric Walberg, in *Postmodern Imperialism: Geopolitics and the Great Games* (New York: Clarity Press, 2011), provides an updated reading of the nineteenth-century 'Great Game,' the imperial rivalry between Russia and Britain, by way of a reading of contemporary global imperialism, in which he offers communism and Islam as two modes, respectively secular and religious, of resistance to imperialism. The notion that 'communism' could have any relevance in the age of transnational and supra-state labor migration, combined with a reading of 'Islam' as a 'religious ideology of resistance' to imperialism (basically a Samuel Huntington theme moving from the right to the left spectrum), is both outdated and analytically flawed. See my *Islamic Liberation Theology: Resisting the Empire* (London: Routledge, 2008) for more details.

37. Alain Badiou, 'The Democratic Emblem,' in Georgio Agamben et al., *Democracy in What State?* (New York: Columbia University Press, 2009): 7–8.

In sum, if the world of the democrats is not the world of everyone, if tout le monde isn't really the whole world after all, then democracy, the emblem and the custodian of the walls behind which the democrats seek their petty pleasures, is just a word for a conservative oligarchy whose main (and often bellicose) business is to guard its own territory, as animals do, under the usurped name *world*.[38]

The implosion of the world that thought itself *tout le monde* is no longer merely political. It is also philosophical. In order to reach for the current world, the world we live in, the world in which people revolt, the world in which Meydan Azadi and Tahrir Square have become emblematic of something else, something beyond 'Western liberal democracy,' something yet to be named, needs to be imagined. In this world, I suggest, demography, labor migration, gender apartheid, and environmental catastrophe are the key operative factors. In this world, Islam will not disappear; it will be sublated into a new cosmopolitan worldliness. For Islam is in continual dialogue with something else. Today it has lost its principal interlocutor, the West, and so is up for grabs. In this world, film, fiction, and poetry will have as much power and panache as people crying in their streets and alleys 'Where is My Vote' and 'People Demand the Overthrow of the Regime'. We have to enable this world via a retrieval of the material evidence for the existing cosmopolitism in film, fiction, art, and poetry, as we raise them to the level of a renewed worldliness that is consciously self-aware. The space of that enduring rally is the simulacrum of our Tahrir Square.

---

38. Ibid.

FIVE

From the Green Movement
to the Jasmine Revolution

To bring an end to 'Islam and the West' as a matrix of animosity and knowledge production, and envision in its place the rise of a new moral map of 'the Middle East' with the capacity to expand its claim within a renewed pact with humanity, is no simple feat. It would mean, among other things, the end of 'Middle East Studies' as a discipline. The idea of that *overcoming* is quite destabilizing; conducive to vertigo, mentally unsettling for the machinery of knowledge production of which we as subjects are at once the product and the consumer, and in which we as agents of our own history are so heavily invested. This revolutionary moment requires that we think outside ourselves.

Other modes of knowledge production have changed drastically under similar circumstances. We must remember that the entire spectrum of modern European social science began with the Enlightenment project in the late seventeenth and early eighteenth centuries, and accelerated in the aftermath of the French Revolution of 1789, when European thinkers, from Auguste Comte (1798-1857) to Karl Marx (1818-1883), began to theorize their societies systematically as a discipline, and universalized their local findings to the entire world. Émile Durkheim (1858-1917) and Max Weber (1864-1920) were the culmination of this Enlightenment-inspired mode of sociological knowledge production. In the aftermath of World War I the European social sciences extended into North America in earnest, and with major sociologists like Talcott Parsons (1902–1979) and C. Wright Mills (1916–1962) the European sociological imagination found conservative or radical reflections in North America. This remained the case until World War II when the horrors of the Holocaust ultimately led to the breakdown of Enlightenment illusions. Poststructuralist thinkers like Michel Foucault (1926–1984) and critical theorists like Jürgen Habermas (b. 1929) appeared either to end or else resume the project of European Enlightenment modernity, a development that in the aftermath of the May 1968 French uprisings assumed more radical postmodern dimensions.

Modes and disciplines of knowledge production have thus always been affected by major, world-historic social movements, from the French Revolution of 1789 to the European revolutions of 1848, the Russian Revolution of 1917, the mass student and labour movements of the 1960s, and the Civil Rights and antiwar movement in the United States. What we witnessed in the last decades of the twentieth century and summarily identified as 'postmodernism' has finally shown itself to be the cul-de-sac of a European project of modernity, which in its European and American manifestations existed as a double bind embedded in a colonial modernity that shaped the world at large.

Throughout these developments, the study of 'the Middle East' had remained more or less within the confines of Orientalism.[1] Soon after the commencement of the Cold War, however, the mode of knowledge production about 'the Middle East' transmuted into 'Area Studies,' by way of producing useful knowledge for the United States intelligence communities (and their European and regional allies) in their endeavors to prevent the spread of Soviet-inspired socialism. That mode of knowledge in turn came ceased with the end of the Cold War, the collapse of the Soviet Union, and the rise of North American think-tanks and political action committees (the example par excellence of which is AIPAC and its intelligence arm WINEP) – a phase I have identified as *knowledge under duress* or

---

1. See Edward W. Said, *Orientalism* (New York: Vintage, 1978).

disposable knowledge in the post-Orientalist phase.[2] Paramount throughout these phases has been the relation between knowledge and power: a mode of knowledge has been manufactured from the position of power that has both justified and sustained that power. What impact will the Arab Spring have on these modes of knowledge production about 'the Middle East'? With the rise of the Arab Spring the colonial construct called 'the Middle East' finally comes to an end, at a time when the onslaught against the European project of 'modernity,' with the rise of the 'postmodern' critique of autonomous reason and subject formation, had already in 1979 sent Michel Foucault to Iran in a self-deluded search for a charismatic outburst that would perhaps announce a new enchantment with the world. Today, however, the rise of democratic uprisings is bound to have a seismic effect on the way we imagine, think, and write about the areas that European and American imperialism calls 'the Middle East.' The existing regimes of knowledge production within the field of 'Middle Eastern Studies' are far from being equipped to deal with the magnitude of events that have unfolded since January 2011. Consider this: by late July 2011, the Syrian government of Bashar al-Assad had drafted a law 'that allows the formation of political parties other than the ruling Baath party.'[3] This was impossible even to imagine, let alone analyze and understand within the epistemic limitations of 'Middle Eastern Studies.' The Baath party had governed Syria for nearly half a century. The mode of knowledge produced and sustained in 'Middle Eastern Studies' was caught entirely unprepared to fathom such cataclysmic events. A change in the regime of knowledge is demanded and will be exacted by events unfolding on the ground. This is a transformative period wherein national boundaries will blur and confuse each other.

The Arab Spring has, I believe, resolved the tension identified in my *Iran, the Green Movement and the US: The Fox and the Paradox* – the paradox being the fact that the Islamic Republic had created

---

2. See Hamid Dabashi, *Post-Orientalism: Knowledge and Power in Time of Terror* (New Brunswick NJ: Transaction, 2008).

3. See 'Syria is to Allow Political Parties, State Agency Says,' BBC News online, 25 July 2011, www.bbc.co.uk/news/world-middle-east-14274891.

a situation whereby whatever the United States did in the stand-off (negotiate or strike) it would strengthen the theocracy. That privileged position is arguably no longer there, precisely because the Arab Spring and the Green Movement have robbed the Islamic Republic of both its habitual friends and its historic foes, and thus drastically altered the geopolitics of the region. Israel, Iran's arch nemesis, is in deep trouble as a consequence of the Arab Spring, as are the Islamic Republic's historic allies Syria and Hezbollah. The dialectical interaction between national and transnational politics has now reconfigured the geopolitics of the region in the form of a permanent revolutionary mood; each affects the other. The habitual politics of despair has been overcome once and for all by the contagious democratic will of multiple nation-states, beyond the tactical or strategic control of counter-revolutionary forces. These events are forcing us all towards a reconsideration of the relationship between a nation and the transnational matrix that embraces it. Beyond all racialized and sectarian divides we are discovering new forms of transnational solidarity, which in turn will demand alternative modes of reading emerging realities. Try as we may to assimilate these realities into what we already now, they will resist, defy, and overcome all such attempts. The facts are all out there – dancing in Tahrir Square – and they will shape their own theories. The combined forces and catalytic impacts of the Green Movement and the Arab Spring have created a new transnationalism. We are on the threshold of a new world that is becoming evident to and conscious of itself.

For the Left to be Right

What sort of knowledge, discipline, geography and language will emerge from the current transformative period remains to be seen. That the ground is shifting under our feet is quite evident. The key factor is that the adoption of traditional political positions is becoming increasingly difficult. We have already seen that both the Arab and the non-Arab left was divided on the Arab Spring as it unfolded, supporting revolts in those countries whose ruling regimes had facilitated American and Israeli interests in the region, whilst being hesitant, suspicious, and even dismissive of revolts in those countries from whose instability they thought the US and its regional allies might actually or potentially benefit. Simon Assaf, focuses the issue in his essay 'Taking Sides in Syria':

> Syria has long been a thorn in imperialism's side. The Baathist regime has given crucial support to the Lebanese and Palestinian resistance movements who depend on Syria for their survival. So those who found themselves on the same side over the revolutions in Egypt and Tunisia have suddenly found sharp disagreement over the movement for change in Syria. At the heart of this disagreement is Syria's opposition to imperialism and the dangers of a revolution finding itself at the mercy of the Western powers. What attitude should revolutionaries take towards the Syrian movement, and how should we assess a regime that, although the victim of imperialism, has unleashed harsh repression on those who have from the onset demanded modest reforms?[4]

The new geopolitics that had both conditioned the Arab uprisings and was deeply affected by them needed fresh thinking, fresh alliances, steadfast determination in order not to lose track of the weakest and most vulnerable sectors of society. The real left – not those museum curators masquerading as the left incapable of thinking beyond the curve – now needed to rebuild from the ground up, from labor unions, women's rights organizations, students assemblies: the very form and substance of a civic life in which civil liberties and social justice were the foundations of a democratic society.

For the left to rethink itself in this environment, the world-historic dimensions of the revolutionary uprisings must be grasped. Rashid Khalidi, the distinguished historian of the modern Arab world, had to reach back all the way to the year 1402 when Ibn Khaldun (1332-1406) met with the Warrior Timur/Tamerlane (1336-1405) to get to grips with the magnitude of the events of the Arab Spring in 2011: 'None of us is Ibn Khaldun,' Rashid Khalidi observed, 'but any Arab historian today watching the Arab revolutions of 2011 has the sense of awe that our forbear

---

4. See Simon Assaf, 'Taking Sides in Syria,' *Socialist Review*, July-August 2011, www.socialistreview.org.uk/article.php?articlenumber=11719.

must have had as we witness a great turning in world affairs.'[5]
This is no mere rhetorical flourish. We are indeed on a blank page
of history. The orchestral expanse and magnitude of these revolts
across multiple Arab counties make for a panoramic view that is
daunting and exceedingly difficult to grasp and comprehend. We
are like spectators sitting in a concert hall, with a baffled and
out-of-practice conductor standing before a versatile and virtuoso
orchestra performing a strangely beautiful symphony. The melody
sounds familiar, the harmony is incredible. It is not just the individual musicians, but the music that they collectively make that
excites and baffles the historian.

Rashid Khalid is convinced that

> what has started in Tunisia and Cairo has opened up horizons that
> have long been closed. The energy, dynamism and intelligence of
> the younger generation in the Arab world has been unleashed, after
> being dammed up by a system which treated them with contempt, and
> which concentrated power in the hands of a much older generation.
> Seemingly out of nowhere, young people in the Arab world have gained
> a confidence, an assurance, and a courage that have made fearsome
> police state regimes that once looked invincible tremble.

This unleashed energy is undoubtedly economically rooted, demo-
graphically driven, and predicated on the profound social anomie
and cultural alienation of preceding generations – ground in which
absolutist Islamism could thrive. But this time around there was
a difference apparent that no one could fail to see:

> What so far distinguishes the revolutionary upsurge that we have
> been watching across the Arab world from its many predecessors? One
> of the apparent distinctions is that in Tunisia, Egypt, Bahrain and
> several other countries, it has so far been largely peaceful: 'Silmiyya,
> Silmiyya' the crowds in Tahrir Square chanted. But so were many of
> the great Arab risings of the past. These included many episodes in
> Egypt and Iraq's long struggles to end British military occupation, and
> those of Syria, Lebanon, Morocco and Tunisia to end that of France,
> not to speak of the first Palestinian intifada against Israeli occupation

5. See Rashid Khalidi, 'Preliminary Historical Observations on the Arab Revolutions
of 2011,' *Jadaliyya*, 21 March 2011, www.jadaliyya.com/pages/index/970/preliminary-
historical-observations-on-the-arab-re.

from 1987–1991. While tactics of non-violence were broadly employed in the recent uprisings in Egypt and elsewhere, this is by no means the first time that Arab uprisings have been largely non-violent, or at least unarmed.[6]

Of course, the absence of violence in the Arab Spring has one fundamental distinction: it was predicated on the absence of an ideology of violence, the absence of an armed extension to the civil uprising. There was no PLO to this intifada, to develop the Palestinian analogy, and it is precisely for that reason that the Arab Spring has frightened Israel more than it has the Arab potentates it has directly targeted. It is not just the fact that people were out in the streets crying *Silmiyya, Silmiyya*. There was no armed wing of the movement in villages, mountains, or urban hideouts blowing up police stations or killing military personnel. The death that initiated the Arab Spring targeted no one other than the body of the person who set himself alight in protest against structural tyranny. Yes, buildings associated with the ruling regimes were burned down, but such acts were few and far between, not systematic, and above all not expressions of a militant ideology. Egyptians were out cleaning, painting, and generally beautifying Tahrir Square the day after they were done ousting Mubarak. This was no Orientalist trope, cooked up by some American journalist; it was a fact on the ground, one that had altered the universal image of Arabs and Muslims – not least the image they presented to themselves – around the globe, and a fact that had outmaneuvered the bloody military interventionism of the US and Israel in the region, from Afghanistan and Iraq to Palestine and Lebanon.

The revolutionary uprisings targeted domestic tyrannies that had feigned revolutionary resistance to foreigners whilst in effect facilitating it. Their power lay in the fact that corrupt tyrannies ranging from the Islamic Republic of Iran to Libya could no longer pretend they were fighting or resisting imperialism while they were abusing their own people. They were exposed for the frauds that they were. Khalidi rightly points out that

---

6. Ibid.

the revolutions that took place from 1800 until the 1950s were primarily directed at ending foreign occupation. These revolutions for national liberation ultimately succeeded in the expulsion of the old colonial powers and their hated military bases in most of the Arab world. These revolutions eventually produced nationalist regimes in most Arab countries. Those in Algeria, Libya, the Sudan, Syria and Yemen still cling to power.[7]

Those revolutions were fought and won for doubtful gain. They succeeded in ending European colonial rule over the Arab world, but resulted in tyrants who abused their own populations and robbed them of their civil liberties, and meanwhile the bedrock of imperialism in the region – Israel – grew more powerful by the day. Against that background, the revolutions that we are now witnessing are seen to be something else, dealing with unfinished business, a form of delayed defiance, embedded in those anticolonial struggles but now running much deeper in their institutional demands for civil liberties. As Khalidi observes, 'What distinguishes the revolutions of 2011 from their predecessors is that they mark the end of the old phase of national liberation from colonial rule, and are largely inward-directed at the problems of Arab societies.' To be sure, Khalidi also warns:

> Of course, with the cold war the old colonialism eventually gave way to a more insidious form of external influence, first of the two super-powers, and for the last two decades of the US alone. The entire Arab regional system was upheld by that hyper-power, whose support was crucial to the survival of most of the dictatorial regimes now trembling as their peoples challenge them. But while this important factor was always in the background, the focus of the 2011 revolutions has been on the internal problems of democracy, constitutions, and equality.[8]

Of course, by no stretch of the imagination can this be construed as playing down such issues as US imperial domination, Israel's theft of Palestinian land, or the Saudi threat to any democratic change in the region, or indeed the Islamic Republic's opportunism in turning any and every event in the region to its advantage.

---

7. Ibid.
8. Ibid.

Nevertheless what has defined the political uprisings is in fact something apolitical, something moral:

> There was another demand in 2011, however. This was for dignity. And this has to be understood in two senses: the dignity of the individual, and the dignity of the collective, of the people, and of the nation. The demand for individual dignity is easily understandable. In the face of frightful police states that crushed the individual, such a demand was natural. The incessant infringements by these authoritarian states on the dignity of nearly every Arab citizen, and their rulers' constant affirmations of their worthlessness, were eventually internalized and produced a pervasive self-loathing and an ulcerous social malaise. This manifested itself among other things in sectarian tensions, frequent sexual harassment of women, criminality, drug use, and a corrosive incivility and lack of public spirit.[9]

Dignity is not a political matter. Dignity is a moral virtue that had now become a political force. As a moral proposition *karamah*, 'dignity,' is a virtue *sui generis*, irreducible to any religion, entirely contingent on its communal summoning and articulation. The innate humanism operative at the heart of an appeal to 'dignity' in effect defines the revolutionary gathering of an inaugural moment for humanity at large. Dignity is an end in itself, caused and conditioned by the revolutionary uprisings. This appeal to dignity posits an agency, maps an unfolding morality, and reclaims the term 'Arab' from years and generations of abuse. As a non-political term entering the political domain, 'dignity' has a catalytic power, an inaugural audacity, announcing the self-conscious start of a world-historic event that was about to discover a world of its own making: announced by the Arab Spring.

Illiberal Neoliberalism

The revolutionary uprisings have opened up the political possibility of looking at events far beyond the Arab world, widening horizons, retrieving what the German philosopher Hans Blumenberg (1920–1996) calls 'the absolutism of reality,' which is the ground zero of renewed (and this time more liberating) myth-making – or

---

9. Ibid.

'absolute myths.'[10] Consider the coincidence (is it a coincidence?): 'In mid-February, the week after Hosni Mubarak was driven from office by the Egyptian revolution, unprecedented demonstrations erupted in the state of Wisconsin opposing the efforts of the newly elected Republican governor to destroy the organizing power of public employee unions.' This is Paul Rosenberg, the senior editor of Random Length News, a biweekly alternative community newspaper, and a contributor to Al Jazeera. He continues: 'Although the specific causes were significantly different, the underlying logic of the people rising up against powerful anti-democratic elites made for more than just a superficial resemblance between Tahrir Square in Cairo, and the capitol building and its environs in Madison, Wisconsin.'[11] This must be the first time that a world-historic event in the Arab and Muslim world has prompted, indeed necessitated, such a – perfectly logical – transcontinental comparison; a comparison that would soon be even more emphatically pronounced following the commencement of the Occupy Wall Street movement.

Paul Rosenberg defines the two occurrences as 'unique, yet related events, like the differing national expressions of waves of protest and revolution that swept Europe in 1848, or that wrapped around the world in 1968.' What is significant here is that for the first time in modern history the axis of world history has shifted. Something has happened in the Arab and Muslim world that prompts Rosenberg to think of 'a prolonged struggle to realize a more just, egalitarian world – a yearning that crosses all manner of cultural boundaries, though it finds unique expression wherever it arises,' in terms of its patience and poise, when compared to previous historic moments:

> Yet, despite the apparent defeat of these waves of revolution [in Europe in 1848 and 1968], they had profound effects, altering the very sense of the possible – even if it wasn't immediately obvious how to make the possible into the real. For example, demonstrations on both sides of

---

10. See Hans Blumenberg, 'After the Absolutism of Reality,' in *Work on Myth*, trans. Robert M. Wallace (Cambridge MA: MIT Press, 1990): 3-33.
11. See Paul Rosenberg, 'Bottom-up Revolution,' Al Jazeera, 17 June 2011, http://english.aljazeera.net/indepth/opinion/2011/06/2011616114013236175.html.

the Iron Curtain in 1968 foreshadowed the decades-long development of movements that helped bring the Cold War to a peaceful end.

Rosenberg offers a similar reading of the revolutions of 1848:

when Otto von Bismarck – one of Europe's leading conservatives of the 19th century – became the architect of Germany's welfare state in the 1880s, he did it in part to co-opt support for the socialist-oriented Social Democratic Party. Yet, that very act of co-option was itself an acknowledgment of how 1848 had profoundly changed the world.

In comparison to this turning point in 1848 or 1968 in Europe, Paul Rosenberg suggests that

The current wave of revolutionary protest, intensely focused in the Arab world, but which echoes from Iran to Spain to the US, shows signs of similar dynamics, though they play out very differently in different situations. One crucial difference from 1848 and 1968 is the role of social media, which gives bottom-up egalitarians a better footing for sustained organizing. It remains to be seen how effective this will prove to be, but at the very least there is a vastly increased potential to sustain a broadly shared sense of what a very different world could look like.[12]

Rosenberg's diagnosis remains rightly focused on the resonances of the Arab Spring in Europe and the United States, which are now witnessing their own versions, or echoes, of the social uprising: 'Things are very different in and around the Euro–US economic core, and the reason for that largely hinges on how the draconian practices of neoliberal economics – forced onto the global south in the 1980s and 1990s – have finally come home to roost in the neo-imperial heartland.' Though the geographical designations of 'global south' and 'neo-imperial heartland' still very much divide the world into old topographies, Rosenberg's comparative assessment nevertheless remains solidly insightful:

Both the Egyptian Revolution and its Wisconsin echo resulted, to different degrees, from the catastrophic failure of the global neo-liberal order in the financial crisis of late 2008, and the followup efforts to

---

12. Ibid.

save those responsible for the crash, rather than those victimized by it. The same is also true of Tunisia, birthplace of the Arab Spring, as well as in Spain, where the 'Real Democracy Now!' movement has brought strikingly similar mass demonstrations onto the European continent.[13]

The binary of 'the West and the Rest' notwithstanding, Paul Rosenberg's equally insightful reference to Latin America widens the frame even more poignantly: 'the explosion of Arab Spring can be seen as a more compressed and complicated version of Latin America's decade-long realignment away from neoliberalism and US hegemony.'[14] This framing within a cross-continental revolt against neoliberalism is insightful but also limiting because the economic factors are both at the heart and at the periphery of the Arab Spring. They cannot define them, nor can they be explained without them. Economically we may, and indeed we must, draw comparisons between what has happened in Latin America and in the Arab World. But the fact that champion of anti-neoliberalism Hugo Chávez offered his 'friend' Gaddafi support when Libyans had revolted against him cannot be totally ignored. Whatever good it is that Hugo Chávez and Evo Morales might be doing in Latin America, the fact that they hold the likes of Gaddafi and Ahmadinejad so close exposes a structural deficiency in cross-continental solidarity and revolutionary uprisings. It is not acceptable to be a champion of the poor in Venezuela or Bolivia and then to support ghastly dictators or theocratic tyrannies in someone else's homeland. The emerging world is at once exposing those hypocrisies and overcoming them.

Rosenberg proceeds to explain the difference between Spain and Wisconsin and Tunisia and Egypt in terms of a 'decades-long struggle between neoliberalism and welfare-state economics around the globe,' thus tracing it back all the way to 'the twin oil shocks of the 1970s' and even the nationalization of oil in Iran in 1953 and Guatemala's attempt to establish a 'New Deal-style welfare state in 1954, [when] CIA operations were used to overthrow both

13. Ibid.
14. Ibid.

democratically elected governments and replace them with dictator-ships, in order to "defend freedom" as defined by the US during the Cold War.' From all of these, Rosenberg then concludes:

> Underlying these particulars is a perpetual clash between the ideo-logical promise of free market rhetoric, and the recurrent reality of oligopolies, oligarchs, crony capitalists and the like who manage to thrive, even dominate, in the name of freedom. First Britain, then the US, have dominated the world for two centuries under this peculiar banner of 'freedom' that gives license to the most predatory forms of capitalism.[15]

This time around, however, millions of people from Morocco to Iran, from Syria to Yemen, are out in the streets and squares of their cities demonstrating against their native tyrannies and foreign abuse at one and the same time. This is the moment at which all the formations of postcolonial ideology have failed, and dictators like Ayatollah Khamenei or Muammar Gaddafi are all it has to show for itself. So, opposing the 'ideological promise of free market rhetoric' is no longer the vacuous rant of one petty dictator or another, but rather the democratic will of nations.

Paul Rosenberg is critical of the European left for having largely 'accepted the neoliberal rhetoric over the past two decades, even while maintaining a theoretical commitment to social and eco-nomic justice to distinguish themselves from parties of the right,' as he is critical of American Democrats largely ignoring the Wis-consin uprising. His conclusion regarding the decline of American power is apt: 'Obama's belated attempts to play catch-up with the Arab Spring are but one facet of a more general loss of previous dominance.' His conclusion sees clearly the road ahead:

> But the true revolution is not to replace US power with another, simi-lar false prophet of 'freedom' defined by the marketplace alone. The true revolution is to make the marketplace the servant of humanity's dreams, rather than their master. This is the cause that Mohamed Bouazizi sacrificed his life for. It is the reason that his spirit lives, not

---

15. Ibid.

just in Tunisia, but also across the Arab world and around the entire globe – even in Madison, Wisconsin.[16]

For Mohamed Bouazizi to remain the martyred witness of a revolution that will not replace one dictator with another, one false prophecy of freedom with another, there is only one logical and lasting measure: the people. As long as Tahrir Square remains open and clear for revolt, that revolution remains open-ended. In late July 2011, tens of thousands of people packed the square, 'after the first call by Islamist leaders for nationwide demonstrations since President Hosni Mubarak was overthrown in February.' The BBC reported that 'Many protesters – dominated by Muslim Brotherhood supporters – are calling for an Islamic state and Shari'a law. Correspondents say the rallies will be a worrying development for secularists.'[17] There has never been a suggestion that Egyptian Islamists should not have a say in their national revolution, or that they should not be allowed to gather at Tahrir Square. The point is for Tahrir Square to be open to those who consider themselves 'secular' to come to the same place if not on the following Friday then on the next Wednesday, if they so wish, to have their say. Fear of the 'Islamists,' whoever they might be, might be a BBC fear of the unknown or a genuine fear of Islamist (or any other kind of) absolutism within Egypt. The opening horizons of the world that is unfolding will reveal these conceptual disturbances as we move forward. But one thing is clear: it is next to impossible to imagine that Islamists in Egypt will maim, murder, silence, imprison, purge the universities, launch a cultural revolution, or force into exile non-Islamists, as the Islamic Republic did more than thirty years ago. The brutal example of the Islamic Republic of Iran stands in Tahrir Square like a tall mirror. This is not to say that Egyptians as Muslims will not or should not have a say in the affairs of their homeland. The open-ended revolution constantly generates its own alterities.

---

16. Ibid.
17. See 'Egypt uprising: Islamists lead Tahrir Square rally,' BBC News online, 29 July 2011, www.bbc.co.uk/news/world-middle-east-14341089.

The Dialectics of Transnationalism

The dialectic between national politics and transnational geo-politics is a formula akin to a nuclear reaction, where no counter-revolutionary force can completely control the colliding political particles as they occupy ever more expansive domains. The democratic wind, to change to a more pleasant and life-affirming metaphor, that is blowing beautifully eastward from North Africa sends refreshing wafts of jasmine across the River Nile, towards the Persian Gulf, beyond the Arabian Sea, over the Indian Ocean and into the farthest reaches of Iran and Afghanistan and then to Central Asia. This is a force of nature, long in the making, and even longer in the unfolding.

The triumph of the democratic will of Tunisians and Egyptians was a simultaneous victory for the identical aspirations of Iranians, who did precisely what we have witnessed in Tunisia and Egypt a year and a half earlier via the Green Movement and yet failed to reach for the dreamlike finale. Iranians within and outside their homeland took vicarious delight in the swift success of the Tunisian uprising and in the heroic determination of Egyptians. Though they are yet to dislodge a far more vicious and entrenched dictatorship, they follow punctiliously the dramatic unfolding of events in Tunisia and Egypt. On Facebook and Twitter, on websites and webcasts, Internet sites and transnational news sites, email listservs and instant text messaging, in Persian, French, English, and Arabic, Iranians around the globe have been posting and sharing, watching and commenting on YouTube clips and Al Jazeera streams, following the unfolding events, offering advice, soliciting details, congratulating their Tunisian and Egyptian friends and colleagues, and have even designed moving posters and graphics uniting their destinies – 'The Future is Ours' reads one in Persian, Arabic, and English.

As these events were unfolding in Tunisia and Egypt, it was imperative that they were not assimilated into the blind retrieval and habitual regurgitation of Arab nationalism, as tempting and perfectly legitimate as the epithet 'Arab Spring' has been. The winds of the Arab Spring have travelled way beyond the Arab world,

indeed have altered the very domain of the Arab world, and projected the revolutionaries beyond their identity politics as 'Arabs.'
It was not merely as 'Arabs' that Tunisians rose against tyranny.
It is not just as 'Arabs' that Egyptians have revolted against corrupt government. Rather, it was as *citizens* of betrayed republics,
which had denied them since the end of European colonialism,
that Tunisians and Egyptians, Yemenis and others in the region
rose up against the tyrants who ruled them – and against the
US and European interests that had kept those tyrants in power
against their peoples' will. The commencement of that postcolonial
disposition of nations was a deferred promise to all those in the
extended shadows of European colonialism.

The Tunisian and Egyptian triumphs were victories also for the
Green Movement in Iran and for democratic uprisings elsewhere
in the region. Whereas the US was deeply troubled by the prospect
of losing its chief allies in the region; the Islamic Republic, for its
part, was losing its main enemies – and in this part of the world
losing enemies is worse than losing friends. The Islamic Republic
has been, since its inception, the sole beneficiary of the politics
of despair that has shaped the region, with the pains of Palestine
the epicenter of that opportunism. There exists a balance of terror
between the US and its regional allies on one side and the Islamic
Republic and its sub-national allies (Hamas, Hezbollah, and the
Mahdi Army) on the other. Any change in that balance would be
potentially damaging not just to the US but, even more so, to the
Islamic Republic – and that is positive for the cause of liberty in
Iran and the region at large.

There is another, equally powerful, way in which the triumphant
rise of the Arab Spring is a cause for joy in the Green Movement
in Iran. The US/Iranian neocon contingent has tried in vain
to hijack the Green Movement, repeating ad nauseam the false
mantra that there can be no democracy without neoliberalism
– that democracy and the free market are two sides of the same
coin. Those forces within the Movement that had fought against
this nonsense had hitherto simply provided sustained theoretical
arguments. But with the spectacular flight of Ben Ali from Tunisia
to Saudi Arabia that delusion lost its aura. The yielding of Ben Ali's

Tunisia to neoliberal recipes was a dream for the World Bank and the IMF. The European Union (Sarkozy's France in particular) was so pleased with Ben Ali's neoliberal policies – more so even than President Bush in his 'fight against terrorism' – that they considered Tunisia an extension of the EU. Never mind that inside this neoliberal haven, a ruthless and corrupt dictator had run the state for the luxurious benefit of himself and his family, entirely unknown to those who upheld the view that 'the cause of the free market is democracy.'

In refusing to satisfy the Islamic Republic's insatiable need for enemies, and in exposing the banality of the assumption that without US aid and neoliberal economics there can be no democracy, the opening out of Tunisia's Jasmine Revolution into the Arab Spring was also a solid victory for the Green Movement, as indeed it was for the democratic will of the entire region.

Transcending Sectarianism:
The Sunni–Shi'i Divide

Let us now turn to the vexed question of sectarianism, the Sunni-Shi'i divide that has always been the source of much strife among Muslims. The overwhelming majority of Muslims are of Sunni (orthodox) persuasion; a small but significant minority (between 10 and 15 per cent) are Shi'i (heterodox). The Shi'a are mainly concentrated in Iran, Iraq, Azerbaijan, Lebanon, Bahrain, and Yemen, but significant Shi'i communities live throughout the Muslim world.[18] The roots of sectarian division between Sunnis and Shi'a go back to early Islamic history and relate to early Muslims' disagreement on the question of succession to Muhammad's prophetic authority. Throughout medieval history there was active or passive hostility between Sunnis and Shi'a. But in the course of European colonial domination of the Arab and Muslim world, and following the old Roman doctrine of *divide et impera*, divide and rule, such sectarian divisions – in common with those between

---

18. For more on the history, doctrine, and contemporary issues pertaining to Shi'ism, see Hamid Dabashi, *Shi'ism: A Religion of Protest* (Cambridge MA: Harvard University Press, 2011).

Muslims and Hindus and between Muslims and Christians – have been systematically abused and instrumentalized for the benefit of imperial domination.[19]

Soon after the US-led invasion of Iraq in March 2003, political strategists and military analysts such as Seyyed Vali Reza Nasr, seeking to divert attention from the principal culprit in the misbegotten war, published essays and books on Shi'ism that attributed much of the violence in the country to sectarian division.[20] Echoing these assessments of a transnational Shi'i uprising against Sunni domination, King Abdullah II of Jordan even spoke of the formation of a 'Shi'i crescent.' In the course of the subsequent revolutionary uprisings, particularly in those countries, such as Bahrain, that have a significant Shi'i population ruled by a small Sunni leadership, once again the question of Sunni–Shi'i hostility and rivalry has resurfaced.

This fear of a 'Shi'i crescent,' or the resurrection of sectarian rivalries in the Muslim world, has proved to be – just like the fear of a renewed militant Islamism – a false alarm, predicated on a flawed reading of Muslims' multifaceted political culture, which certainly includes Islam and its sects but is not limited to them. The factual evidence of recent regional history unequivocally discredits the assumption of a transnational Shi'i solidarity against Sunnism. For eight long and bloody years Iran and Iraq, two major Shi'i countries, were at each other's throats – Shi'a killing Shia on two sides of a national divine. Shi'ism (and Islam in general for that matter) has never been the sole determining factor in people's political identity. Today in Bahrain, over which until recently Iran had territorial claims, people are infinitely more attuned to Arab nationalism and even pan-Arabism than they are to Shi'ism. Within specific Shi'i countries, loyalties and identities fracture along many intersecting lines. In Iran, a major Shi'i country, we are witness to a massive civil rights movement (now galvanized and radicalized by the revolutionary uprisings in the region), in which Shi'a are

---

19. For an excellent study of the abuse of the Indian caste system for the benefit of British colonialism, see Nicholas B. Dirks, *Castes of Mind: Colonialism and the Making of Modern India* (Princeton NJ: Princeton University Press, 2001).

20. See Vali Nasr, *The Shia Revival: How Conflicts within Islam Will Shape the Future* (New York: W.W. Norton, 2006).

engaged in street demonstrations against the Islamic Republic, run by a government based on Shi'i doctrines. This points to the fact that Shi'ism is just one among many factors that determine people's political persuasions and social actions.

What we are seeing in much of the Arab and Muslim world is not a reenactment of Sunni–Shi'i rivalries but, far from it, the defiant retrieval of a vast and variegated cosmopolitan culture – the assertion of a syncretic worldly identity that is the cumulative result of distant and recent history. This vibrant and multifaceted culture is reducible to no sectarian or ideological persuasion.

It is imperative for the world at large to understand what is happening in the course of the Arab Spring in the uprising's own terms and not reduce events to cliché and imagined bifurcations. Political cultures are neither reducible to their constituent factors and forces nor fixed and stagnant in history. The historical circumstances of people have primacy, not the generic abstractions that would claim them. People from Morocco to Oman, from Yemen to Iran are determined to change their destiny from a politics of despair to an open-ended moral imagination that navigates entirely uncharted courses for liberty and dignity. In this process, every aspect of their religions and cultures will come forward only to the degree that they can help restore a sense of pride of place and historical agency in shaping their new world. This does not mean that the ethnic, sectarian, and chauvinistic proclivities that have divided and ruled will disappear over night. But the melting pot of the revolutionary uprisings has a temperature and purpose of its own – and the course of history will be altered.

SIX

The Center Cannot Hold

The general panorama of the revolutionary uprisings across the Arab and Muslim world, which date from 18 December 2010, can seem chaotic and confusing. By autumn 2011, revolutions had overthrown the ruling regimes in Tunisia, Egypt and Libya – though NATO's bloody bombing under the rubric of 'humanitarian intervention' had marred the victory of the Libyans. Syria, Yemen, and Bahrain saw peaceful masses of people pouring into their streets demanding democratic change, only to be met by brutal suppression and denial. Major protests had broken out also in Morocco, Algeria, and Jordan, forcing the regimes to promise drastic reform. Relatively minor rallies had broken out in Oman, Kuwait, Lebanon, Mauritania, Saudi Arabia, Sudan, and Western Sahara.

Each of the countries in the region has a special significance, and no two countries are alike. For example, Saudi Arabia is the most recalcitrant and hence the hardest to change through peaceful means; the regime is relentlessly violent and the fact that the two most sacred Muslim sites, Mecca and Medina, are located there grants the country a certain aura of sanctity. But even Saudi Arabia has witnessed a major movement: that of middle-class women who, contrary to the law of their homeland, assert their equal right to drive a car. This may appear to be a trivial

matter in the wider context, but it could have serious and enduring implications far beyond women's demand to enjoy a basic
civil liberty. Iraq is an interesting example, in that it differed
from the rest of the Arab world, being still under US and allied
military occupation and as such stand as a glaring example of the
catastrophic consequences of trying to 'export democracy.' If the
US had not invaded Iraq and Saddam Hussein was still around,
Iraqis might well have been among the first nations to join the
Arab Spring. Instead, they remain under military occupation with
their homeland destroyed

What was driving all these revolts? When the Egyptian revolution began both the ruling clergy in Iran and their American
neoconservative counterparts asserted that this was an 'Islamic
revolution.' But to deploy a simple analytic of influence – especially
of the Islamic Revolution in Iran – to explain the revolutionary
uprisings was and remains misleading. The dynamics of the revolutions were intrinsic to each country and demanded deciphering.
These events are not extended responses to a violently Islamized
(not Islamic) revolution in Iran more than thirty years ago; nor is
there any indication that an Islamic ideology is the driving force,
(although of course Islamic organizations such as the Muslim
Brotherhood in Egypt were not totally absent from the political mobilization for collective action). The democratic uprisings
demand a wider frame of historical explanation – for today not
just militant Islamism but all forms of ideological absolutism have
lost their legitimacy.

As we have seen, the major argument of this book is that the
events in the Arab and Muslim world generically referred to as the
'Arab Spring' represent the end of postcolonial ideological formations as we have known them for the past two hundred years. By the
end of postcoloniality I mean the cessation of ideological production in colonial contexts and terms – the terms determined by the
European colonial domination of the region, and the tyrannical
'postcolonial' states left behind when the Europeans collected their
flags and left. Anticolonial nationalism, socialism, and Islamism
are the ideological formations that historically have confronted
European colonialism and shaped the modern nation-states that

emerged in the former colonial territories. These forces finally won their anticolonial battles, but only to produce catastrophic postcolonial state formations, the key examples being the ghastly theocracy that rules the Islamic Republic of Iran, the ruthless and violent Baathist regime in Syria, the tyranny that has ruled Libya, the patrimonial tribalism that has held sway from Saudi Arabia and Jordan to Kuwait to Morocco, and the neoliberal autocracies of Egypt and Tunisia. These countries fought their anticolonial battles, secured their postcolonial states, but ended up with incompetent tyrants ruling a disenfranchised and disaffected citizenry whom they treated like domesticated ungulates. Thus the ideological matrix constructed during colonial domination, but dispensed with in the postcolonial period, was exhausted.

The end of postcolonial ideological formations does not mean that colonialism itself has ended or that imperialism does not generate resistance. Today we look at countries like Bahrain, Saudi Arabia, and Yemen as the central axis of American imperial projects in the region, an axis that forces us to think far beyond the limited (racialized) implications of an 'Arab Spring' and towards the vaster global configuration of power in the heart of Africa and around the rim of Asia. As three major allies of the United States and Israel in the region, these tyrannical regimes expose the Palestinian predicament as the emotive universe from which the Arab Spring has finally blossomed. Today the United States remains the single persistent promoter of imperial domination, while Israel is the last remnant of European colonialism in the region. But precisely because the United States has lost the imperial game of hegemony and ideological domination, and because Israel is exposed for the naked colonial project it is, resistance to them is no longer ideological as such. The United States lacks the hegemony required to generate counter-hegemonic ideologies. Israel is identified as an apartheid settler colony and garrison state and does not require Arab nationalism, militant Islamism, or Soviet-inspired socialism to oppose it. Opposition to the United States and Israel is thus no longer articulated in postcolonial ideological terms, but rather inhabits the material, moral, and imaginative realms.

Consequent upon this exhaustion of postcolonial ideologies is a sweeping turn to societal modernities. Thus the battleground involves a *civil rights movement* rather than ideological contestation. People are fighting for their civil liberties, embedded in which are the delayed democratic institutions that postcolonial ideological and state formations had miserably failed to deliver.

Who is History's Master?

The seismic change in the region, with the lowering of ideological banners, was not only there for Arabs and Muslims to see and celebrate. The new world was coming to full self-consciousness, its dominant ideologies challenging people's perceptions. 'Something fundamental has changed. I grew up believing that we – Americans and Jews – were the shapers of history in the Middle East. We created reality; others watched, baffled, paralyzed, afraid.' This is Peter Beinart, senior political writer for *The Daily Beast*, associate professor of journalism and political science at City University of New York, and a senior fellow at the New America Foundation. He continues:

> In 1989, Americans gloated as the Soviet Union, our former rival for Middle Eastern supremacy, retreated ignominiously from the region. When Saddam Hussein tried to challenge us from within, we thrashed him in the Gulf War. Throughout the 1990s, we sent our economists, law professors and investment bankers to try to teach the Arabs globalization, which back then meant copying us. In a thousand ways, sometimes gently, sometimes brutally, we sent the message: We make the rules; you play by them.[1]

'They' never made the rules and thus 'others' did not play by them. That has been a self-perpetuating, triumphalist, delusion. But more than a delusion (which a Palestinian child with a stone in his hand could shatter at any time), the sense of entitlement to that 'We Americans and Jews' is perhaps the most powerful index of

---

1. See Peter Beinart, 'Israel's Palestinian Arab Spring,' *The Daily Beast*, 15 May 2011, www.thedailybeast.com/articles/2011/05/16/israels-palestinian-arab-spring-jews-and-americans-losing-ability-to-shape-mideast.html.

where the world was before the rise of the Arab Spring. That phrase 'We Americans and Jews,' which immediately becomes just 'We' and 'us,' is where the world was when that 'we' conquered, stole, dominated, and wrote the history, and when anyone who dared to write or say otherwise was chastised, branded anti-Semitic, anti-American, a terrorist, and thus sought to be silenced, or else dismissed from his or her employment. That 'we' failed to silence anyone – not Mahmoud Darwish, Edward Said, Mona Hatoum, or Elia Suleiman. Books wait to be written, poems composed, plays performed, movies made, and libraries filled with the horrors experienced by those who dared to think differently from those like the triumphalist (but now wiser and reflective) Beinart. He summarizes in just a few words the terror that generations of Palestinians, Arabs, and Muslims have experienced by simply saying 'No' to the terrorizing power of self-entitlement.

Beinart gives a bravura summary of Jewish triumphs and Arab defeats, ending with the Zionist cliché that 'We went from strength to strength; they never missed an opportunity to miss an opportunity.' But he then seeks to redeem himself, declaring with a hint of nostalgia:

> That world is gone. America and Israel are no longer driving history in the Middle East; for the first time in a long time, Arabs are. In Tahrir Square, Egypt's young made a revolution. President Obama bowed to reality and helped show Hosni Mubarak the door; Benjamin Netanyahu stood athwart history, impotently yelling stop. Now Egypt's leaders are doing its people's will, bringing Hamas and Fatah together in preparation for elections. Hamas and Fatah are complying because they fear their own Tahrir Square ... For American and Israeli leaders accustomed to Palestinian autocrats and Palestinian terrorists, this is something new. Netanyahu and his American backers are demanding that Obama rewind the clock, but he can't.

The terms are still triumphalist, but substitutional – 'we Americans and Israelis' had our turn and now it is 'the Arabs' turn.' No epistemic shift, no moral lessons, no overcoming of the cycle of 'we' and 'them,' no inroad into a world in which 'we' and 'they' resolve into the far more urgent issues – concerning the environment, demography, poverty – faced by humanity at large. But by the end of his essay, Beinart has lost that lingering overconfidence of a triumphalist Zionist, confronting his own insight that 'the more America sticks by Netanyahu, the less relevant America will become.' His conclusion promises to be liberating – for him and for his relationship with Zionism:

> The Palestinians are taking control of their destiny because Israel has not. Zionism, which at its best is the purposeful, ethical effort to make Jews safe in the land of Israel, has become – in this government – a mindless land grab, that threatens Jewish safety and Jewish ethics alike. Once upon a time, when the Arabs were hapless and America was omnipotent, Israel could get away with that. Not anymore. If Barack Obama cannot get Benjamin Netanyahu to endorse – and work toward – a Palestinian state near 1967 lines, events will pass them both by. Others will take the initiative; in the Middle East, the U.S. and Israel will increasingly find their destinies in other nations' hands. For those of us raised to believe that Americanism and Zionism were can-do faiths, it is harder to imagine any crueler irony than that.[2]

Palestinians and other Arabs are not taking control of their destinies 'because' Israel has not. Israel has done and can continue to do whatever it wishes. The force of history has left Israel and Zionism behind. Jewish lives and Jewish ethics were not just threatened but sacrificed long before Beinart wrote these sentences. From the every moment that Theodor Herzl laid a finger on the map of Palestine and said he wanted it, Jewish lives and Jewish ethics were sacrificed; and they continued to be sacrificed until the day of the so-called 'Tent Movement,' when tens of thousands of Israelis finally poured into their streets and hinted to the world that they may in fact join the Arab Spring. Two months after the publication of Beinart's words, Israel itself was in revolt against Netanyahu. The action was prompted by a crisis in housing but, according to many Israelis, including Gideon Levy, the distinguished *Haaretz* columnist, also by more than that:

> It was the night that Benjamin Netanyahu was tossed out of the Prime Minister's Office in disgrace. ... The protests went up a notch last night. Chants about high rents were rare. 'The people demand social

---

2. Ibid.

justice,' was the most common, followed by 'Hoo ha, mi zeh ba? Medinat harevaha' (Who's that coming? It's the welfare state). Socialism, today? Yes, with choked throats and emotional tones. The protest took flight last night. Forget the housing protest, it's no longer alone. Those who feared that the protest was too narrow, too spoiled, yesterday watched it expand. Its goals are already way beyond a small rented apartment.[3]

This is still a far cry from Israelis bringing down the apart-heid walls – physical and mental – that they have built around themselves and away from the hopes and aspirations of the Arab Spring. But no social movement was ever in complete control of its causes and consequences. Even Zionism, the last European colonial settlement, was asking questions of itself. Israelis were coming down from their Massada.

The East is West, the West is East

The end of postcolonial ideologies means a return to (and of) history – and not just in the former colonies. When the multiple worlds that make up the periphery go their own way, the center (self-designated) cannot hold. If, as I argue, the age of postcolonial ideology formation has come to an end in the former colonies, the former colonizers too have hit the plateau of the postmodern politics of indifference precisely because the principal cause of those ideological formations (code-named 'the West') no longer exists. Consider: if in the Arab and Muslim world democracy has been denied, in Europe and North America it has been deboned (Arendt's distinction between the French and American revolu-tions no longer exists in the age of political postmodernity that characterizes late capitalism); these two facts bring together the people in Tehran's Azadi Square and Cairo's Tahrir Square with those in Madrid's Puerta del Sol and Syntagma Square in Athens, and with those across the Atlantic in the Occupy Wall Street movement in the US and around the globe. Egypt, Spain, and the US may appear to be vastly different from each other, but what

---

3. See Gideon Levy, 'Israeli Protesters Must Remain in Tents until Time is Right,' *Haaretz*, 31 July 2011, www.haaretz.com/print-edition/news/gideon-levy-israeli-pro-testers-must-remain-in-tents-until-time-is-right-1.376113.

brings them together is a corroborating history of democratic will being veiled by tyranny and the stripping from democracy its point and purpose.

In Tahrir Square and Puerta del Sol we return to the origins of democracy – when the idea was yet again to find its name. If the idea of democracy was born in Athens, that city has itself now joined Tahrir Square in a renewed pact with history. As Stathis Gourgouris, Professor of Classics and Comparative Literature and director of the Institute for Comparative Literature and Society at Columbia University in New York, puts it, 'there is no doubt that the events of Tahrir played a crucial role in the Syntagma formation. So, for that matter, what happened in Athens in December 2008 helped to radicalize youth in various parts of the Arab world.'[4] The Muslim mystics have a saying that when there was Sufism there was no name for it and when there was a name for it there was no Sufism. The same is true about democracy. In the delusion called 'the West' the reality called 'democracy' has long since found a name; in the reality called Egypt the rebellious ideal of liberty is yet to find a name. In Spain they have the name but they lack the euphoria to discover it; in Egypt they do not have the name but they thrive on the ecstasy of looking for it, while practicing it. Tahrir has retrieved Syntagma, and with it Cairo has retrieved Athens, for a renewed rendezvous with history.

Consider the case of Islamic sectarian strife between Shi'i and Sunni communities. This sectarianism helps to posit Islamism as the single most important ideological formation in Arab and Muslim countries. That posited Islamism works in turn to legitimize the Jewish state, for that is the only way that Israel makes sense, not just in terms of its presence in the neighborhood but even more so to itself: as a Jewish state against militant Islamism. There was, to be sure, a Jewish state in the neighborhood some three decades before there was an Islamic Republic. Compound sectarianism – Jewish, Christian, Islamic, Hindu – strengthens Islamism and falsely privileges it as the defining moment of political culture

---

4. See Stathis Gourgouris, 'Democratic Dreams Rage in Athens,' Al Jazeera, 21 July 2011, http://english.aljazeera.net/indepth/opinion/2011/07/201171985335665864. html.

in the region. But the catastrophic record of Islamism as practiced over the last three decades in the Islamic Republic of Iran stands as a warning to the Arab world not so much to reject Islamism but to embed it within the larger context of their political culture. This contextualization frames Islamism as part of the larger political culture, which includes nationalism and socialism; this process, predicated on the exhaustion of Islamism as an ideology, cleans the slate, producing a ground zero of history.

The systemic dissolution of Islamism within the larger political cosmopolitanism that has historically embraced it thus clears the way for the post-ideological ground zero of history. But, and here is the rub, 'the West' has been so contingent on 'the Rest' that when 'the Rest' decouple from it to discover their own renewed pact with history, 'the West' will not know what to do with itself. So the glory of Syntagma and Tahrir come together to rename 'democracy' on an Athens–Cairo axis. On that basis, the very idea of 'the West' will disappear from the face of the earth.

False Anxieties

Let us now consider the exhaustion of Islamism in greater depth. From the commencement of the Egyptian revolutionary uprising in late January 2011, it became something of a cliché to compare it to the Iranian Revolution of 1979. The mass demonstrations in Egypt against a US-backed dictator evoked a certain sense of déjà vu among certain observers, who had witnessed similar scenes in Iran three decades before. This led them to believe that perhaps another 'Islamic revolution' was in the making. This was a mistaken reading of the Iranian Revolution of 1977–79, however; and an even more mistaken reading of the Egyptian revolution of 2011.

The trend in comparing the two revolutions is usually predicated on an ulterior ideological motive. The pro-Israeli neocons in the United States and their Zionist counterparts in Israel choose to compare the Egyptian and Iranian revolutions because they are frightened of a massive revolutionary uprising in a major Arab country that may challenge the colonial settlement called 'Israel.' The Israeli prime minister wasted no time in raising the alarm:

'What happened in Iran could happen in Egypt ... Benjamin Netanyahu said ... after meeting with German Chancellor Angela Merkel,' *Haaretz* reported on 31 January 2011.[5] The Israeli prime minister seems to have received his signal from Abbas Milani, an Iranian employee of the Hoover Institution think-tank in California, who just a day before Netanyahu's warning had issued precisely the same counsel in a pro-Israeli pamphlet, *The New Republic*, published in New York. Milani, too, feared that the Muslim Brotherhood might take over the Egyptian revolution and create an Islamic republic. Of course both the Israeli prime minister and his likeminded Iranian ally habitually ignore the fact that more than sixty years ago a 'Jewish Brotherhood' had created a Jewish republic in the same neighborhood.[6] Soon after what was in effect a joint statement by Netanyahu and Milani, Ali Khamenei, the leader of the Islamic Republic, celebrated events in Egypt as a reflection of the late Ayatollah Khomeini's legacy and duly hailed the commencement of an 'Islamic awakening.'[7] Not so fast, interjected the Egyptian Muslim Brotherhood almost instantaneously: this is not an Islamic revolution, but an Egyptian revolution that belongs to all Egyptians – Muslims, Christians, and others of different ideological persuasions.[8]

Between Zionist propaganda and Islamist wishful thinking a myriad other views measured the success of the Egyptian revolution, in one way or another, by the influence exerted by the example of the Islamic Revolution in Iran. This assumption is false first and foremost because what took place in Iran was not an 'Islamic revolution' but a violently and systematically 'Islamized revolution.' It was a brutal and sustained course of repression,

5. See 'Netanyahu Warns Outcome of Egypt Revolution Could be like Iran's,' *Haaretz*, 31 January 2011, www.haaretz.com/news/diplomacy-defense/netanyahu-warns-outcome-of-egypt-revolution-could-be-like-iran-s-1.340411.

6. See Abbas Milani, 'A Note of Warning and Encouragement for Egyptians,' *The New Republic*, 30 January 2011, www.tnr.com/article/world/82450/egypt-riots-iranian-revolution-1979.

7. See 'Iran's Supreme Leader Calls Uprisings and Islamic "Awakening",' *Los Angeles Times*, 4 February 2011, http://articles.latimes.com/2011/feb/04/world/la-fg-khamenei-iran-egypt-20110205.

8. For the response of the Muslim Brotherhood to Khamenei's statement, see 'Muslim Brotherhood Rejects Khamenei Calls for Iran-style Islamic State,' The Green Voice of Freedom, 4 February 2011, http://en.irangreenvoice.com/article/2011/feb/04/2724.

perpetrated under the successive smokescreens of the American hostage crisis of 1979-81, the Iran-Iraq War of 1980-88, and the Salman Rushdie affair of 1989-99. A cruel crescendo of university purges, cultural revolutions, mass executions of oppositionists, and the forced exile of survivors have taken full advantage of domestic and regional crisis over the three decades to turn a multifaceted and cosmopolitan revolution into a banal and vicious theocracy. The CIA-sponsored coup of 1953, the massive arming of Saddam Hussein to wage war against Iran, and the creation of the Taliban as a bulwark against the Soviet occupation of Afghanistan (all engineered by the United States) and the continued armed robbery of Palestine by Israel have formed the regional context within which the Islamic Republic first destroyed all ideological and political alternatives and then consistently and systematically abused regional crisis to keep itself in power. What happened in Iran between 1977 and 1979 was not an 'Islamic revolution' and cannot serve as a model for Egypt in 2011. In this regard, it is crucial to remember that historically Egypt has had far more enduring influence on Iran than the other way around.

No false analogy or undue anxiety regarding the influence of 'Islamism,' real or demonized, can be allowed to mar the joyous and magnificent uprising of Tunisians and Egyptians to reclaim their dignity in a free and democratic homeland. And there is no reason to believe that they will allow any such kidnapping of their dreams and aspirations by one or other fanatical absolutism. There is no doubt that the Muslim Brotherhood in Egypt, and indeed Muslim political affiliations in other countries, were integral to the revolutionary uprisings. But such organizations and networks should not be demonized – although, of course, neither should they (or any other absolutist force) be trusted to lead the revolution forward uncontested.

Under no circumstances should we limit our understanding of the rich and effervescent political cultures of the region to militant Islamism of one sort or another, for this particular revolutionary politics has never been the only source of ideas and action in the region. Anticolonial nationalism has had catalytic consequences beyond any colonially manufactured national boundary. The same is true of revolutionary socialist movements. The Popular Front for the Liberation of Palestine (PFLP), for example, has had a far-reaching impact on Marxist movements in the region. This cross-fertilization (and cross-metaphorization) of a defiant politics of hope and struggle is evidenced in the regional solidarities that have developed and informed the revolutionary uprisings, whose scope reaches far beyond any colonially manufactured and racialized nationalism. That these ideologies were produced and spread under specific historical circumstances is evidenced in historical memory and documentation. Required now is the theoretical versatility to see them sublated into a new revolutionary politics.

From Tehran to Tunis to Cairo and beyond, innate cosmopolitan cultures are being retrieved, hidden worlds discovered, above and beyond any anxiety regarding negative influences. Egyptians have achieved a collective future. Although this was not to be the outcome for Iranians in 2009, the victories of Tunisians and Egyptians in 2011 will have consequences for the Iranian opposition, as it will for all other democratic and national liberation movements in the region. We must open our eyes: these are the same people; their democratic will has the versatility to play a long game with a criminal theocracy in Iran while suddenly dismantling the ruling regimes in Tunisia and Egypt!

The Islamic Republic in Bahrain

Let us now examine another myth: that the Islamic Republic is supporting the democratic uprising in Bahrain because the vast majority of its population are Shi'i and thus natural allies of the ruling clergy in neighboring Iran.

Soon after the commencement of the Bahraini democratic uprising, in solidarity with Egyptians and Tunisians, much was made of the Shi'i link to the Islamic Republic. Both the regime in Bahrain and the Saudi invading force, leading the Gulf Cooperation Council (GCC) move to keep the ruling elite in power, accused the Islamic Republic of fomenting revolt in the tiny but strategically significant kingdom. 'The Sunni royal family in Saudi Arabia,' reported the *Telegraph*, 'fears the growing influence of Shi'ite Iran in the Middle

East, and is helping Bahrain's Sunni rulers retain power.'⁹ The clerical rulers of the Islamic Republic deny any involvement. The same *Telegraph* report indicates that 'the [UK] Ministry of Defence has now admitted that members of the Saudi Arabian National Guard sent into Bahrain may have received military training from the British Armed Forces in Saudi Arabia.' So we learn that the British armed forces had trained the very military force that was crushing the democratic uprising in Bahrain, whilst Britain was accusing the Islamic Republic of interference. This astonishing hypocrisy on the part of the British, however, does not mean that the Islamic Republic is the champion of liberty here.

In the meantime, Bahraini democracy activists were being brutally suppressed. 'After severely curbing news coverage of its crackdown on opposition groups by foreign reporters,' reports Roy Gutman of the *Miami Herald* from Dubai, on 25 May 2011, 'Bahraini authorities have begun an assault on local journalists working for international news agencies – with arrests, beatings and, apparently in one instance, electric shock.'¹⁰ Cutting through the hypocrisy and duplicity that cloud the true picture, it is clear that the influence of the Islamic Republic in Bahrain is not what the ruling regimes in Bahrain and Saudi Arabia, and their supporters in London and Washington DC, wish us to believe: namely that the ruling clergy in Iran has supported the democratic uprising in Bahrain. Such support would be very odd indeed. Why would the Islamic Republic help a democratic uprising in Bahrain, while viciously suppressing one of its own? Just because the protestors in Bahrain are Shi'i? These competing claims notwithstanding, what the Islamic Republic and Bahrain have in common is not just that the majority of their populations is Shi'i but that both are ruled by brutal and intolerant dictatorships.

The Arab Spring is the return of the Islamic Republic's repressed, the recovery of the universal euphoria of a moment three decades

9. 'Saudi Troops Sent to Crush Bahrain Protests "had British training",' *Telegraph*, 25 may 2011, www.telegraph.co.uk/news/worldnews/middleeast/saudiarabia/8536037/Saudi-troops-sent-to-crush-Bahrain-protests-had-British-training.html.

10. Roy Gutman, 'In Bahrain, a Candlelight Vigil Can Land You in Jail,' *Miami Herald*, 25 May 2011, http://article.wn.com/view/2011/05/30/Bahrains_official_tally_shows_cost_to_Shiites_of_crackdown/.

ago, whereafter the militant clergy hijacked a revolution and turned it into a vindictive and vicious theocracy. In this sense, then, the Islamic Republic did indeed have a direct influence in Bahrain – as model of tyranny. As such, it could not have played any part in the events that followed the massive democratic uprising in the tiny archipelago, home of the US Fifth Fleet, in which that great advocate of democracy, the US, turned a blind eye to the murderous regime in Bahrain, while the UK-trained Saudi military intervened to crack down on the uprising. The only influence the Islamic Republic has had on Bahrain is to teach the ruling regime, by example, how to quell a democratic revolt – the same role it had for the even more bloody crackdown of Bashar al-Assad in Syria. There is no ideology, religious or otherwise, at work here, only brute force and self-survival. The same holds for Saudi Arabia and the other Persian Gulf states, for Israel, and for the United States and its European allies. The ideological gloves were now off.

In a revealing piece in the *Independent*, Patrick Cockburn reports of the atrocities the ruling regime in Bahrain is committing to murder its own citizens, identifying their victims as Shi'a, instigated by the Islamic Republic, by way of dissociating their democratic will from the rest of the Arab uprising:

> The repression is across the board. Sometimes the masked security men who raid Shia villages at night also bulldoze Shia mosques and religious meeting places. At least 27 of these have so far been wrecked or destroyed, while anti-Shia and pro-government graffiti is often sprayed on any walls that survive.[11]

He details the scope of the government's violent crackdown and of its purging of Shi'i professionals:

> Nurses and doctors in a health system largely run by Shi'is have been beaten and arrested for treating protesters. Teachers and students are being detained. Some 1,000 professional people have been sacked and have lost their pensions. The one opposition newspaper has been closed. Bahraini students who joined protests abroad have had their funding withdrawn.

---

11. Patrick Cockburn, 'Bahrain Is Trying to Drown the Protests in Shia Blood,' *Independent*, 15 May 2011, www.independent.co.uk/opinion/commentators/patrick-cockburn-bahrain-is-trying-to-drown-the-protests-in-shia-blood-2284199.html.

These and other atrocities committed by the regime in Bahrain are straight out of the handbook of the Islamic Republic. Are Mir Hossein Mousavi and Mahdi Karroubi, two of the principal founders of the Islamic Republic and now the leaders of the Green Movement, who are being kept incommunicado and under house arrest, not Shi'a? Were Neda Agha Sultan, Sohrab A'rabi, Amir Javadifar, along with scores of other innocent demonstrators murdered in cold blood by the security forces of the Islamic Republic, not Shi'i? The major human rights organizations have reported widely on the systematic torture of Shi'i protestors in the dungeons of the Islamic Republic. Mahdi Karroubi has detailed the rape of young Shi'i men and women in custody. Why would the Islamic Republic, capable of treating its own Shi'i citizens in this way, care about the Shi'i population of Bahrain? The ruling regime in the Islamic Republic is the role model for the rulers of Bahrain and other repressive regimes in how to brutally repress democratic uprisings; it is not on the side of those who launch them.

The democratic uprising in Bahrain was integral to the Arab Spring, and the Arab Spring shared its aspirations and demands with the Green Movement in Iran. Neither a Sunni–Shi'i divide in Bahrain nor a Muslim–Christian divide in Egypt could halt the dramatic events in the Arab world and beyond. Born of the same economic malaise, social anomie, political stalemate, and cultural alienation, these social uprisings extended across two continents and had nothing to do with interreligious or religious–secular divides. They were not the consequence of any ideological mobilization. Instead they were mobilized *against* ideologies – both dominant and outdated.

It is vital to remember how the Shi'i factor entered the current geopolitics of the region. It was soon after the US-led invasion and occupation of Iraq that US military strategists like Seyyed Vali Reza Nasr began to divert attention from the principal party responsible for the bloodshed and introduced the idea of the Sunni–Shi'i conflict as the key problem. It was also at this time that King Abdullah II of Jordan spoke of a 'Shi'i Crescent' as a threat to the stability of the region. The idea of sectarianism was thus a US military psy-op rather than anything integral to the politics of the region. This does not mean that the US invasion of Iraq did not exacerbate the Sunni-Shi'i bifurcation, in the same way that the Israeli invasion of Lebanon in 1982 was the catalyst for the formation of Hezbollah. But this politically engineered sectarianism does not equate to a valid or dominant Islamist ideology, historically formed in contestation with European and American colonial and imperial domination.

Regardless of whether the Shi'i factor was initiated by US military strategists to distract from the pain inflicted on Iraqi national sovereignty or imagined by outdated Arab rulers afraid of their own people, the fact is that Shi'a and Sunnis, Muslims and Christians, religious or not, Asians and Africans – and even Europeans – have now all revolted against identical sets of economically dysfunctional and politically alienating circumstances. People in Spain are now calling for a Tahrir Square of their own. Are they also Shi'i? The Sunni-Shi'i conflict is thus a red herring – strategic maneuvering to distract attention from the real issues, which are demographic, economic, women's rights issues, civil liberties. These are the stuff of which histories are made, and worlds altered.

The abuse of the Shi'i-Sunni divide also points yet again not just to a manufactured sectarianism that would discredit the democratic uprisings but also to the banal racialization of transnational, revolutionary movements that in fact cross all such colonially engendered tensions and hostilities. The fact remains that the Arab Spring cannot turn a blind eye to the brutalities of the Islamic Republic just because the US is its enemy. It remains imperative that the criminal atrocities of the Islamic Republic be brought fully into the purview of the Arab Spring. The Arab Spring will not fully blossom unless and until it includes the green pastures of Iran.

Decolonizing a World

In the classic study *Colonising Egypt*, Timothy Mitchell does for that country what Foucault himself could not have achieved: he extends Foucault's ideas into a non-European context. Mitchell dissects the manner in which Egypt (as both an idea and a territory) was colonially engineered and exhibited – from its cities to its schools to its military, dividing its people between their bodies and souls, and the spaces they occupied between private and public, their existential whereabouts between their native Orient and the European modernity they faced. Central to Mitchell's study is the idea that Egypt was 'exhibited' – not as a reality that was staged, but as an exhibition *sui generis*, one that kept exhibiting itself. There is an echo of Guy Debord's *Society of the Spectacle* (1967) in Mitchell's Foucauldian reading of Egypt as exhibition:

> If the world outside the exhibition was in this sense not a simple original, not reality itself, but a further series of representations, then the distinction between an exhibit and the real thing was not, after all, something absolute. The clear discernability between a representation and an original, promised by the exhibition, actually consisted only of representations standing for representations. Life was to be lived as though the world were an exhibition of reality; but the exits from the exhibition led not to reality itself, but only to further exhibitions.[12]

This was not just Egypt; it was also Europe. Europe itself, 'the West,' was the exhibition par excellence: it was like an onion, layer upon layer of representation, until you came to the core, and there was nothing there. Europe exhibited the colonized Egypt the way it was modernizing itself – not to mimic realities but to superimpose frameworks of meaning upon them and thus make them meaningful in a colonial setting. Europe made Egypt in its own image: its past was cast upon Egypt's present, while it hid its own inner anxieties. Europe became a disciplinary power that ordered the reality of Egypt. It modernized as it museumized it. The Oriental was thus manufactured by way of contrast to the modern.

---

12. Timothy Mitchell, *Colonising Egypt* (Stanford: University of California Press, 1991): 173. In his *Colonial Effects: The Making of National Identity in Jordan* (New York: Columbia University Press, 2001), Joseph Massad offers a similar study of Jordanian identity through the institutions of law and the military, whereby national identity is territorialized as a mode of Foucauldian effect of power – albeit in a colonial context.

SEVEN

The End of Postcolonialism

It is now time to give a more detailed account of my central proposition that in the rise of the Arab Spring we are witness to the end of postcoloniality as a condition and mode of ideology formation. This judgment is based on an argument that I have carefully constructed over a period of almost thirty years, in reference to various contexts. It didn't suddenly dawn on me when I saw Hosni Mubarak packing his belongings and leaving the presidential palace on 11 February 2011 that the period of postcoloniality was over. I will now explain in some theoretical detail what I mean by this proposition and how I arrived at that particular judgment.

The Genealogy of an Argument

At the commencement of the Green Movement in Iran in June 2009 I went on record as identifying it a post-ideological civil rights movement.[1] This assessment, picked up by many and contested by others, was not a spur-of-the-moment reaction to post-electoral crisis in Iran. Rather, it was predicated on a longstanding pre-occupation with both the intellectual history of and the rise and fall of ideological thinking in the Iranian (and by extension Muslim)

---

1. See Hamid Dabashi, *Iran, the Green Movement, and the USA: The Fox and the Paradox* (London: Zed Books, 2010) for more details.

encounter with colonial modernity in general, and in particular since the establishment of the Islamic Republic in the aftermath of the Iranian Revolution of 1977-79.

Just a year before the Green Movement emerged, and when the false alarm of Samuel Huntington's 'clash of civilizations' thesis had been sounded in the aftermath of the events of 9/11, I developed in *Islamic Liberation Theology: Resisting the Empire* (2008) the theoretical underpinning of my thesis that 'Islamic ideology' had run its course.[2] The book gives a detailed account of the rise of Islamism in ideological contestation with European colonialism across the Muslim world, with particular comparative reference to the Latin American context of Christian liberation theology. My argument is simple. Historically, Islam had developed in conversation with an interlocutor: Greek philosophy, Jewish theology, Christian asceticism, Persian imperial culture being chief among the intellectual and political forces with which Islam had dialogically articulated itself. Over the past two hundred years, I argue, European colonialism has been the chief interlocutor for Muslim thinkers and thus they systematically turned their own religion into a site of ideological contestation with the code-name for colonial modernity, 'the West.' Contrary to all appearances, at the crucial juncture of 9/11 Islam was no longer up against 'the West'; the dangerous liaison between 'Islam and the West' had run its course, in fact, and Muslims had entered a new phase in their history. For 'the West' had by then – in the aftermath of the collapse of the Soviet Union, the unification of Europe, and the rise of military, strategic, and economic differences between the US and the EU – conceptually imploded. Hence 'Islam' as the signifier that had been its principal Other was now up for grabs: in its new dispensation it would have to appeal to a mode of *theodicy* of liberation rather than remain entrenched in a monological theology.

In this new phase, when not just political Islamism but also all other postcolonial ideological formations have reached the point of epistemic exhaustion, what we witness flourishing is 'societal

2. See Hamid Dabashi, *Islamic Liberation Theology: Resisting the Empire* (London: Routledge, 2008).

modernity' rather than 'political modernity' as the ideal aspiration of combative ideologies. This is an entirely new project that has emerged in the aftermath of a collapse of ideological thinking that had in its entirety paradoxically served a colonial project extending into the postcolonial period.

We now turn to consider what specifically I mean by 'post-ideological': the end of the postcolonial condition of ideology production.

What Does Post-ideological Mean?

The theoretical underpinning of my scholarly disposition has remained very much informed by my training as a sociologist deeply rooted in the sociology of knowledge, a seminal text of which (after Max Scheler's pioneering work) was and remains Karl Mannheim's *Ideology and Utopia* (1929). The period between the publication of Karl Marx and Friedrich Engels's *The German Ideology* (1845) and that of Mannheim's text is formative in the history of the sociology of knowledge: the social conditioning involved in knowledge production lies at the heart of our understanding of the nature of ideological formations – an insight which, incidentally, had prepared my generation of sociologists for the appearance of Edward Said's *Orientalism* (1978) long before it took the discipline of Middle Eastern Studies, and indeed the emerging field of Post-colonial Studies, by storm.[3]

Paul Ricoeur gave a series of lectures on Mannheim in 1975 at the University of Chicago. Following Mannheim, Ricoeur's organizing hypothesis is that 'the very conjunction of these two opposite sides or complementary functions [ideology and utopia] typifies what could be called social and cultural *imagination*.' He further observes, trying both to combine and to contrast the twin ideas, that 'Ideology ... designates initially some distorting, dissimulating process by which an individual or a group expresses its situation but without knowing or recognizing it'; while 'utopia ... has a pejorative reputation too. It is seen to represent a kind of

---

3. I have dealt with this point extensively in the first chapter of *Post-Orientalism: Knowledge and Power in Time of Terror* (New Brunswick NJ: Transaction, 2008).

social dream without concern for the real first steps necessary for movement in the direction of a new society.[4] From which juxta-position, Ricoeur concludes, 'it is within their common aspect of noncongruence with actuality, of discrepancy, that they diverge.'[5] He also observes that 'ideology' is something we ascribe to others, while 'utopia' is something we claim for ourselves. Ricoeur's refer-ences to 'cultural imagination' served as a clue to my generation of immigrant scholars adjusting to its postcolonial condition to think of the colonial disposition of that imagination, which was radically different from, indeed was inimical to, the dominant ideology that had conditioned imagination in the presumed centers, the so-called metropole, of the colonial universe. Ricoeur's insights were all predicated on Mannheim's initial observation that ideol-ogy was basically a stabilizing and utopia a destabilizing mode of knowledge production.

> The concept of 'ideology' reflects the one insight that has emerged from political conflict, namely that ruling groups can become so intensively interest-bound in their thinking about a particular situation that they simply lose sight of certain facts that can undermine their dominance. Implicit in the word 'ideology' is the awareness that in certain situations the collective unconscious of certain groups obscures the real condition of society both from itself and from others and thereby stabilizes it. ... The notion of utopian thinking, for its part, reflects the contrary insight arising from political struggle, namely that certain oppressed groups are intellectually so strongly interested in the destruction and transformation of a given aspect of society that they unwittingly see only those elements of the situation that tend to negate it.[6]

From Marx to Mannheim, the notion of 'the dominant ideology' was heavily influenced by the stabilizing effect of the existing social order and the hegemonic discourse of the class that benefited from it. But this was never the case on the colonial edges, where ideologies were utopian dreams of change, change that was desired, indeed paradoxically necessitated, by virtue of the encounter with

---

4. Ibid.: 1.
5. Ibid.: 2.
6. See Karl Mannheim, *Ideology and Utopia*, trans. Louis Wirth and Edward Shils (New York: Harcourt Brace Jovanovich, 1936 [1929]): 40.

European colonialism. At the furthest extent of the dominant European ideologies' reach, they possessed absolutely no stabilizing force; indeed, on the contrary, they were the first thing to be suspected. For example, the Pahlavi regime's aspiration to fashion a monarchic ideology was the principal target of revolutionary ideologies that competed with each other to topple it.

That ideologies were utopian on the colonial edges of European modernity, and thus utopias ideological, was the paradox that sustained the production of revolutionary ideologies and made them at once politically combustive and thematically short-lived. My principal argument has always been that all these ideologies, including those that posited themselves as 'secular' as opposed to 'Islamic,' were in fact the side effects, the by-products, even the unanticipated consequences, of colonialism, extended into postcolonial ideology and state formations, and thus paradoxically colonial. If you take 'the West' away from 'Islamic ideology' it will fall; it cannot stand on its own. All such ideologies – not just militant Islamism, but equally anticolonial nationalism, and Third World Socialism – were invented in combative conversation and contestation with and against a colonial modernity, a colonizing interlocutor, that coded itself, and was thus called, 'the West.' In the age of globalized capital, that 'West' has imploded, so the dialogical modus operandi that it had set in motion has dissolved. The center of that imaginative geography and the matrix of ideology and knowledge production that it had occasioned cannot hold anymore, but instead of mere anarchy there has been a retrieval of the multiple worlds that existed before the insatiable abstraction that was 'the West' consumed them voraciously under the binary opposition 'the West and the Rest.'[7]

On the colonial edges of capitalist modernity, thus ideologically peripheralized, the ideology/utopia imbalance was always fluid and interchangeable. There was no stabilizing ideology and all utopian propositions were ideological in language and disposition, so one

---

7. That the wingnut British historian Niall Ferguson continues to spin 'the West and the Rest' in his cumbersome tomes so late in the game places them more in the genre of obituary than of panegyric. For his latest spin on Bernard Lewis's mantra, see Niall Ferguson, *Civilization: The West and the Rest* (London: Penguin, 2011).

had a structurally unstable paradigm that kept negating itself. Thus the proposition of post-ideological qua post/colonial means the collapse of the post/colonial paradigm altogether, and the epistemic end of both the grand dictator and the grand intellectual – the interchangeable ideologue and utopian – that were coterminous in their constituting of the paradigm. It is this collapse of the ideology/utopia (dictator/intellectual) binary that finally results in the birth of republican citizenship.

As a mode of knowledge production for political mobilization, ideology was always the trace of something else, always a contingent term, a mark of the absence of what it wishfully presented. An originary lack of historical referent has always been definitive of the condition of being and hope that presented itself as ideological. Ideology is a contingent condition, *ipso facto* a critique of the societal condition that gave birth to it. As a political proposition, ideology has always carried within itself the necessity of its own undoing, always already exposing its inner contradictions and thus positing a meaning different from that ostensibly signified. The metaphysics that ideology posited was one of pure self-negational presence, an exposure of the transcendental signified that at once made it possible and yet exposed the impossibility of its promises. Ideology was always a wishful lie that sought to overcome brutal truths.

At the end, Islamism turned itself in, as the Islamic Republic became the death of its own ideology, as well as the demise of the confluence of adjacent ideologies it had to devour to survive. We observe in the Islamic Republic the skeletal structure of a once healthy and robust ideological body politic. Today from Tahrir Square in Cairo to Meydan Azadi in Tehran, we are witness to the birth of the first post/colonial person, the citizen who has left the very condition of post/coloniality behind, and who celebrates the exhaustion of the post/colonial episteme, of which all absolutist ideologies of the colonized world were the supreme manifestation and the master code. The brute force that these postcolonial states – from Iran to Bahrain, Yemen, Saudi Arabia, Syria, to Libya – have had to show to survive each day of their existence gives the lie to their claims to ideological legitimacy. All ideologies,

Islamic or otherwise, have come to a conclusion in a condition of globality of capital where there is no center to oppose, no pole to take out, no master code to codify, no metropole in the world that amorphous capital vaguely wishes but systematically fails to control.

The Point of Ideological Meltdown

This ideological meltdown of a once potent claim on reality is the point of no return, where no government can have any claim to governmentality and where the region has degenerated into a group of garrison states trying to rule societies of camps that map its territory. The end of an 'Islamic ideology' marks the end of ideology as a colonial project in a postcolonial world where the imperial condition both necessitates and dismantles its own claims to empire. Under these global circumstances, then, the postcolonial states have effectively become a mockery of their own ideology, faking a warring posture in relation to imperialism (Iran, Syria, Libya), while assuming the status of fortified states.

The apparent affliction of Iran, Syria, and Libya with a kind of Tourette's Syndrome, running amuck with a Schmittian conception of 'the Enemy' as the cornerstone of their state apparatus, has been the most evident sign of their ideological bankruptcy. The summer of 2009 in Iran and the Arab Spring of 2011 will go down in the languid history of the ignominies of the postcolonial states as the season when theorists such as Max Weber, Talcott Parsons, Jürgen Habermas, and Richard Rorty were summoned to a kangaroo court in Tehran and made to wear those unseemly prison pajamas and sit shoulder-to-shoulder with the intellectual elite of the reformist movement on the defendants' seats, to be charged with plotting a velvet coup to topple the Islamic Republic. In the opening statement of the prosecutor general during the first session of the public trial of the leading reformists arrested in the aftermath of the post-electoral crisis of 2009, the defendants were accused of reading, inviting to Tehran, and disseminating the ideas of Jürgen Habermas by way of intellectually paving the way for the coming velvet revolution against the Islamic Republic.

With a straight face, and without the slightest awareness of the astounding mendacity of the charges, the Islamic kangaroo court tried and indicted Habermas *in absentia*. The purpose of the reformist movement, the state prosecutor charged, was none other than to promote secularism, camouflaged as the rule of law and democracy.

> The invitation of Habermas to Iran in 2003 was precisely for this reason. In a secret meeting at the residence of Mr. Kadivar, which included such figures as Said Hajjarian and Shabestari, the process of secularization is examined in detail and certain new guidelines are also provided. Mr. Habermas returns to his country convinced of his advisory capacity in the objective of the reformists to establish secularism in Iran.

Political theorist John Keane, the author of, among other books, *Global Civil Society* (2003), was accused of a similar plot, and presented as 'a major theorist of velvet revolutions and a member of the British Intelligence community MI6'.[8] As such, he was held up as one of the chief villains trying to bring down the Islamic Republic.

A similar fate awaited Max Weber, when, in what Ervand Abrahamian has aptly called 'tortured confessions,' Said Hajjarian, the leading reformist strategist, recanted his interest in Max Weber and averred that the German sociologist's conceptualization of Sultanism was in no shape or form applicable to Iran:[9] 'The regime based on Velayat-e Faqih derives its legitimacy from the Imam of the Age (May God Almighty Hasten His Return), and as a result is not applicable to Max Weber's theory of Sultanism.' He added: 'I was ignorant and without a critical perspective extended his ideas to our country.' Hajjarian further asserted that Max Weber had managed to execute this treacherous act of distorting Iranian politics (some ninety years after his death in 1920) because the cultural revolution had not been carried forward properly and

---

8. For the original text of the indictment (in Persian), see www.fardanews.com/fa/pages/?cid=87772.

9. See Ervand Abrahamian, *Tortured Confessions: Prisons and Public Recantations in Modern Iran*, Berkeley, CA: University of California Press, 1999.

the authorities were not sufficiently attentive in their vigilance. Hajjarian was reported to have said that it was not just Max Weber, but also poststructuralism, post-Marxism and feminism that were equally treacherous in their design to topple the Islamic Republic. Through the intermediary of Professor Hossein Bashiriyeh, a distinguished professor of political theory who had been forced to flee his homeland, Hajjarian had also come under the influence of John Keane.[10]

Militant Islamism had by now degenerated into psychotic delusion – rightly fearful of the mere suggestion of an idea which could expose the charlatanism and buffoonery of Iran's clerical leadership, pulling the strings like a latter-day Wizard of Oz.

Dismantling a Colonized Mind

The hallucinatory language and psychotic semiosis of fact and fantasy at the heart of the public prosecutor's indictment in that kangaroo court in Tehran are the historical record of the final fate of Islamic ideology and the depth of delusional fear and fantasy to which it had sunk in trying to defend the Islamic Republic it brought into the world and was now seeing off to its grave. If the healthy and robust prose of Ali Shari'ati's French sojourn, telling of the European encounters of a Muslim revolutionary, represented the authority of an Islamic ideology in combative mode, then the public prosecutor's document prepared by the latter-day ideologues of the beleaguered Islamic Republic sounded the death knell of that very encounter. Like a page from Gabriel García Márquez's *The Autumn of the Patriarch* (*El otoño del patriarca*, 1975), the indictment reads more like the death certificate of Islamic ideology itself than as the account of a plot to topple the Islamic Republic it has created by its manufacturing of factual, figurative, and fictive enemies. Hence the power to topple the Islamic Republic lay in the document itself, not with those it targeted.

---

10. For a complete transcript of Said Hajjarian's 'confessions' (in Persian), see www.dw-world.de/dw/article/0,,4596669,00.html.

In the aftermath of 'Islamic ideology' and the rise of post-ideological movements across the 'Muslim world,' we witness the birth of the first post/colonial person. Post-ideological here means post/colonial, the end of coloniality as a condition of knowledge production, in the sense that the formation of all the competing and overriding ideologies against both domestic tyranny and foreign domination were in response to colonialism and thus colonial in their paradoxical disposition. The Green Movement and the Arab Spring, perhaps two hundred years in the making, are the overcoming of that history of ideological post/coloniality, and as such are the first effectively post-ideological uprising in the course of the Muslim encounter with post/colonial modernity. Those among the 'left' who oppose the Green Movement and the Arab Spring – in a bizarre combination of a politics of despair, political Orientalism, and nihilistic anti-imperialism – are trapped inside their sclerotic, retrogressive imaginations.

The gradual release from the post/colonial condition of knowledge production in terms of utopian ideologies was a historical process and hard fought. What is ahead will be no stroll in the park either. To this day the categories 'secularity,' 'secularism,' and 'secularization' remain for oppositional intellectuals an aggressive resonance of that condition of coloniality. As Albert Memmi recognized in *The Colonizer and the Colonized* (*Portrait du colonisé, précédé par Portrait du colonisateur*, 1957) only too well, decolonization of the colonized is no easy task, for the psychological consequences of the violence outlast its political impacts. Memmi saw the process as involving various stages, ranging from xenophobic nativism to reversed racism directed against the colonizer. In specifically ideological terms, anticolonial nationalism and a 'return to self' (religion, culture, past) are also contingent on the selfsame process. These stages, in both political and psychological terms, are categorically negational, reactive, and targeted against colonial mythologies that have denied the colonial agency, and in defiant opposition to the culture of colonial domination. But the overcoming of alienation will commence only in the wake of such negational responses.

Societal Modernity and Aesthetic Reason

The condition of post-ideological knowledge production that has overcome postcoloniality is above all worldly: it retrieves the world it had lost to post/coloniality by once again learning how to dwell in it. The two defining moments and abiding aspects of this post-ideological stage of worldliness are (1) its pointing to the active formation of a *societal modernity* that bypasses and leaves behind the ideologically mandated *political modernity* that all of those ideologies combined kept promising but could never attain, and (2) its doing so via the working of an *aesthetic reason* that circumvents the colonially conditioned preemption of *public reason*. Neither societal modernity nor aesthetic reason is any longer ideologically mitigated. They are both worldly, by way of their effectively retrieving the cosmopolitan worldliness that had been ideologically suppressed.

While post-ideology means an end to the condition of post/coloniality, and thus the extended domination of European master narratives, of the hermeneutic immanence of a transcendent interpretation of history, the proposition of societal modernity points to a circumventing of the cul de sac of political modernity. In the 'Muslim World' (which will thus be forced to recover its former position as *avant la lettre*), in three distinct eras, which have overlapped and cross-fertilized, ideological formations have competed in the making of political modernity. After two hundred years of such ideological formations, and one tyranny after another, we have finally (and rightly) reached the point of the de-sedimentation of post/colonial ideology and knowledge production. The master code of European post/colonial modernity had very much determined the master narrative of political modernity, while the mimetic absolutism of this modernity, predicated on Hegelian transcendence, was entirely incongruent with the post/colonial condition of intransigent mimesis that was the *conditio sine qua non* of anticolonial aesthetics. At the presumed centers of the imposition of that colonial modernity, poststructuralists have sought to dismantle that master code, while the neo-Marxist critique of poststructuralism insists on preserving it, and thus both remain, in their negation of each other, Aristotelian in their mimetic fixations. Ideology as a form of immanent transcendence, a metanarrative interpretation of the world that distorted the world, has lost (for good) that transcendence for European continental philosophy – though it never had that transcendence for, or in, the rest of the world anyway. Ideology as a hermeneutic master code of history played a historic role for Europe, for 'the West,' as its transcendental signifier. But 'Ideology' as the transcendent interpretation of history, using power as the master code of the world it crafted, had but a tenuous hold on the history of the rest of the world, which was in fact ultimately saved by being precisely 'the rest' of that world.

A societal modernity thus predicated on that embedded intransigent mimesis is the passage to citizenship – a citizenship not hoped for or promised in any ideology, but rather implicated in the retrieval of a cosmopolitan worldliness that is at once integral and definitive to being-in-the-world. The Green Movement began with the slogan 'Where is My Vote?,' and the Arab Spring echoed with the rallying cry 'People Demand the Overthrow of the Regime,' both as the death sentence on all preceding ideological movements that failed to provide citizenship rights, and as the emancipatory proclamation of the birth of that citizenship. Precisely in the competitive manufacturing of ideological narratives, social revolutions before the Green Movement and the Arab Spring dreamt in their manifestos of citizenship, including what they called their 'constitution,' but they failed to interpret citizenship in enduring institutional terms, planted in their worldly disposition. All the tyrannical states in the 'Muslim World,' and with them Islamic ideology, and indeed ideology as such, are disintegrating before our eyes in Tahrir Square and beyond, the dusted-off debris revealing the skeletal structure of our emerging citizenship. There is nothing wrong with the notion of citizenship in the ideological document we know as 'the constitution' of these tyrannies: with minor revisions here and there they compare well with any other constitution. But with the first cries of 'Where is My Vote?' and 'People Demand the Overthrow of the Regime,' these tyrannies scrapped those documents and transformed themselves into killing machines defending garrison states. The notion of 'citizenship' is ideological only to the extent that it is articulated within an ideologically driven constitution; it is no longer ideological when it is predicated on the material formation of a societal modernity that has banked on the historical forces of social formations – women's rights movements, labor unions, student organizations, professional associations, expatriate communities, and other kinds of voluntary associations. Citizenship is loudly proclaimed in dialogical terms, but is quietly practiced in societal institutions.

These systematic social formations, the societal modernity they implicate, and the aesthetic basis of their practice will no longer be wasted on any 'total revolution.' They will act as fragments of an emerging picture and stay that way. If, in accordance with the Eurocentric conception of revolt, we were awaiting a 'total revolution,' we would be disappointed as we watched the Arab Spring unfold.

One message and one message only is being communicated loud and clear from Morocco to Iran, from Syria to Yemen, and everywhere in between: *Al-Sha'b Yurid Isqat al-Nizam*, 'People Demand the Overthrow of the Regime.' These uprisings are neither 'specific' nor 'based on immediate regional concerns.' They are precisely 'a globally expanding chain of revolt,' and not mini- or aborted revolutions, signs of a postmodernity that has run ahead of itself. These are signs of an entirely different system – yet to emerge into a semiotics. If the ideological grid within which 'Muslims' as citizens began contemplating in defiant terms is defined as colonial, and thus the proposition of post-ideology is *ipso facto* the overcoming of postcoloniality, then narratively we hark back to the proposition that modernity as a European project in and of itself was a colonial enterprise, which duly renders the post-ideological realm postmodern in the abiding sense that the colonial person has never inhabited the domain of Reason and Progress, being instead at the receiving end of what passes as reasonable and progressive in the colonized world. But 'postmodernity' in this proposition means approximation to aesthetic reason as opposed to public reason, whereby the working of semiotic intransigence supplants the mimetic absolutism that in the false consciousness of the colonial condition has defined the ideological matrix of a globalized mode of knowledge production. The problem with Hardt and Negri, as observed in Chapter 1, is that they demand 'total revolution' while offering a 'postmodern' theory of Empire – which is of course a perfectly normal thing to do for a European or American revolutionary thinker. But what we witness in the Arab Spring is 'open-ended revolutions' (as opposed to 'total revolutions'), and we watch them unfold within an imperial syntax that enables the postmodern Empire (through the agency of the US, the EU, NATO, the UN, etc.) to team up with the premodern Saudi Arabian sheikdom, and permits the navel-gazing European philosopher to befriend Libyan tribal fighters to ensure the emergence of a post-Gaddafi Israel-friendly Libya.

The idea of an 'aesthetic reason,' as I propose it here, is predicated on what Christoph Menke, in *The Sovereignty of Art* (1998), calls 'aesthetic negativity,' by way of carving out for art a *terra incognita* of its own and beyond philosophical reason. 'Only by conceiving of works of art in their negative relationship to everything that is not art,' he suggests, 'can the autonomy of such works, the internal logic of their representation and of the way they are experienced, be adequately understood. ... What art actually is is contradiction, rejection, negation.'[11] It is precisely in those qualities – contradiction, rejection, and negation (pure and simple) – that works of art (from Elia Suleiman's cinema, to Mohsen Namjoo's music, to Mona Hatoum's art, to Sun'allah Ibrahim's fiction) posit an *aesthetic reason* that works beyond ideological reasoning and speaks of a societal modernity that cannot be arrested, tortured, and murdered in the dungeons of any postcolonial tyranny. Art is not real, and its signs point to nothing but themselves; precisely in its irreality it suspends the reason of the real, by virtue of what art is, and thus subjects everything else to an aesthetic defiance, thereby always suggesting the suspension of reality. Art does not complement, Menke rightly observes; it just negates, *ipso facto*, without pointing anywhere. The lyrics and semiotics of defiance are the misbehaving signs of an *aesthetic reason* that will dis-

11. Christoph Menke, *The Sovereignty of Art: Aesthetic Negativity in Adorno and Derrida*, trans. Neil Solomon (Cambridge MA: MIT Press, 1998): 3.

mantle, that has already dismantled, the regimes of knowledge and power, and destroy the entire archive of ideological thinking that constituted its foundation.

Semiotic Intransigence

By 'semiotic intransigence' I therefore mean the revolutionary aesthetic condition in which the defiant signs refuse to succumb to the belligerent signifiers, and the intellectual and the ideologue are made redundant. In this condition of semiotic defiance, beyond the reach and remit of both ideology and utopia, signs mean not just temporarily but temporally – there is not even a Derridian *trace* in this always foreplay of signs; for even the detection of, and the insistence on having noted or discovered, the Derridian *trace* is in and of itself a residue of Hegelian transcendence, from which Derrida could not completely free his deconstructive runaway. We on the colonial edges of his deconstruction needed no *trace*. Signs, for us, mean nothing. And that is what we call the condition of post/coloniality – the condition that in the Arab Spring we have now overcome and been delivered from, to be born. When Derrida insists on the *trace* as the 'mark of the absence of a presence, an always-already absent present,' his entire project to avoid yielding to metaphysics remains contingent on the Hegelian presence that he sought to overcome. But in the intransigent semiotic that delivered us from our post/coloniality, there is no need to mark such a *trace*, for there is no assumption of a presence that is now absent. Hasan Agha the Butcher is not Imam Hossein in any old Ta'ziyeh performance. He has no pretension to be the real thing, the Imam Hossein. He is just there to act; and the acting does not prevent him from turning and waving to his buddy in the audience and saying, right in the middle of his 'lines': *Mokhles Agha Majid?* 'What's happening Majid?' – while at the same time fighting the bastard Shimr.

Our condition of postcoloniality overcome, in open-ended revolutions, we now understand that there is no room, no need, for a 'total revolution.' What is needed, for an open-ended conception of revolution, is to exercise vigilance with regard to Tahrir

Square, resting assured that events are no longer predicated on the exhausted and depleted paradigm of postcoloniality. However, the end of postcolonialism as a matrix of political action and ideological formation does not mark the end of the globalized conditions of predatory capitalism that occasioned colonial and imperial adventures in the world in the first place, and that have now, perforce, generated newer forms of domination. The exhaustion of ideological formations in the postcolonial mode (as an epistemic matrix) will not preempt the rise of a newer *régime du savoir* that will seek to dominate – which is where resistance to those modes of domination becomes so critical in the revolutionary process. Islamism is gone, but Muslims qua Muslims will continue to populate the public sphere. Third World socialism will have to reconfigure itself in fresh modes of resistance in the absence of any socialist camp. Anticolonial nationalism will, equally, yield to modes and manners of solidarity in this transnational chorus of revolutionary uprisings. The role of *violence* as the cornerstone of the state – to the degree that in the name of stopping violence the state reaches for violence: military invasion masquerading as 'humanitarian intervention' – is the central political means that must be radically reconsidered. As the world begins to reconfigure its new geography of liberation, we need to rethink the very notion of *humanity*, beyond the violent despair that, informed by Hobbes and Rousseau, has long defined the theoretical terms of politics, and that, since Marx and Weber, has become the cornerstone of our reading of state formation.

EIGHT

Race, Gender, and Class in Transnational Revolutions

As the historic trial of Hosni Mubarak got under way early in August 2011, some Egyptian revolutionaries were worried that what appeared to them as the combined forces of the military and the Muslim Brotherhood, allied with the literalist and puritanical Salafis, long repressed and ostracized, would snatch their revolution away from them. The trial of Mubarak, they feared, would be 'the last concession' that the military would give to the revolutionaries. Responding to this fear, Khalil al-Anani, a scholar of Islamic politics at the Middle East Institute at Durham University and the author of *The Muslim Brotherhood in Egypt: Gerontocracy Fighting against the Clock* (2008), wrote a piece for *Almasry Alyoum*, in which he argued that the fear of Salafism (and political Islamism in general) was in fact misplaced. 'Salafism is becoming the new bogeyman in Egyptian politics,' al-Anani warns:

> The Islamist mass rally in Tahrir Square on 29 July, which was dominated by Salafis, showed just how intolerant some political forces in post-Mubarak Egypt can be. No, I don't mean the Salafis, but rather some liberal and secular groups that are keen on excluding Islamist voices from Egypt's new political arena. These groups not only demonize Salafis as a regressive current that aims to destroy the revolution

and build a new dictatorship, they also deny their right to share Tahrir Square, a space of public dissent for all Egyptians.[1]

The fear of another 'Islamic Republic' in the region is the deep (or not so deep) context of this anxiety – an anxiety that is indeed felt by some Egyptians but that is fueled particularly by American (and Israeli) neoliberals and neoconservatives (who of course would never refer to 'the Jewish Republic' as the paramount threat to democracy in the region for the last sixty years). Sympathetic to the cause of the Salafis, al-Anani argues that Egyptian Islamists were long suppressed under the Mubarak regime and they had every right to use the newly liberated Tahrir Square to air their views and display their power. 'Sure,' he admits,

> the overwhelming presence of Salafis (many of whom opposed the revolution at the start) can be provocative. But there's nothing that shocking about Salafis raising conventional Islamic slogans, like 'Islamyyia, Islamyyia', or calling for the implementation of Sharia Law. Such chants are within the bounds of their freedom of speech. What's more striking, indeed frustrating, is when some liberals and secularists use the same fear-mongering tactics as the Mubarak regime to demonize Islamists, rather than engage with them.[2]

Al-Anani calls this fear of the Salafis 'Salafobia,' and as such believes it obscures 'significant transformations taking place within the Salafi movement.' He points to internal schisms within the Salafi movement and insists that they had adopted 'democratic political views' and that they were 'willing to reach out to secular and liberal forces.' 'True,' he concedes, 'some Salafi leaders take a hostile stance towards democracy and secular parties, but others – especially younger Salafis – tend to be more moderate and pragmatic.' They are now willing to be part of the political process. Al-Anani then judiciously warns that, 'by excluding them, they may adopt more aggressive means to assert their political presence. There's a need to pull Salafism from the ideological periphery into the political center. If this happens, Egyptian Salafism can become less dogmatic and more open.' He concludes:

---

1. See Khalil al-Anani, 'Salafobia,' *Almasry Alyoum*, 5 August 2011, www.almas-ryalyoum.com/en/node/483504.
2. Ibid.

The conflict between secularists and Islamists is not just ideological, but also social. Salafis and their supporters come mainly from the Egyptian lower middle class, especially in smaller towns and rural areas that has been alienated from official politics for the past three decades. Like any other political group, they're now fighting for their fair share in the post-Mubarak era. The Salafi-secularist divide represents a conflict of interests over how to re-construct Egypt's political system, rather than an irreconcilable clash of ideologies. For this reason, Egypt's Salafis should be talked to, not feared.[3]

The fear of militant Islamism among some Egyptian revolutionaries is thus balanced by others (equally committed to the democratic aspirations of the revolution) who argue for tolerance and dialogue, though still along the false Islamist–secular binary, entirely disregarding the *public space* (Tahrir Square itself) in which these and other political positions would be absorbed into the future of Egypt. Those who have warned against militant Islamism scarcely raised their voices against the more pernicious encroachment of American neoconservatives and neoliberals; nor have they warned against the defeatist and conspiratorial elements within the Iranian left who dismissed the entire Arab Spring (as indeed they did the Green Movement before it) as a plot by the Obama administration. Fear, anxiety and suspicion became rampant. There was no way to assure those who called themselves 'secular and liberal' that Egyptian Islamists would abide by democratic principles; nor was there any way to deny the Islamists their fair share of the Egyptian revolution.

Amidst these fears and suspicions, two issues were paramount in the secular–Islamist debate: gender and class. The call for the full implementation of sharia implies frightful consequences for the status of women, while at the same time the Islamists had an obvious appeal to certain strata of society – extending from the poor to the middle class. A further issue is race, which also became evident in the opening weeks of the Arab Spring. After a lifetime of living under authoritarian dictatorship, Egyptians were

---

3. Ibid.

suddenly singing a different tune – the question was whether they were willing to improvise their lyrics.

Changing the Lyrics

During the spring of 2011 Ramsy Essam was catapulted from being an ordinary Egyptian student to one of the most popular revolutionary singers in his homeland. 'The melodic chant had become an anthem of the revolution,' the BBC reported of one of Essam's most famous revolutionary songs: '"Irhal, Irhal" or "leave, leave" they cried, calling for Mr Mubarak to step down.' And then one day the world, and the song, changed:

> 'Irhal' was a song he cobbled together from the protest chants of the revolution's early days. As he stepped up to perform it once again he realized the words were redundant – Mubarak had gone. He quickly scribbled down new lyrics, changing the cry from 'leave' to a demand for the end of military rule. 'I will never forget, there was a mother of a martyr who was with us all the time and she never laughed or smiled. ... It was at that moment when she looked really happy and started smiling because she heard that the words of the song had changed.'[4]

Despite the lingering fears, Egyptians were quickly learning to sing new lyrics. The question was how quickly they could change the lyrics and catch up with the new tune – or vice versa. Hannah Arendt's warning about the French Revolution – that there would never be any limit to social demands in any revolutionary uprising if they were constantly fed into the political domain – remained critical here. But the open-ended nature of those demands had posited a different time frame within a *longue durée* that had immediate and instant dis/satisfactions, opening up the horizon for longer-term engagements. The political culture of Egypt was changing, and the changes were seismic though still imperceptible – all other political demands and changes would be registered against that foregrounding of a sublated politics yet to surface.

---

4. See Stephanie Hegarty, 'Ramy Essam: Singer Catapulted to Fame on Tahrir Square,' BBC News online, 11 July 2011, www.bbc.co.uk/news/world-middle-east-14254564.

The fear of militant Islamism was as natural as it was misplaced. There was no possibility that militant Islamists could do in Egypt in 2011 what they did in Iran in 1979, unite their forces, defeat their opponents, conspire with the military and its American backers, establish an Islamic Republic, fully implement the sharia, purge the universities, lead successive cultural revolutions, force dissidents into exile, murder the rest, and thus manage to create the diabolic inferno of the Islamic Republic of Iran anew in Egypt. Yet the fear that fueled this anxiety was good for the revolution – it made its democratic metabolism more efficient. Militant Islamism was not the only threat that Egyptian revolutionaries were facing. Exclusionary and jingoistic nationalism, a fully fledged military coup, sectarian violence, American/Israeli/Saudi interference, and a fossilized left that had stayed on the sidelines – such were the threats that, to varying degrees, would agitate and exercise the democratic intuitions of the revolutionary uprising. And yet their effect was positive for the revolution, serving to tone its democratic muscles.

We need to broaden the frame of reference of the Arab Spring in order to see beneath and beyond the inherited geography of the Arab or Muslim world; for example, to detect the multiple patterns of labor migration into and from North Africa, a phenomenon that reveals the wider economic and demographic implications of the uprisings. Such labor migrations inevitably raise the question of class, and with it issues of race and gender – an understanding of which will give us a much better reading of the Arab Spring than one demonstration or another in Tahrir Square, which might serve to skew the analysis. We of course need to pay close attention to these reactions on the street, but we must also adopt a perspective that is able to detect and analyse the deeper, more muscular, flexing of societal formations in the abiding intersections of race, gender, and class.

Race and Racism

Soon after the brutal crackdown on the post-electoral uprising in Iran in June 2009, rumors began circulating in cyberspace and among ardent supporters of the Green Movement that some among the security forces of the Islamic Republic that had been recruited to attack demonstrators were in fact not Iranians at all, but in fact 'Arabs.' Photographs of security forces began to circulate with darker-skinned individuals circled in red, and Arabic-sounding names attributed, denoting them as members of the Lebanese Hezbollah or Palestinian Hamas. Iranians like me who come from the southern regions of our homeland, who look like those circled in red, and who remember being derogatively dismissed as 'Arabs' by our whiter-looking northern brothers and sisters, were not convinced by the allegations. We also recalled that in the aftermath of the Soviet invasion of Afghanistan and the subsequent Afghan refugee influx into Iran, all sorts of crimes and misdemeanors were attributed to 'Afghanis'.

Then, almost two years later, 'the mercenaries' allegedly deployed by the Gaddafi regime to crush the revolutionary uprising engulfing Libya were reported to have been 'African.' 'As nations evacuate their citizens from the violence gripping Libya,' Al Jazeera reported, 'many African migrant workers are targeted because they are suspected of being mercenaries hired by Muammar Gaddafi, the Libyan leader.' The report further specified that 'dozens of workers from sub-Saharan Africa are feared killed, and hundreds are in hiding, as angry mobs of anti-government protesters hunt down "black African mercenaries," according to witnesses.'[5]

These traveling metaphors of racially profiled acts of violence – violence that is always perpetrated by 'others,' and not by 'oneself' – metamorphosing as they moved and racialized the transnational revolutionary uprisings in Arab and Muslim lands, were a nasty remnant of ancient and medieval racism domestic to these cultures, deployed to demean and subjugate them by European colonialism to further its own interests, and now come back to haunt and mar the best and most noble moments of a collective uprising against domestic tyranny and foreign domination alike. The manifestations of this racism were multifaceted and not limited to the revolutionary momentum of street demonstrations or the anonymity of web-based 'activism.' They extended well

---

5. See 'African Migrants Targeted in Libya,' Al Jazeera, 28 February 2011, http:// english.aljazeera.net/news/africa/2011/02/201122286581437854l.html.

into the cool corners of reasoned analysis and deliberation. The racist identification of 'Arabs' among the security apparatus of the Islamic Republic by some pro-democracy activist Iranians was reciprocated by certain leading Arab public intellectuals who were on record as having dismissed the massive civil rights uprising in Iran as a plot by the United States and Israel and funded by Saudi Arabia, condescendingly equating it with the 'Cedar Revolution' in Lebanon. Such expressions of inanity were in turn echoed, even amplified, by some Iranian activists, who ridiculed and dismissed the Egyptian and Tunisian revolutions as a 'glorified military coup,' or else boasted that 'Arabs' were doing now what 'we' did thirty years ago, concluding that 'they' were therefore three decades behind the times.[6]

This closed-circuit cycle of racism fed on itself, and its cancerous cells spread over the body politic of nations and their nationalisms. The roots of such racism, directed by Arabs and Iranians at each other and by both against 'black Africans' go deep and are troubling. Aspects of these pathologies point to the necessity for collective emancipation from the snares of racism transmuting into cycles of racializing violence. On the Arab side, as Joseph Massad has demonstrated in his *Desiring Arabs* (2007), in the course of Arab nationalism, the trope of 'Persian' was systematically racialized and invested with all sorts of undesirable and morally corrupt and corrupting 'sexual perversions,' and thus a 'manly' and 'straight' heteronormativity was manufactured for 'Arabs.'[7] Massad's insight has been borne out by the derision heaped upon the Green Movement in Iran, in which estimation Iranians were considered to be too 'feminine,' too pretty, too weak, too bourgeois to have their own uprising, and therefore – like all women – in need of help from the superpower. Imperialism, for its part, was real power, hence masculine. Revolutions too were real power, therefore also masculine. Whilst the Iranian Green Movement was thus feminized by way of dismissing it as feeble, flawed, and

---

6. I have attended to this matter in some detail in Hamid Dabashi, 'The Left is Wrong on Iran,' *Al-Ahram Weekly*, 22 July 2009, http://weekly.ahram.org.eg/2009/956/op5.htm.

7. See Joseph Massad, *Desiring Arabs* (Chicago: Chicago University Press, 2007): *passim*.

manipulated by 'the West,' the Egyptian and Tunisian revolutions were assimilated aggressively into a decidedly masculinist Arab nationalism. The homophobic anxieties of masculinist Arab nationalism – to extend Joseph Massad's crucial insight – thus protested too much by dismissing the Green Movement as something effeminate, soft, middle class, bourgeois, and above all supported by the 'superpower.'

The pathology of Iranian racism has a different genealogy. Engulfed in the banality of a racist Aryanism, a certain segment of the Iranian population, mostly (but not exclusively) monarchist in political disposition, has been led to believe that they are an island of pure-bred Aryans unfortunately caught in a sea of Semitic ruffians, and that, marred by Arab and Muslim invasion, they need to reconnect with their European roots in 'the West' to regain their former glory. Predicated on the historic defeat of the Sassanid Empire (224-651) by the invading Arab army in the Battle of al-Qadisiyyah (636), in particular, this national trauma has always been prone to xenophobia of the worst kind. It is not only 'Arabs' but also 'Turks' and 'Mongols' – corresponding to successive invasions of Iran from the seventh to the thirteenth centuries – who have been the repository of Iranian racism. The internal manifestation of this racism has been the derogatory and condescending attitude of self-proclaimed 'Persians' towards racialized minorities like Kurds, Azaris and Baluchis. External and internal racisms come together to manufacture a fictitious 'Persian' marker that is the mirror image of its 'Arab' invention. The binary Persian/Arab, rooted in medieval history and exacerbated by colonialism, in turn becomes a self-propelling metaphoric proposition and feeds on itself.[8]

Predicated on these dual acts of racialized bigotry, pan-nationalist political projects have been the catastrophic hallmark of postcolonial history over the past century. As pan-Iranism competed with pan-Turkism in Central Asia and exacerbated pan-Arabism in West Asia and North Africa, their combined calamity – while they at once mimic and loathe 'the West' they collectively

---

8. I have attended in more detail to this racism in Hamid Dabashi, *Iran: A People Interrupted* (New York: New Press, 2007): *passim*.

helped manufacture – comes together and coalesces in an identical expression of bigotry against 'black Africans.'

The proclivity towards the racialization of transnational revolutionary uprisings played a systematic part in that ghastly history; were this not to be addressed, the revolutionaries would be engaged in a wild goose chase just when they thought they were being liberated. As the Zimbabwean journalist and filmmaker Farai Sevenzo has noted,

> In the violence of the last fortnight [mid-February 2011 in Libya], the colonel [Gaddafi]'s African connections have only served to rekindle a deep-rooted racism between Arabs and black Africans. As mercenaries, reputedly from Chad and Mali fight for him, a million African refugees and thousands of African migrant workers stand the risk of being murdered for their tenuous link to him.[9]

Farai Sevenzo also reports: 'One Turkish construction worker told the BBC: 'we had 70–80 people from Chad working for our company. They were cut dead with pruning shears and axes, attackers saying: "you are providing troops for Gaddafi." The Sudanese were also massacred. We saw it for ourselves.'[10] That ghastly manifestation of racialized violence could not be the reason why millions of people from Senegal to Djibouti, from Morocco to Afghanistan, and from Iran to Yemen were dreaming of better days for their children. But the fact that it has been aired, discussed, criticized, and made integral to the discourse of emancipation is a vital aspect of 'the Arab Spring.'

Racializing violence was also the very last remnant of colonial racism, which was only too familiar with the Roman, and later Old French Republic, logic of 'divide and conquer,' or 'divide and rule' (*divide et impera* or *divide ut regnes*), a dictum that was ultimately brought to perfection by Machiavelli in his *Art of War* (1520). The criminal record of European colonialism in Asia and Africa is replete with examples of this treacherous strategy. Germany and Belgium both put the dictum to good use in Rwanda by appointing

---

9. See 'African viewpoint: Colonel's continent?' BBC News online, 25 February 2011, www.bbc.co.uk/news/world-africa-12585395.

10. Ibid.

members of the Tutsi minority to positions of power. The Tutsi and Hutu groups were re-manufactured racially, an atrocity at the heart of the subsequent Rwandan genocide.[11] The British had a similar use for the colonial maxim when they ruled Sudan and sustained a divide between the North and the South, which in turn resulted in successive Sudanese civil wars. The colonial history of the rest of Africa abounds with similar divides, as does the history of Asia, not least in India where the British were instrumental not only in reinscribing the caste system to their colonial benefit, but also in fomenting hostility between Muslims and Hindus, which ultimately resulted in the catastrophic partition of India and Pakistan along religious lines.[12]

It is Aimé Césaire, in *Discourse on Colonialism* (1955), who systematically thought through the link between racism and colonialism and connected them to the rise of Fascism and Nazism in the very heart of Europe. Colonialism and racism were integral to the operation of capitalism, Césaire proposed, and a sign of its 'collective hypocrisy.' The so-called civilizing mission was a mask for systematic exploitation, inflicting 'covetousness, violence, [and] race hatred,' thereby causing 'a universal regression.' Colonialism, Césaire suggested, 'thingified' human beings as instruments and raw material of production.[13] The French in Africa, the British in Asia, the Spanish in Latin America, succeeded by the United States around the globe, were all in the business of 'thingifying' human beings. That overriding proclivity either manufactured racialized divides or else used and abused existing racism on the ground that had been conquered.

Beyond the reach of colonial and imperial treachery, Arabs and Muslims were destined to renew their rendezvous with history. Were today's revolutions to be reassimilated to the outdated and

---

11. For more details, see Mahmood Mamdani, *When Victims Become Killers: Colonialism, Nativism, and the Genocide in Rwanda* (Princeton NJ: Princeton University Press, 2002).

12. Nicholas Dirks, in *Castes of Mind: Colonialism and the Making of Modern India* (Princeton NJ: Princeton University Press, 2001), has demonstrated how the Indian caste system is in fact the by-product of the colonial relationship between India and British imperial rule.

13. Aimé Césaire, *Discourse on Colonialism* (New York and London: Monthly Review Press, 2001): 10, 13, 21.

racializing elements of pan-Arab, pan-Iranian, pan-Turkic, and similar frames of references, we would be back where we were two centuries ago – and all of the heroic sacrifices would be for naught. However, the younger generation of Arabs, Iranians, and Africans now speak an entirely different language. The transnational solidarity of the Arab Spring is what has ignited the uprising and will sustain it for years to come. For example, in reaction to anti-Arab sentiment in the Green Movement, activists wrote articles on the Palestinian artist Naji al-Ali's character Hanzala, and soon the Palestinian cartoon hero appeared with green scarf keeping demonstrators company in Tehran;[14] and on the day Mubarak left office, the first young Egyptian interviewed by the BBC expressed solidarity with his Iranian counterparts, and predicted that Iran would be next, a position supported by Wael Ghoneim, the young Egyptian Internet activist, who, sporting a green wristband when addressing the rallies in Tahrir Square, said he was delighted that Iranians recognized this as solidarity with their cause. From their economic foundations to their political aspirations, the revolutionary uprisings were the initial sketches of a whole new atlas of human possibilities – beyond the reach of racialized violence, gender apartheid, and class division.

Racism does not operate in isolation; it is intimately linked to issues of gender and class. The gendering of racialized and colonial attitudes is well examined by Ashis Nandy in his exquisite study *The Intimate Enemy: Loss and Recovery of Self under Colonialism* (1989) in which he demonstrates how colonizers effectively infiltrate and alter the consciousness of the colonized. 'The political economy of colonization is of course important,' he stipulates, 'but the crudity and inanity of colonialism are principally expressed in the sphere of psychology and, to the extent the variables used to describe the states of mind under colonialism have themselves become politicized since the entry of modern colonialism on the world scene, in the sphere of political psychology.'[15] This altering

---

14. See Hamid Dabashi, 'The Arab Roaming the Streets of Tehran,' Tehran Bureau, 7 July 2009, www.pbs.org/wgbh/pages/frontline/tehranbureau/2009/07/the-arab-roaming-the-streets-of-tehran.html.

15. See Ashis Nandy, *The Intimate Enemy: Loss and Recovery of Self under Colonialism* (Oxford: Oxford University Press, 1989): 2.

of the consciousness is of course predicated on the material basis of power upon which the colonizer and the colonized find themselves connected. Nandy specifically identifies the manner in which this alteration occurred in the Indian case:

> The change in consciousness that took place can be briefly stated in terms of three concepts which became central to colonial India: *purusatva* (the essence of masculinity), *naritva* (the essence of femininity) and *klibatva* (the essence of hermaphroditism).[16]

Predicated on societal formations prior to European colonial onslaught, this gendering of domination is thus localized, written into the normative and moral fabric of the colonized consciousness. Nandy explains in details how the reordering of Indian culture was in fact performed by a number of leading Indian authors who sought to reevaluate Hindu traditions by way of coping 'with the modern concepts of mature, adult normality as opposed to abnormal, immature, infantile primitivism.' These authors

> tried to contain within the Indian world view Western concepts of the male and the female, and the adult and the infantile, and thus to make the Western presence in India seem natural in a context where the West had seemingly come to represent, for many Indians, the more valued aspects of Indian culture.[17]

Colonial domination is at once racialized and gendered, but not *ex nihilo*, and is predicated entirely on existing conditions, which are recast to the advantage of colonial domination. It is precisely in that context, where local traits and colonial stratagems come together, that the Arab Spring saw one of its most fundamental changes: namely, to the globalized perception of Arab and Muslim women.

Gender

Recall, if you can, the image of the Muslim woman manufactured by US and European Islamophobes and their native informers:[18] passive, docile, incarcerated inside a repressive religion, denied

16. Ibid.: 7–8.
17. Ibid.: 18, 22.
18. I have dealt with this matter extensively in my *Brown Skin, White Masks* (London: Pluto, 2011).

a public presence. They were sent off to hideouts to read *Lolita* in Tehran while waiting to be liberated by US marines – and the inanity that popularized that image become a national bestseller in George W. Bush's North America and Tony Blair's and Silvio Berlusconi's Europe.[19] They were said to be participating in communal orgies when they joined political protests.[20] They were invariably portrayed in cages, desperately peering out through the bars – and this by women's studies scholars and publishers[21] and the publishers of fake memoirs of Arab princes and honor killings alike.[22] Even when they were coming out in their millions in Iran to participate in public rallies, there were still some among the Arab, Iranian, and North American 'left' who ridiculed their dresses, sunglasses, or scarves – not having an inkling that their sisters were about to join them from one end of the Arab and Muslim world to the other.[23]

Now consider the pictures of these women defying the odds, domestic and foreign, defying tyranny, homegrown and imposed; look at them closely. Half of them would be denied the dignity of choosing their own clothes from one end of Europe to the other – particularly those who choose the veil in France, Germany or the Netherlands, upsetting the racist sensibilities of European mass murderers like Anders Behring Breivik. These women would be denied full citizenship in Europe and yet they are at the forefront of a world-historic succession of revolutions in the Arab and Muslim world. That alone should tell us where the world is today – and

---

19. For more details, see Hamid Dabashi, 'Native Informers and the Making of American Empire,' *Al-Ahram Weekly*, 1-7 June 2006.

20. Pardis Mahdavi, *Passionate Uprisings: Iran's Sexual Revolution* (Stanford CA: Stanford University Press, 2009).

21. For a typical example, see the cover of Janet Afary's *Sexual Politics in Modern Iran* (Cambridge: Cambridge University Press, 2009), www.amazon.com/Sexual-Politics-Modern-Janet-Afary/dp/0521727081. For one of the earliest clichéd Orientalist tropes to which this cover is an allusion, see the opening shot of the Hollywood production *The Adventures of Hajji Baba* (1954), available on YouTube: www.youtube.com/watch?v=5pYnRRMxrgc&feature=related.

22. Nourma Khouri's *Forbidden Love: A Harrowing Story of Love and Revenge in Jordan* (New York: Bantam Books, 2003) is the most infamous of these fake memoirs. For an account of how the lie was discovered, see Phil Mercer, 'Doubts over "honor killing" Book,' BBC News online, 26 July 2004, http://news.bbc.co.uk/2/hi/asia-pacific/3925791.stm.

23. For details, see Hamid Dabashi, 'The Left is Wrong on Iran.'

where it is headed. 'Among the most prevalent Western stereotypes about Muslim countries,' notes American political activist and social critic Naomi Wolf, in a piece for Al Jazeera, 'are those concerning Muslim women: doe-eyed, veiled, and submissive, exotically silent, gauzy inhabitants of imagined harems, closeted behind rigid gender roles.' And then she rhetorically asks: 'So where were these women in Tunisia and Egypt?' Her response:

> In both countries, women protesters were nothing like the Western stereotype: they were front and centre, in news clips and on Facebook forums, and even in the leadership. In Egypt's Tahrir Square, women volunteers, some accompanied by children, worked steadily to support the protests – helping with security, communications, and shelter. Many commentators credited the great numbers of women and children with the remarkable overall peacefulness of the protesters in the face of grave provocations.

Naomi Wolf also notes that in the course of the revolutionary uprisings women were at the center of the action, and

> not serving only as support workers, the habitual role to which they are relegated in protest movements, from those of the 1960s to the recent student riots in the United Kingdom. Egyptian women also organized, strategized, and reported the events. Bloggers such as Leila Zahra Mortada took grave risks to keep the world informed daily of the scene in Tahrir Square and elsewhere.[24]

Much has happened in the Arab and Muslim world that has not made it into the global limelight. Chief among these changes on the ground has been the massive presence of women in the labour force and higher education. As Wolf notes,

> The greatest shift is educational. Two generations ago, only a small minority of the daughters of the elite received a university education. Today, women account for more than half of the students at Egyptian universities. They are being trained to use power in ways that their grandmothers could scarcely have imagined: publishing newspapers – as Sanaa el Seif did, in defiance of a government order to cease

---

24. See Naomi Wolf, 'The Middle East Feminist Revolution,' Al Jazeera, 4 March 2011, http://english.aljazeera.net/indepth/opinion/2011/03/201134111445686926.html.

operating; campaigning for student leadership posts; fundraising for student organisations; and running meetings.

Predicated on these subterranean and enduring changes in the status and achievements of women, what we have witnessed is a seismic change that prompts Naomi Wolf to compare it to other major shifts in history:

> Just when France began its rebellion in 1789, Mary Wollstonecraft, who had been caught up in witnessing it, wrote her manifesto for women's liberation. After educated women in America helped fight for the abolition of slavery, they put female suffrage on the agenda. After they were told in the 1960s that 'the position of women in the movement is prone', they generated 'second wave' feminism – a movement born of women's new skills and old frustrations.

Her conclusion:

> since feminism is simply a logical extension of democracy, the Middle East's despots are facing a situation in which it will be almost impossible to force these awakened women to stop their fight for freedom – their own and that of their communities.[25]

These women did not appear out of nowhere. That 'the war on terror,' predicated on a whole history of Orientalism, had manufactured a docile image of Arab and Muslim women, waiting to be 'liberated' by the US Army, the way they were liberated in Afghanistan and Iraq, was not their problem. This was the treachery of a propaganda machine fed by native informer and career opportunists. Arabs and Muslims were now risking their lives for their collective liberties in a manner that the world (awash with Islamophobic and Orientalist nonsense) was unprepared to witness. They of course paid a very heavy price for their acts of heroism. As Elizabeth Flock notes in 'Women in the Arab Spring: The other side of the story,'

> Much has been written about the women who have protested, organized, blogged and conducted hunger strikes throughout the Arab Spring. An opposition newspaper in Libya recently headlined a story about the role women have played in the uprisings this way: 'She is the Muslim,

---

25. Ibid.

the mother, the soldier, the protester, the journalist, the volunteer, the citizen.' But the other piece of the story is the anguish countless women have had to endure, in the form of rape, detention, or simply a lack of appreciation of their role in the protests.[26]

Women were not only at the forefront of the revolutionary uprisings. They were also its first and foremost victims – the first targets of the brutal repression that those in power launched against the uprising. Flock again: 'In Syria, for example, rapes and other assaults on women have increased during the past few months, indicating an escalation of violence by the government and its allies.' The raping of women as a tactic of repression was not limited to Syria: 'In Libya, a similar story of rape as a weapon of war has played out. An investigation by the International Criminal Court in early June found evidence that Libyan leader Moammar Gaddafi ordered mass rapes.'[27]

These revolutionary roles for women were not unprecedented or unusual of course. In an excellent article in *The Nation*, Juan Cole and Shahin Cole provide some historical context:

> To start with Tunisia, women there have, in fact, been in the vanguard of protest movements and social change since the drive to gain independence from France of the late 1940s. Tunisian women have a relatively high literacy rate (71 percent), represent more than one-fifth of the country's wage earners, and make up 43 percent of the nearly half-million members of eighteen local unions. Most of these unionized women work in the education, textile, health, city services and tourism industries. The General Union of Tunisian Workers (French acronym: UGTT) had increasingly come into conflict with the country's strongman, Zine el-Abidine Ben Ali, and so its rank and file enthusiastically joined the street protests. Today, the UGTT continues to pressure the government formed after Ben Ali fled to move forward with genuine reforms.[28]

---

26. See Elizabeth Flock, 'Women in the Arab Spring: The Other Side of the Story,' *Washington Post*, 21 June 2011, www.washingtonpost.com/blogs/blogpost/post/women-in-the-arab-spring-the-other-side-of-the-story/2011/06/21/AG32qVeH_blog.html.

27. Ibid.

28. See Juan Cole and Shahin Cole, 'An Arab Spring for Women,' *The Nation*, 26 April 2011, www.thenation.com/article/160179/arab-spring-women.

Nevertheless, women faced much criticism for their presence in the movement: 'On April 15, Yemeni president for life Ali Abdullah Saleh scolded women for "inappropriately" mixing in public with men at the huge demonstrations then being staged in the capital, Sanaa, as well as in the cities of Taiz and Aden.' This reaction was in response to the overwhelming presence of women in public spaces. 'They came out in unprecedented numbers throughout the country, and even in the countryside, day after day, accusing the president of "besmirching their honor" by implying that they were behaving brazenly.'[29]

Women appeared in the demonstrations alone, with members of their families, and even with their children.

> In Syria ... women have shown their strength and bravery, turning out in forceful demonstrations – sometimes without men, but with their children in tow. Near the town of Bayda, for instance, thousands of women shouting 'We will not be humiliated!' cut off a coastal road to protest a heavy-handed government policy in which the secret police of President Bashar al-Assad had arrested their demonstrating male relatives.

And rallies composed exclusively of women had also been evident: 'On other occasions, Syrian women have staged all-female marches to demand democracy and changes in regime policy.' These revolutionary women were of course not always welcomed by revolutionary men:

> Patriarchal forces such as Muslim fundamentalist groups and clergy are determined that women's rights should not be expanded in the wake of these political upheavals. As an omen in the wind, when a modest-sized group of 200 women showed up at Tahrir Square on March 8th to commemorate International Women's Day, they found themselves attacked by militant religious young men who shouted that they should go home and do the laundry.[30]

Cole and Cole challenge the idea that the uprisings could lead to a worsening of women's rights. They conclude:

---

29. Ibid.
30. Ibid.

The Arab Spring has proven an epochal period of activism and change for women, recalling the role of early feminists in the 1919 Egyptian movement for independence from Britain, or the important place of women in the Algerian Revolution. The sheer numbers of politically active women in this series of uprisings, however, dwarf their predecessors. That this female element in the Arab Spring has drawn so little comment in the West suggests that our own narratives of, and preoccupations with, the Arab world – religion, fundamentalism, oil and Israel – have blinded us to the big social forces that are altering the lives of 300 million people.[31]

To be sure, much structural inequality persists:

The Arab Spring was not about gender equality. Women in all countries involved say that. But many are alarmed that their efforts risk going unrewarded, and that men who were keen to have them on the streets crying freedom may not be so happy to have them in parliament, government and business boardrooms.[32]

But the battleground was now theirs, and battle lines were drawn. Ahdaf Soueif, the distinguished Anglo-Egyptian novelist and political and cultural commentator, became a leading and eloquent vice in the course of the Egyptian revolution. She wrote regularly for the *Guardian*,[33] travelled to Egypt and was a force at Tahrir Square, as indeed was Noha Radwan, a professor of Arabic and Comparative Literature at the University of California, Davis. Radwan, a mother of two young children, took leave of absence from her teaching duties in California and travelled to Cairo to be there, right in the middle of Tahrir Square, for the duration of the revolution. She reported for the leading American progressive news outlet Democracy Now. After filing one such report she was attacked and savagely beaten by Mubarak's security forces.[34] Like

---

31. Ibid.
32. Ibid.
33. For an example, see Ahdaf Soueif, 'Egypt's Revolution Is Stuck in a Rut, but We Still Have the Spirit to See It Through,' *Guardian*, 12 July 2011, www.guardian.co.uk/commentisfree/2011/jul/12/egypt-revolution-rut-military-obstacles?INTCMP=SRCH.
34. For more details about this incident, see 'California Professor Beaten by Pro-Mubarak Forces Minutes after Interview on Democracy Now!' www.democracynow.org/appearances/noha_radwan.

their sisters two years earlier in Iran, Egyptian and other Arab women would not be denied their democratic rights.

The excitement felt by progressive American and European academics, journalists, and activists on watching Arab and Muslim women pouring into the streets in their masses and demanding civil liberties is perfectly understandable given the negative portrayal of these women (and of Arabs and Muslims in general) in the mass media, particularly over the last few decades. But we must not allow that excitement, any more than the deliberate distortion it attempts to correct, to distract from the more fundamental issue, which is the sustained struggle by Arab and Muslim women to alter the course of their national and regional histories. Those women on Tahrir or Azadi Square, active agents in a world-historic succession of events, did not emerge from nowhere. They are the voices and visages cultivated in the public domain for decades and centuries. It has taken relentless and tireless work to enable these women and girls to show the courage, the imagination, and above all the audacity to come out on the streets to demand their rights. It is a North American and Western European calamity that these women are thought of only in Oriental harems, presided over by a professor of English literature deciphering *Lolita* for them in Tehran – that is, when they are done with their sexual orgies in a nearby public bath. These are the perverted banalities of a corrupt warmongering culture that would manufacture consent when sending in its marines to 'liberate' Muslims from their own tyrannies.[35]

To be sure, the manufacturing of the image of Arab and Muslim women as passive and inert has not been limited to the periodic political abuse on the part of the US or its European allies when waging war on Muslim lands; it was endemic, for instance, in generations of scholarship in the field of women's studies before the emergence of postcolonial and transnational feminism. The distinguished feminist theorist Chandra Talpade Mohanty, in a groundbreaking essay 'Under Western Eyes: Feminist Scholarship

---

35. For an excellent critique of this genre of literature, see Lila Abu-Lughod, 'Do Muslim Women Really Need Saving? Anthropological Reflections on Cultural Relativism and Its Others,' *American Anthropologist*, vol. 104, no, 3, September 2002.

and Colonial Discourses' (1986), finally broke the silence on the working of this colonial (and postcolonial) gaze and exposed the categorical flaw in this sort of scholarship. In her pioneering essay, Mohanty systematically exposes the specific ways in which '"women" as a category of analysis is used in Western feminist discourse on women in the Third World,' illustrating 'the construction of "Third World women" as a homogenous, "powerless" group often located as implicit victims of particular socioeconomic systems.'[36] Of course the issue is not limited to 'Western feminism' looking at 'Third World women'; many 'Third World' scholars working in North American and Western European universities have reiterated those terms in their works. So, being a 'Third world woman' scholar or activist does not mean you are free from such self-colonizing categories. In fact you may authenticate and corroborate with them.[37]

The fact that, against this background in both the public domain and on university campuses, progressive scholars and activists are now correcting those images, based on the factual evidence of what they are seeing, should not, however, muddy the water and lead us to disregard the reality that successive generations of women's rights pioneers, social historians, imaginative theorists, community organizers, public educators, political activists, revolutionary leaders, poets, filmmakers and artists have paved the way for their daughters in Tahrir and Azadi Squares. The gradual and systemic making of a collective conscience (to use Durkheim's term) has been at work creating the necessary historical agency that is alive and active in every single women and girl in those squares, an agential confidence from which they draw courage beyond the tyrannies women have faced at home, the indignities they have suffered during the colonial conquests, the disappointments of postcolonial state building – and, above all, the patriarchy and misogyny that have informed them all.

---

36. See Chandra Talpade Mohanty, 'Under Western Eyes: Feminist Scholarship and Colonial Discourses,' in *Feminism without Borders: Decolonizing Theory, Practicing Solidarity* (Durham NC: Duke University Press, 2003): 23.

37. For two such examples, see Pardis Mahdavi, *Passionate Uprisings: Iran's Sexual Revolution* (Stanford, CA: Stanford University Press, 2008); and Janet Afary, *Sexual Politics in Modern Iran* (Cambridge: Cambridge University Press, 2009).

We need to shift our perspective away from the globalized media under the influence of imperial powers and towards local and regional modes of alternative knowledge production, where revolutionaries and artists alike have been busy for generations. In her classic book, *Women of Algiers in Their Apartments* (2002), the Algerian novelist and filmmaker Assia Djebar explores in probing prose and exquisite detail the predicament of women during the anticolonial struggles and postcolonial liberation – paying insightful attention to issues and tropes of silence and invisibility. She demonstrates how the Algerian War of Liberation (1954-62) was in fact liberation for men only. Noting the role of women as active fighters during the war, she explains how this was only a temporary measure, for after the war a new cycle of repression ensued. Revealing these struggles, we are told: 'I was a voiceless prisoner. A little like certain women of Algiers today, you see them going around without the ancestral veil, and yet, out of fear of the new and unexpected situations, they become entangled in other veils, invisible but very noticeable ones.' Defying the imposed silence, Djebar proclaims:

> For Arabic women I see only one single way to unblock everything: talk, talk without stopping, about yesterday and today, talk among ourselves, in all of the women's quarters, the traditional ones as well as those in housing projects. Talk amongst ourselves and look. Look outside, look outside the walls and the prisons! ... The Woman as look and the Woman as voice ... not the voice of female vocalists whom they imprison in their sugar-sweet melodies ... But the voice they've never heard ... the voice of sighs, of malice, of the sorrows of all the women they've kept walled in ... The voice that's searching in the opened tombs.[38]

It was *the image* that needed to be changed – 'The image of women (as the Orient) is still perceived no differently, be it by the father, by the husband, and, more troublesome still, by the brother and son'[39] – and women had started changing that image long before Azadi and Tahrir Squares. The genealogy of that

---

38. Assia Djebar, *Women of Algiers in Their Apartments* (Charlottesville VA: University of Virginia Press, 2002): 48, 50.
39. Ibid.: 138.

change must be traced domestically and regionally, where women have waged their battles, and not based solely on the alternating images of the repressed or revolutionary women where the power of representation has hitherto resided.

Generation after generation – in both colonial and postcolonial eras – women have entered the public space and changed it; in so doing assigned gender roles have been consistently challenged. The body politic of the dominant regime of knowledge and power has been challenged via a sustained course of defying the gendered body – where and what it was to appear and to do. As Judith Butler has demonstrated, the gendered body is never a 'mute facticity.' The gendered 'fact' of the human body is manufactured – socially, psychologically, culturally, politically – through the repetition of 'received notions' that soon assume the function of being perceived as 'natural.' Butler rightly questions 'the natural' in order to expose the 'foundational categories' that are at work in making of sex, gender, and desire sites and formations of power. There are extended political stakes in designating as '*origin* and *cause*' those identity categories that are in fact the *effects* of institutions, practices, discourses with multiple and diffuse points of origin.[40] There is a revolutionary dimension to Judith Butler's ideas here that must be traced to the public space that women occupy to alter their gendered roles. Gender is performance, not existence.

Gender is the repeated stylization of the body, a set of repeated acts within a highly rigid regulatory frame that congeal over time to produce the appearance of substance, of a natural sort of being. A political genealogy of gender ontologies, if it is successful, will deconstruct the substantive appearance of gender into its constitutive acts, and locate and account for those acts within the compulsory frames set by the various forces that police the social appearance of gender.[41]

---

40. See Judith Butler, *Gender Trouble: Feminism and the Subversion of Identity* (New York: Routledge, 1999): 48, 164, 29.
41. Ibid.: 43.

Class and Labor

The issue of class, labor, and migration is no longer just a national, or even transnational, concern; it has assumed intercontinental proportions – countries and cultures seeming to moving around with the same ease as legal and illegal laborers. In consequence, the class dimensions of the Arab Spring link the revolutionary uprisings to the thorny issues of labor migration and racism, whose varied manifestations in recent times have included mass murder in Norway, riots in the UK in the summer of 2011 and in France in the autumn of 2005, and are camouflaged as 'multiculturalism' and Islamophobia' in Western Europe, North America, and Australia.

Within the domain of the Arab Spring proper, labor as a force was present but not definitive to the revolutionary uprisings, in the same way that women were present in but women's rights were not definitive of the mass rallies. This does not mean that labor issues and economic factors (or indeed demands for women's rights) were not integral to these movements. The class-conscious working class is perfectly capable of organizing mass rallies and is now demanding and exacting gains. Labor strikes were as critical to the success of the Egyptian revolution as acts of civil disobedience. Indeed the labor strike that was held in Suez on 8 February 2011 was a key – perhaps even the decisive – pressure on Hosni Mubarak's regime. Yet long before the rise of the Arab Spring, labor issues were rampant in the Arab and Muslim world. As Professor Ahmed Kanna, a scholar of the modern Middle East, notes, 'before these rebellions came others, arguably more modest in their aims and undeniably less noticed by the world media. For years, workers, predominantly South Asians, have been taking to the streets in the United Arab Emirates.' He observes:

> It is important to point out that these revolts, while often led by merchants, technocrats, or students, also often involved, instrumentally, the participation of workers. Saudi workers, for example, rebelled against ARAMCO's Jim Crow style policies in the 1940s and 1950s. In recent months ... Omani workers in Salalah, Sohar, and Sur agitated en masse against stagnant wages, runaway inflation, and exclusion from

jobs, which they accused the Qabus bin Sultan regime of handing out to favored Muscatis and foreigners. The regime ... met these protests with live ammunition and tear gas, killing a fifteen-year-old boy.[42]

The presence of 'foreign workers' in the Gulf states is endemic to the entire region: workers come from Asia and Africa in search of temporary jobs, and lead a miserable, slave-like existence working for the oil-rich potentates. Yet, while these workers are 'marginalized and exploited, [they] are far from the silent, passive wage slaves of popular imagination.' Whilst there is no direct link apparent between such endemic labor unrest and the rise of the Arab Spring, there certainly exists a structural affinity between the two. As Kanna puts it:

> Admittedly, while the mass actions in Egypt, Tunisia, and the other countries of the Arab Spring are political protests, the actions in the UAE are labor strikes. We should not conflate the two: the stakes in each kind of demonstration are different. The foreign workers of the UAE are citizens of another country and they will eventually return to their own countries. Yet while foreigners – whether workers or middle class – in the UAE do not envision being part of the imagined community, their protests nevertheless resonate in some important ways with those of the Arab Spring ... Both the Arab Spring and Gulf worker actions are, broadly, about dignity and justice; both challenge the status quo of unaccountable family/security-states; and both are met with ferocious responses by those states. Yet, the Gulf worker actions are ignored. Why?[43]

This perfectly legitimate question Kanna answers by way of referring to Georgio Agamben's notion of 'bare life' or *Homo sacer*:

> in Dubai, for example, they live either in a vast system of labor camps on the peripheries of the city or within the domestic sphere of the household, perpetually in informal and temporary status and subject to any of the aforementioned privations of national-citizenship or economic rights, arbitrary acts that deprive them of full humanity

---

42. Ahmed Kanna, 'The Arab World's Forgotten Rebellions: Arab Workers and Biopolitics in the Gulf,' *Jadaliyya*, 2 June 2011, www.jadaliyya.com/pages/index/1735/the-arab-worlds-forgotten-rebellions_foreign-worke.
43. Ibid.

and reconstitute them, for the duration of their stay in the Gulf, as bare life.

From which he concludes that

> both cognitively and spatially, it seems, the foreign worker in the contemporary Gulf societies constitutes the limit of sovereignty, the figure in relation to whom both citizens and, in some instances, more privileged foreigners take on the role of the sovereign.[44]

The issue of 'national sovereignty' with regard to these mass labor migrations in fact becomes entirely secondary to the social alienation and cultural anomie that the migrant laborers endure, and the brutal measures of repression they face. Nevertheless within this general contour of transnational labor migration, the national scene is of course still crucial – though it must be transnationally contextualized. On Labor Day 2011, the world was witness to the first gathering of labor unions at Tahrir Square in the aftermath of Mubarak's fall and the rise of the new Egypt.

> Red flags were waving yesterday as thousands of Egyptians celebrated Labor Day in Cairo's Tahrir Square. Workers from different factories across Egypt, the newly founded Federation of Independent Labor Unions as well several leftist parties rallied to celebrate their new freedoms. Ahmed El-Borai, Egypt's minister of manpower and immigration, announced last month that Egyptian workers will have the right to establish independent labor unions. This marks an unprecedented level of organizational freedom in Egypt's long history of labor struggles.[45]

Serious challenges lay ahead for Egyptian laborers of course. Some revolutionaries feared 'communism.' Others were curious. 'I think I am rather leftist,' Noha Wagdi, a pharmacy student said, 'and I am here to inform myself about the political parties so that I can decide which party I would like to join.'[46] Socialist political

44. Ibid. For Agamben's notions of 'bare life' and *Homo sacer*, see Giorgio Agamben's *Homo Sacer: Sovereign Power and Bare Life* (Stanford CA: Stanford University Press, 1998).

45. See 'Labor Day in Tahrir: New Freedom and Challenges Ahead,' *Bikiya Masr*, 2 May 2011, http://bikyamasr.com/wordpress/?p=33320.

46. Ibid.

parties were popping up rapidly. 'Whereas the Workers Democratic Party pledges for the re-nationalization of large parts of the formerly privatized industry, others are demanding a limited role of the private sector in autonomous development.' Expectations were high. 'One of the key demands is to raise the monthly minimum wage, currently set at 400 Egyptian pounds (about $70) to 1,200 Egyptian pounds (about $200). Wages should be tied to the rising inflation, they argued.' A new political culture was forming. 'While the radicalization of millions of Egyptians during the revolution offers an unprecedented opportunity for the Left to mobilize, it also struggles to connect to the large sections of protesters that remain deeply distrustful of political organizations.'[47] Speeches were celebratory:

> Today, we celebrate with the whole world the 1st of May, world Labor Day, the symbol of labor solidarity for so many decades worldwide, and the reminder of their struggle. This day comes to acknowledge that it is laborers who make life; it is their hands that make the edifices of the society; and it is their sacrifices that draw the path for future generations.[48]

What was different about these expressions of hope and articulation of demands was the new horizon of possibilities and the fact that the repressive regime had caved in.

> This [May day celebration] is made more poignant by the fact that Mubarak used to use Tahrir Square for his official celebration. 800 people lost their lives at the time of the 25 January revolution and mothers were there with pictures of their children who died in the fighting. Bumper stickers and satirical montages celebrate the revolution. Mubarak's cronies are mercilessly denounced in these popular mementoes.[49]

These national scenes were the domestic markers of the more seismic changes that had completely blurred the boundaries

---

47. Ibid.

48. As reported in 'Beyond the Media Radar, Egypt's Arab Spring Pushes Forth,' *In These Times*, 4 May 2011, www.inthesetimes.com/working/entry/7269/beyond_the_media_radar_egypts_arab_spring_pushes_forth.

49. See 'May Day in Tahrir Square,' *Right to Work*, 1 May 2011, http://righttowork.org.uk/2011/05/may-day-in-tahrir-square.

between a domestic and a foreign labor force. What Ahmed Kanna maps out in the Persian Gulf region has a more global resonance, which is best captured by political economist Behzad Yaghmaian.[50]

> While millions in the world are celebrating the popular uprisings in North Africa, Europe is watching with skepticism and fear. The fall of the African dictators will deprive Europe of valuable allies in the fight against irregular migration. The political vacuum and the social and economic instability that follows will create a new wave of desperate migrants daring the high seas to reach the coast of Europe. This will deepen the immigration crisis Europe has been trying hard to manage in recent years. Europe is responding with an increased use of force. A new humanitarian crisis is looming.[51]

Yaghmaian is wary of the regional and transnational consequences of the Arab Spring and what it means for the flow of labor north into Europe.

> Devastated by war and poverty, thousands of Sub-Saharan Africans have been leaving home on a torturous and long journey north every year. Arriving in Morocco, Tunisia, or Libya, they recuperate from the journey fatigue, pay human smugglers, and climb aboard flimsy boats heading to Italy or Spain.

This assessment places the Arab Spring right in the middle of a labor drama between Africa and Europe. It would be foolhardy to imagine the Arab Spring in terms of a racialized geography that disregards this intercontinental crossover. 'In a bilateral agreement with Zine Al-Abidine Ben Ali,' Yaghmaian reports, 'Italy pledged financial support in exchange for help in preventing African transit immigrants and Tunisians from leaving for Europe. Zine Al-Abidine Ben Ali's fall ended the agreement. Border control collapsed in Tunisia and 5000 Tunisians arrived in the Italian port of Lampedusa.' This phenomenon is not limited to Tunisia.

---

50. See Behzad Yaghmaian, *Embracing the Infidel: Stories of Muslim Migrants on the Journey West* (New York: Delacorte Press, 2005).
51. See Behzad Yaghmaian, 'The Specter of a Black Europe,' *Counterpunch*, 23 February 2011, www.counterpunch.org/behzado2232011.html.

In a 2003 agreement between Spain and Morocco, Moroccan authorities pledged full cooperation in migration control in return for $390 million in aid. Two years later in September 2005, Moroccan soldiers and Spanish guards fired at hundreds of Africans trying to enter the enclaves of Ceuta and Melilla. Gun shots killed 11 migrants and injured many more.

From Morocco to Tunisia, central to this pattern of labor migration was Libya:

> The most notable of the bilateral agreements with North African dictators was the 'Friendship Pact' signed between Italy and Libya on August 30th, 2008. The two countries pledged increase cooperation in 'fighting terrorism, organized crime, drug trafficking, and illegal immigration.' Muammar Gaddafi agreed to keep African migrants from leaving its frontiers for Italy, and readmit to Libya those intercepted in international waters. The price tag for this service was $5 billion Italian investment, and six patrol boats to police the waterways between Africa and Europe.[52]

The wave of labor migration northward to Europe included the mighty Egypt. 'Although in much smaller numbers, Egyptians have been leaving their homes and heading to Italy.'[53] So, as Egyptian workers were celebrating their May Day in Tahrir Square, homeless laborers, with no Tahrir Square to their names, over 200 million of them, were roaming the globe in search of jobs: African laborers moving north to the Arab World and from there into Europe – carrying some Arab laborers with them. Europe, the Arab world, and Africa are linked like never before by labour migration. There are of course other routes and flows, such as from South Asia, specifically the Philippines and Thailand. Sex workers from Eastern Europe, meanwhile, are going south to the Persian Gulf states for temporary work. The Arab Spring is very much implicated in this tracing of the patterns of labor migrations:

> [Gaddafi's] fall will be, however, an irrevocable blow to Europe's current migration policy. The loss of Europe's hired gun in the fight against irregular migration will lead to a more open confrontation between the

---

52. Ibid.
53. Ibid.

EU armed guards and the African migrants in high seas. How far will Europe go to stop the African from reaching its frontiers?

The unfolding events soon verified Behzad Yaghmaian's assessment: 'About 1,000 North African migrants on a dozen boats have reached the Italian island of Lampedusa overnight,' the BBC reported early in March 2011; 'Others have been sighted approaching the island, off the coast of Tunisia. Most of the migrants are said to come from Tunisia amid turmoil there and in neighboring Libya.'[54] The destination was obvious:

> Several thousands have arrived on the Sicilian island since mid-February. Italy has sought EU help as it copes with the influx amid fears of a larger exodus from North African countries. Prior to this arrival, more than 6,000 Tunisians had reached Lampedusa, reports say.

These labor migrations are crossing national boundaries, coming up from former European colonies in Asia and Africa to European capitals (giving a whole new meaning to Malcolm X's famous reference to 'chickens coming home to roost'), and on their way paying a visit to the Arab Spring, with some even passing through Tahrir Square and bringing some Egyptian revolutionaries along with them. According to the International Organization for Migration, an estimated 214 million migrants are roaming around the globe. That is 3.1 per cent of the world's population. That number would constitute the fifth most populated country in the world. Some 49 per cent of these migrants are women.[55] These labour migrations define a global condition that marks 'postcoloniality' as a mirage, which, notwithstanding two centuries of knowledge, power, and production of ideology (of both domination and resistance), now appears for what it always was.

The end of postcolonialism as the ideological machinery that colonialism left behind also means the end of the two binary oppositions that had created and sustained it: 'the West and the Rest.' It is not just 'the West' but also its origin in the notion of 'Europe'

54. See 'Migrants Fleeing North Africa Turmoil Land on Lampedusa,' BBC News online, 7 March 2011, www.bbc.co.uk/news/world-europe-12662756.

55. These and other related statics are available from the International Organization for Migration, www.iom.int/jahia/Jahia/pid/241.

that is ending. 'Europe,' as both an idea and an identity, is ending – and that is a good thing: Europeans will be freed from Europe; Muslims are being freed from being among 'the Rest.' 'Europe,' as Frantz Fanon noted, was the invention of 'the Third World'. Now that 'the Third Word' has risen, it is un-inventing itelf.

God is Great – So is Freedom

Sandy Tolan, a professor of communication and journalism, wrote an essay for Al Jazeera in late July 2011 in which he describes a tense moment in Tahrir Square when the Islamists and the secularists engaged in a historic face-off at Tahrir Square. Mamdouh Hamza, 'an Egyptian civil engineer, businessman and longtime government critic ... [was] sitting in a plastic chair in an outdoor café at Tahrir Square, puffing on a water pipe ... with his cadre of young revolutionaries, to whom he'd become a kind of beneficent godfather.' We learn that an anonymous caller was hired to kill Hamza, and that the would-be assassin had changed his mind, because he liked the aging revolutionary. Hamza was warned, however, not to take part in the mass rally scheduled for the following Friday, 29 July 2011. 'Now came Wael Ghoneim, he of the social media revolution, with his own followers, to say hello to Hamza. He engaged the older man about finding common ground with the Islamists.' But Ghoneim insisted that the conversation not to be recorded on any reporter's camera. It was a pregnant night. Things were brewing. Tolan continues:

> At two in the morning we headed back downtown to catch a few hours sleep. As we climbed into the taxi, the bearded Salafis, bussed in from all over the nation, were pouring single file into the square: a stream of white robes and skullcaps, part of a planned show of force by Islamists. They would be spending the night in the square, ready with their banners and chants as the sun rose on Cairo three hours later.[56]

---

56. See Sandy Tolan, 'Visions Collide in a Sweltering Tahrir Square,' Al Jazeera, 30 July 2011, http://english.aljazeera.net/indepth/opinion/2011/07/2011730142651302182.html.

There were signs and slogans: 'Red and white, and black and white banners, and modified Egyptian flags all carried the scrawled message: There is one God but God. Other signs called for the implementation of Sharia law.' These were the Egyptian Islamist revolutionaries, exacting a fair share of their Tahrir Square, though they seem to have broken an agreement with their secularist counterparts. They were not supposed to brandish divisive slogans. The secularists were offended. 'Here and there, posters of Bin Laden were raised.'

> Nevertheless, secular voices were heard in large numbers: Alongside the chants for an Islamic state came calls for democracy, freedom, social justice and accountability. '*Islamyyia, Islamyyia*' rang out, but so did 'Muslim-Christian unity,' and denunciations of Mubarak, US aid, and the Israeli occupation. Still, the clear force in the square was Islamic.[57]

Two groups of Egyptian revolutionaries – Islamists and secularists – had alternative visions of their revolution, and here these visions were colliding, confronting, disputing. But Tahrir Square had a logic of its own, overriding them both:

> By now it was time for Friday prayer. A sea of humanity stretched out below us: Hundreds of thousands of Egyptians, folding in unison, then rising together, then folding forward again, placing foreheads to the earth. It was powerful to watch; beautiful. 'God is great,' came a surge of voices. They retreated like a wave, giving way to another chorus: 'Change, freedom, social justice...' 'God is great,' came the new crashing wave. Change, freedom, social justice... God is great... Change, freedom, social justice... God is great... Change.... [58]

Egyptians were home. Negotiating democracy in their liberated Tahrir Square, the Egyptian revolutionaries were laying down historic markers, strengthening the democratic muscles of a nation finding its way, though all predicated on phantom fears, in the face of the onslaught of the real issues – race, class, and gender. What is bringing these depleted states down is their outdated tyrannies,

---

57. Ibid.
58. Ibid.

their imperial hubris, in a situation that is no longer determined by the coloniality of their history or by the depleted paradigms of a postcoloniality that has exhausted its mobilizing metaphors. In the heart of night, Egyptians were searching, for new metaphors, for the entire Arab world to renew itself.

Beyond the enduring anxiety of Islamism versus secularism, there are women in the Arab and Muslim world who are deeply concerned about the forceful imposition of sharia law. There are other women for whom the sharia is not an imposition but a blessing. At the same time, labor migrations override national boundaries and procure a racialized politics that targets migrant laborers. The engendering of social relations is stabilized or challenged by the historic entry of women into the labor force, as they expand into and occupy the very definition of the public sphere, symbolized by Tahrir Square. As a consequence of the Arab Spring, a fuller definition of that public space is being created, both conceptually and spatially. National boundaries remain, but the contradictory forces of labor and capital will inevitably generate and sustain labor migration in and out of the Arab world. Gender, class, and race relations will all be affected by this overriding fact, facilitated by the Arab Spring and formed within the emerging public space. No debate regarding the imposition or embracing of sharia, no racialized politics, and no class formation will be left unaffected by the expansion of the public space. The Arab Spring is the crucible of that space.

NINE

Libya: The Crucible
and the Politics of Space

Early in August 2011, in one of his regular updates on the Arab Spring, Marwan Bishara, the senior political analyst for Al Jazeera, sought to explain the militant endurance of the beleaguered regimes in Syria, Libya, and Yemen, as compared with the relative ease of the collapse of the regimes in Tunisia and Egypt. His explanation, this time, was in terms of the nature and function of the military in these regimes:

> The transformations in Egypt and Tunisia raised expectations of swift change elsewhere, but when the Arab Spring turned into a hot summer, it led to disappointment and doubt. In reality, the early Arab Spring was exceptional by all standards when it led to the ousting of a combined 54 years of dictatorship in Tunisia and Egypt within the course of a few weeks. While the military sided against the dictators in Egypt and Tunisia, the situation in Libya, Yemen and Syria is complicated by the fact that their regimes' militia, special forces and republican guards have been better organized, better armed and better financed – and hence more potent and in control of their national armies.[1]

But the evident distinction did not mean success for these regimes. On the contrary, they were digging their own graves: 'Libya,

---

1. See Marwan Bishara, 'A Rude Arab Awakening,' Al Jazeera, 1 August 2011, http://english.aljazeera.net/indepth/opinion/2011/08/201181131751785145.html.

Yemen and Syria face complete economic shutdown, economic sanctions, and poor supplies. There is a limit to their resources.' In other words, under popular pressure these regimes were now reduced to garrison states, military dictatorships – desperate, maniacal, out of touch with reality, dangerous. They lacked even the slightest pretension to legitimacy. 'Every state is founded on force,' to be sure, as Max Weber observed (quoting Leon Trotsky at Brest-Litovsk), in his famous essay on 'Politics as a Vocation' (1919).[2] But that force is predicated on two complementary parameters: 'inner justification and external means.'[3] The 'external means' are the means of coercion at the disposal of the state, its claim to 'legitimate violence,' but the 'inner justification' is something to which the citizens of a republic must consent – and the ruling regimes of Syria and Iran (hostile to the United States and its regional allies) and of Yemen and Libya (accommodating to those forces and their interests) had obviously lost all claims to 'inner justification' on the part of their people.

What the naked military apparatus of these illegitimate states faced was the expanded public space that was now fully conscious of itself. 'Once people dare to rise in defiance against dictators, as is the case in Libya, Yemen and Syria,' Bishara observes, 'it means that the regimes have lost their deterrence, their hegemony and their capacity to instill fear or command loyalty.' That amounts to the people, hitherto the subjects of a ('postcolonial') tyranny, becoming, *ipso facto*, the citizens of the republic they wish to populate and thus expand into the public space they must thus define and designate. It also gives the lie to the ludicrous assumption that these ruling regimes are part of the 'resistance' to Israeli and American imperialism in the region. They offer no 'resistance' to domination; they are the condition of this domination. The loss of legitimacy for states like Syria and Iran also means that the United States, Israel, and Saudi Arabia are exposed for the sustained and unabashed imperialism that they still practice in the region.

---

2. See Max Weber, 'Politics as a Vocation,' in Hans Gerth and C. Wright Mills, eds, *From Max Weber: Essays in Sociology* (Oxford: Oxford University Press, 1946): 77-128.
    3. Ibid.: 78.

However, on the front line of the legitimacy battles are the corrupt 'postcolonial' states themselves. 'Once force is used and fails to tame or silence protesters, but rather brings them out in greater numbers, it [further] diminishes the regime's power.'[4]

As people come out on the streets in greater numbers the more they become aware and increasingly confident of their reclaimed public domain, and the more the regime loses legitimacy. This dialectic has a direct impact on the moral, normative, and political legitimacy of the state: 'Such violence represents the government's *de facto* abdication as the recognized authority and their transformation to being just another rogue element in the state.' It is precisely in the course of acts of civil disobedience, in which the state effectively 'abdicates,' that the social fabric of the emerging political culture is measured and woven. It is crucial to keep in mind that the foundation of that future civil society and the public space that it needs are being constructed on those heroic days when citizens of the future republic revolt against their illegitimate state. 'The good news is that despite the terrible violence, pluralistic city- and town-based associations and regional coordination committees are being established to help the resistance in all three countries. Such civil cooperatives are the best guarantees for ploughing forward and ensuring a popular-based, post-conflict future.' Society and its political culture must have been ready to hit the ground running for these 'civil cooperatives' to have popped up so swiftly.

Yet the threat of violence is two-way, for as Bishara notes:

> [The] challenge is no longer limited to the removal of the expired and bloody regimes, but also to try to ensure that the transition is not excessively long and costly. The challenge for the Arabs is to define their conflict through peaceful protest, and to not be dragged into bloody conflicts that tend to change people for the worse. If I could end with an analytical cliché, I would say change must be defined by the motivation for sacrifice, not the bitterness of the fight; defined by the dream of a peaceful and prosperous future, not by the nightmares of a violent past.[5]

---

4. Bishara, 'A Rude Arab Awakening.'
5. Ibid.

The transition had become bloody in Syria, Yemen, and above all in Libya, where 'Gaddafi's idiotic and bombastic threats against his people provided the pretext to rush in UN Resolution 1973, which effectively authorized the use of airpower to protect civilians. All of this means that the regimes' viciousness, terror, and shows of force are signs of weakness, not strength.'[6]

The specific case of Libya and how it offered the US and its European and regional allies the pretext for a military foothold points to the more extensive battle being waged between illegitimate state apparatuses and the expansion of the public space that confronts them. This initially counter-revolutionary development (brute and naked imperialism using the pretense of 'humanitarian intervention' to find a foothold in the democratic uprising of a people) will in effect undermine the viability of the very military power that has descended upon Libya, and that is poised to act against Syria and Iran. In other words, the US and its NATO allies are not just destroying the military equipment that they sold to Libya in the first place; they are also challenging the very logic of military intervention in a democratic uprising – by virtue of its being defined by non-violent acts of civil disobedience.

This systematic occupation of the public space is predicated on a history of colonial and postcolonial tyranny that regressively extends back to the Ottoman Empire. Bashar al-Assad, for example, has been in power in Syria since November 2000 when his father died. Hafez al-Assad himself came to power in 1970 when he overthrew president Nur al-Din al-Atasi and imprisoned his rivals. These postcolonial agitations date from 1920, when in the aftermath of the San Remo Conference Syria and Lebanon became French colonies. As early as 1925-26, there was already a major nationalist uprising against the French, who eventually left in 1946; and from 1947 the postcolonial state formations basically consisted of one military coup after another until 1958 when Syria and Egypt joined together to form the United Arab Republic (UAR). This was not successful and within a couple of years the Syrian Baath party had broken the union. It held power until the

---

6. Ibid.

1967 Arab–Israel war, in which Syria lost the Golan Heights to Israel, after which Hafez al-Assad assumed power. Syria has thus never experienced anything remotely resembling a democratic space. Obviously today's massive demonstrations and sacrifices are projected in that direction.

The contours of that public space are very much contingent on what happens in Libya. The counter-revolutionary forces that can potentially pose a threat to the revolutionary uprisings gathered at the crucible of Libya, where US and NATO forces were siding with the Libyan rebels. The emergence of the Mediterranean basin as a new theater of operations for NATO reveals in particular the necessity to reconfigure its military muscles in order to control not just the radical implications of these revolutions but also their demographic and economic (especially labor migration) implications.

What we have witnessed above all in the region, from the Green Movement of 2009 to the Arab Spring of 2011 and beyond, is a systematic and expansive reclaiming, by one massive demonstration after another, of the public space that the postcolonial era had left vacant. These transnational uprisings have had a catalytic impact on each other, generating their own tempo. No matter what the states do, the ever-expanding public space is restricting the scope of the ruling regimes' operations.

Selling the Sea to Stay in Power

In Gabriel García Márquez's *The Autumn of the Patriarch* (1975) one of the (literally) outlandish antics of the General of the Universe is the selling of the Caribbean Sea to the Americans who have kept the demented monster in power.

> Your excellency, the regime wasn't being sustained by hope or conformity or even by terror, but by the pure inertia of an ancient and irreparable disillusion, go out into the street and look truth in the face, your excellency, we're on the final curve, either the marines land or we take the sea, there's no other way, your excellency, there was no other way...

They took away the Caribbean in April, Ambassador Ewing's nautical engineers carried it off in numbered pieces to plant it far from the hurricanes in the blood-red dawns of Arizona, they took it away with everything it had inside general sir. [7]

Why is it that the Generals of the Universe, East and West, South and North, never read the novels that are written for them? It's tragic. Like his fictive prototype in *The Autumn of the Patriarch*, the Libyan 'Brother Leader of the Revolution' Muammar Gaddafi would have sold the Mediterranean to the Americans and their European allies, if only he could have done, in order to stay in power. His trouble was that they were no longer buying – at least not from him. Magical realism is ahead of history. We are catching up with it. The world community – the real world community, not the diplomatic charade code-named the UNSC (United Nation Security Council) – is thrown into a psychosomatic stupor and forced into a moral dilemma: choosing between letting a psychotic tyrant maim and murder a nation or standing by and witnessing the hypocritical abuse of that fact by the US and its European allies in order to carve out a role for themselves in the events in North Africa and beyond. This dilemma, however, presents false choice: the answer is 'none of the above.'

By luring the US into leading yet another war against a sovereign nation-state Gaddafi has given the US and its allies a military foothold in the region and effected the meltdown of state power and national sovereignty in Libya. By this act, and thanks to the revolutions that now sweep through two continents, we are back not to *la vita nuda* of Georgio Agamben but to a renewed *asabiyyah* of Ibn Khaldun. We are not helpless in the face of these tribal and postmodern acts of escalating violence; we are in the process of retrieving a collective consciousness of commitment and identity that can and will judge these atrocities – of Gaddafi and of those who initially sold and subsequently sought to destroy his arms. We will do so with historical agency, political prerogative, and above all moral rectitude.[8]

---

7. Gabriel García Márquez, *The Autumn of the Patriarch* (New York: Harper Perennial, 1999): 232.

8. For an account of UK arms sales to Libya, see 'The "Dirty Secret" of British Arms

Seeing through the thicket of these events is no easy task – but we must be able to do so. Leading Arab intellectuals struggled to strike a balance between support for the Libyan uprisings and appearing to endorse or condone the US-led action. Just shy of two years before the Libyan uprising, if President Obama so much as mentioned the name of Neda Aqa Soltan, the young woman who was cold-bloodedly murdered by the security forces of the Islamic Republic during the heyday of the Green Movement, many on the left were quick to read the reference as an indication that the movement was in fact the handiwork of the CIA and financed by the Saudis. Now the same people found themselves in the rather embarrassing situation where President Obama was using his military might (along with that of the EU and NATO) to bomb Gaddafi's army in support of the democratic uprising in Libya. Another, earlier, embarrassment for them was the fact that the Egyptian army became instrumental in the success of the Egyptian revolution. The money that the CIA had evidently allocated for regime change in the Islamic Republic was insignificant compared to US investment in training the Egyptian army to police its imperial projects in the region. But did either of these two cases destroy the legitimacy, veracity and grassroots authenticity of the Egyptian revolution or the Libyan uprising? The answer: not a whit. The Egyptian revolution remained exemplary for the whole Arab world, and that world could only have expressed identical support for the Libyan uprising against domestic tyranny and foreign domination alike, regardless of the actions of US and EU imperial elements in wanting to abuse it. The only embarrassment that remained was for what passes for 'the left' to recognize the limits of its own moral and political imagination.

To be fair, the left has not been the only bloc of thinkers and activists in a sectarian stupor – be it for or against the US-led action

Sales to Libya Just Months before Gaddafi Slaughtered Pro-democracy Protesters,' *Mail Online*, 5 April 2011, www.dailymail.co.uk/news/article-1373444/Libya-The-dirty-secret-UK-arms-sales-Gaddafi.html. For similar deals between the US and Libya, see 'Obama Administration Approved $40 Billion in Private Arms Sales to Countries including Libya and Egypt,' *Mail Online*, 12 March 2011, www.dailymail.co.uk/news/article-1365523/Obama-administration-approved-40billion-private-arms-sales-countries-including-Libya-Egypt.html.

in Libya. A group of mostly American scholars and think-tank employees wrote an open letter to President Obama urging him to 'recognize, arm, and support the National Coalition Government in Libya.'⁹ No such letter was written by any one of these individuals asking the US president to 'recognize, arm, and support' Hamas, for example, or Hezbollah, in resisting the brutalities of Israel. Meanwhile, Shaykh Yusuf al-Qardawi's dismissal of the Bahrain democratic uprising as merely sectarian was yet another clear indication that moral and political bankruptcy was not just a feature of leftist or right-wing sectarianism and had an equally prominent role in aging, stale Islamism.[10]

In the crucible of Libya all the fat of a politics of despair was melting. What all these positions on Libya and beyond illustrate is a fundamental fact, as Marwan Bishara has noted, about the 'abdication' of legitimate authority on the part of states that had nothing but violent contempt for their citizens – and the corresponding opening up of a public space in which to express their freedom and liberty. In the Libyan crucible the US, NATO, Gaddafi, and the rebels alike were burning to use and abuse their military power – at once contradicting and depleting each other's logic. Vox populi – the voice and power of a people – remained triumphant, even (or particularly) when their voice was silenced by the roaring of jet fighters and machine guns.

The categorical denunciation of violence – whether perpetrated by Gaddafi, Sarkozy, or Obama – is a moral position and not a political proposition. The unwavering solidarity with the democratic will of a people who have put their lives on the line – from Tehran to Syria to Libya and beyond – never fluctuates on account of any political consideration or because American neocons or French Zionists are doing their best to hijack it. In a famous articulation of

---

9. The text of this letter is available at: www.csidonline.org/index.php?option=com_petitions&view=petition&id=141. Among those who was 'unabashedly cheering' the UNSC Resolution 1973 and the US and NATO military strikes was the prominent American blogger Juan Cole. See 'An Open Letter to the Left on Libya,' *The Nation*, 28 March 2011, www.thenation.com/article/159517/open-letter-left-libya.

10. For more on how Shaykh Yusuf al-Qardawi dismissed the democratic uprising in Bahrain as sectarian (meaning it was Shi'i in disposition and thus offended his Sunni sensibilities), see 'Qardawi Says Bahrain's Revolution Sectarian,' *Al-Arabiya News*, 19 March 2011, www.alarabiya.net/articles/2011/03/19/142205.html.

the 'categorical imperative,' in his *Groundwork of the Metaphysic of Morals* (1785), Immanuel Kant proposes that we are 'never to act otherwise than so that I could also will that my maxim should become a universal law.'[11] This is a moral maxim, not a political dictum – a mandate by which a moral imagination can form a society of citizens and citizenship, and not the political proposition by which a polity might be formed or, in its absence, deformed. States are not moral propositions, they are political machines; as such they still function in very much the same way that Max Weber defined them early in the twentieth century, as a political machine that claims a monopoly of 'legitimate' violence.[12] Weber always considered that 'legitimacy' parenthetically: a polity might grant or withdraw it from a state apparatus. Investing a state – a tyranny like Libya or a democracy like the United States – with legitimacy is a political contract predicated on a moral choice; shooting your own citizens or invading another sovereign nation-state is a political atrocity that *ipso facto* suspends that moral pact, whereby the state 'abdicates' (in Bishara's precise word) its own legitimacy. We as citizens, as 'the people,' must never presume to have the political prerogative to order a military strike or to drop a bomb, for that would be at the heavy price of forfeiting our moral agency to invest or withdraw legitimacy from the state apparatus that is supposed to represent our moral will. We, the people, were never consulted when millions of dollars' worth of arms were sold to Gaddafi by the US or the UK; as we, the people, were never consulted when UNSC Resolution 1973 was ratified. So why must we, the people, be put in a position to condone or approve the US-led invasion of Libya? We are not, have never been, in a position to decide. But we are, and we remain, in a position to bear witness, to judge, and to act accordingly – and what we are witnessing from one continent to another is first and foremost a moral rebellion, and thus we persist in calling it for what it is, a demand for 'dignity.'

---

11. See Immanuel Kant, *Fundamental Principles of the Metaphysics of Morals* (New York: Prentice Hall, 1949): 26.

12. Max Weber, 'Politics as a Vocation,' in Hans Gerth and C. Wright Mills, eds, *From Max Weber: Essays in Sociology* (Oxford: Oxford University Press, 1946): 78.

Holding our ground as moral agents, for us, the people – Libyans, French, British, Americans, and so on – the US and its European allies, as well as Gaddafi, are the losers in this game – or will be, sooner or later. The democratic will of the Libyan people will remain triumphant and will overcome this debacle. The only question is how. Gaddafi's bloodying of this democratic uprising cannot be allowed to shape the post-Gaddafi choices. The Libyan people – a collective term that cannot be reduced to those 'rebels' who have taken up arms but must extend to the civic foregrounding of a democratic future – must think of and build enduring institutions, in a realm quite different from the obscene 'doctorate' in democracy bought from the London School of Economic for Saif al-Islam al-Gaddafi, the man who would be king.[13]

Clichéd and outdated forms of solidarity or opposition no longer make sense. Neither blind solidarity with no eye to the formation of enduring institutions of democracy, nor the degeneration of opposition to imperialism into a suspicion of democratic uprisings, will form part of the texture and contours of this long-awaited revolutionary moment. We need to keep our eye on the prize, which is the democratic will of people, rising to demand and exact enduring institutions of civil liberty and social justice. The UN functions as the diplomatic arm of the US and its European allies and their imperial warmongering, and by no stretch of imagination represents the will of the people around the globe. The US lacks any moral authority to pose on the side of these democratic uprisings, and NATO has abused Gaddafi's slaughter of his own people to reclaim the Mediterranean Sea and environs as its theater of operations.

The revolutionary uprisings are realities *sui generis*; their legitimacy is intrinsic to what and where they are. They must not be reduced by loss of their agential autonomy, and hence legitimacy, by the hypocritical and opportunistic attempts by military powers to embrace or repress them. What Egyptians have achieved

---

13. For more details on Saif al-Islam al-Gaddafi's Ph.D. from the London School of Economics and the £1.5 million gift the School received from the Gaddafis, see 'Libya: LSE "should strip Gaddafi's son of PhD",' *Telegraph*, 28 February 2011, www.telegraph.co.uk/news/worldnews/africaandindianocean/libya/8350867/Libya-LSE-should-strip-Gaddafis-son-of-PhD.html.

in Tahrir Square reconvenes the very notion of 'democracy.' As Georgio Agamben observes about his contemporary Europe,

> Today we behold the overwhelming preponderance of the government and the economy over anything you could call popular sovereignty – an expression by now drained of all meaning. Western democracies are perhaps paying the price for a philosophical heritage they haven't bothered to take a close look at in a long time.

He adds: 'To think of government as *simple executive power* is a mistake and one of the most consequential errors ever made in the history of Western politics.'[14] Tahrir Square is today the symbolic site of rethinking the entire gamut of a political philosophy that can, happily, overcome the meaningless catastrophe code-named 'the West' as it redefines government in terms much closer to popular sovereignty, even before it is translated into enduring institutions of civil liberties. It is likely that neither 'government' nor 'economy' (the paramount issues in Hannah Arendt's conception of revolution) is in fact the ultimate objective or even purpose of these revolutions, which may instead be the political positing of the will of the people, its social institutionalization, and its philosophical and theoretical conceptualization.

The Making of a Transnational Civil Rights Movement

Ever since the emergence of the Green Movement in Iran in June 2009, I have referred to it as a 'civil rights movement.'[15] This assessment is coupled with two provisos: one, that the question 'Where is my vote?', which pre-dates the Islamic Republic, will outlast it; two, that either the Islamic Republic will accommodate this civil rights movement and survive or else will not accommodate it and be swept aside. The revolutionary potential of the

---

14. See Georgio Agamben, 'Introductory Note on the Concept of Democracy,' in Georgio Agamben, et al., *Democracy in What State?* (New York: Columbia University Press, 2911): 4; emphasis added.

15. For a selection of my earliest essays on the Green Movement in Iran, see Hamid Dabashi, *The Green Movement in Iran*, ed. with an Introduction by Navid Nikzadfar (New Brunswick NJ: Transaction, 2011). For a more comprehensive treatment, see Hamid Dabashi, *Iran, the Green Movement, and the USA: The Fox and the Paradox* (London: Zed Books, 2010).

Green Movement lies in its demanding and achieving civil liberties – the American side of Hannah Arendt's bifurcation between the French and American Revolutions. The existence or destruction of the Islamic Republic is entirely irrelevant in this regard. The Islamic Republic reads the movement's target as *barandazi*, 'regime change'; the American neocons and liberals recruited by the Islamic Republic also read the purpose as regime change, one in admiration and support, the other with derision and ridicule. 'Regime change,' then, is a coded political term in Washington newspeak, and at once a term dear to the Islamic Republic, which uses it to discredit the Green Movement and annex it to the US and Israel. Yet, at its core, the Green Movement remains a civil rights movement, whose reformist and revolutionary wings give it either a more modest or a more radical proclivity.

This was my assessment of the Green Movement before the rise of the Arab Spring, which I suggested as early as June 2011 could be seen in part as a response to the Green Movement[16] – and it remains my assessment. The Arab Spring is changing the imaginative geography of the region by way of bringing all these 'horizontal' (Hardt and Negri's term) movements closer together and categorically de-racializing revolts along Arab–Iranian, Sunni–Shi'i, nationalist–socialist, and secular–Islamist divides. That Al Jazeera is a crucial communication link among the Arab countries and a major catalyst in these revolutionary uprisings is indisputable. Iran is not an Arabic-speaking country (with the exception of segments of southern Iran), and thus is not party to the effects of this crucial factor. Al Jazeera English has been very important in the regional universalization of the democratic uprisings.

The revolts are *transversal*, moving from one country to another and back, altering governments from the ground up, and thus citing new sites of self-subjection, defying stabilized governmentality (in fact the Arab Spring makes the whole Foucauldian notion of governmentality oddly structural-functional), and thereby necessitating

---

16. See Hamid Dabashi, 'Middle East is Changed Forever,' CNN, 20 July 2009, http://articles.cnn.com/2009-07-20/world/dabashi.iran.domino_1_geopolitics-iran-middle-east?_s=PM:WORLD.

alternatives modes of knowledge production – that is to say, the *New York Times* no longer stands as the (self-proclaimed) 'paper of record'. Opposition to secrecy (e.g. WikiLeaks' Palestine Papers), to disinformation, to mystifying representation via propaganda has now become definitive of our critical readings of reality. What all this questions is not just the production but also the circulation of knowledge. The *régime du savoir* associated with that politics is being altered, by way of altering the worlds we inhabit, and not merely by way of resistance to power. The transversalism of these revolutionary uprisings, as a result, generates its own synergy by systematically and consistently expanding the public space they implicate for the exercise of civil liberties.

The expression 'civil rights movement' needs some qualification, for the term has been heavily whitewashed over the last half-century and a benign middle-class idiomaticity ascribed to it. As Thomas F. Jackson has demonstrated in his groundbreaking *Civil Rights to Human Rights: Martin Luther King, Jr., and the Struggle for Economic Justice* (2006), the American Civil Rights Movement, as it was led morally and politically by Martin Luther King, was far more radical in its demands for economic justice, praise for Scandinavian social democracies, and radical critiques of American capitalism. Were we to revisit the rise and crescendo of the American Civil Rights movement with Thomas Jackson, we would see how, through the progression of such iconic events as Montgomery, Albany, Birmingham, and the Washington marches, a far more radical conception of these iconic event emerges. In the case of the current democratic uprisings on multiple sites in Asia and Africa we are witness to a transnational civil rights movement, one that is mitigated by demands for institutional guarantees of economic justice – something that has eluded these countries for the last half-century of the 'postcolonial' period.

I have suggested that the Iranian wing of the democratic uprising in the regions is dialectically radicalized. This position has confused both those sympathetic to my reading and those opposed to it. The Green Movement had become radicalized in response to the Arab Spring, in which the demand for civil liberties were set out on a more urgent and radical platform, and thus it had to embark on an organizational phase involving labor, women, and student voluntary associations. The democratic uprisings had a galvanizing effect – a transnational synergy affecting all national events. So by 'radicalization' I mean that the demand for civil liberties – including on the part of independent labor unions, women's rights organizations, and student assemblies – had been radicalized, and the need had become ever more urgent for the Green Movement to cultivate an active relationship with the Arab Spring – and for both movements to deepen their social formations into these specific sectors.

The radicalization of the democratic uprisings does not mean the movements will resort to blind acts of violence, which the ruling regimes will brutally suppress – a response we have seen in Iran, Syria, Bahrain, and Libya. These are desperate times – in Europe, in North America, and in the Arab and Muslim worlds – and we need to rethink radically what it might mean, and through what specific mechanisms, to recast a more just and balanced world. The continued and sustained resistance of unarmed people – of the kind we have witnessed in Syria in particular since March 2011 – with its nonviolent disposition but radicalized demands, extending from constitutional reform to the overthrow of the regime, is paving the way towards that democratic future via the cultivation of a public sphere and civic discourse. As much as blind violence is ineffective and flawed, nonviolent civil disobedience will never be successful unless and until the movements begin to interface with the grassroots social formations of labour, women, and student movements. The mobilizing of these formations is precisely the factor that can guarantee the success of the revolutionary uprisings. For the ousting of a dictator here or a sheikh there does not equate to democracy or justice; what is needed are enduring, grassroots, voluntary associations that will demand and achieve civil liberties and democratic rights in particular and detailed terms. The formation of these associations will not only safeguard democratic gains but also shift the terms of engagement with the larger frames of military thuggery involving the United States and its regional allies. The nonviolent character of such formations robs the US and its regional allies and nemesis alike of their means of repressing or derailing the democratic uprisings.

The nonviolent character and disposition of the democratic uprisings and the foundations of public space they are now inaugurating have implications far beyond the eventual demise of corrupt potentates and the collapse of their regimes. The emerging sites of public space and the introduction of civil liberties will render the whole gamut of US military bases useless. This applies not just to the US Fifth Fleet in Bahrain, the massive US military operations in Afghanistan and Iraq, and the biggest US military base in the region, Israel. The entire network of bases from Diego Garcia in the Indian Ocean, around the Arabian Sea, the Persian Gulf, all the way to the northern coasts of Africa and up to and including Israel and then up north to Central Asia and the caucuses – in short, the very foundation of the American empire – is now in question. The bases are in jeopardy not on account of the Taliban in Afghanistan or of al-Qaeda challenging it here and there, but as a consequence of the glorious model of Tahrir and Azadi Squares, where the nonviolent democratic will of peoples are challenging the banality of the tyranny that rules them. Consider the heroic standoff between the Syrian people and Bashar al-Assad's dictatorship. Syrians have stood up to the vicious military crackdown on their democratic and nonviolent uprisings week after week, month after month, with thousands of deaths and tens of thousands of arrests, and a major humanitarian crisis on the Syrian–Turkish border. What is being defeated in Syria with the bare hands of its people is not just Assad's diabolical dictatorship, but the violent logic of Israeli and American military might in the region.

TEN

Delayed Defiance

In an essay written for Al Jazeera in early September 2011 address-ing the 'Intricacies of Bahrain's Shia–Sunni Divide,' the Middle East specialist Shirin Sadeghi shifts attention on the unfolding events in Bahrain away from the dominant discourse on sectarian division and towards the colonial and imperial history and disposi-tion of the small Arab country and its aspiration to join the Arab Spring. 'Bahrain, like so many other countries in the region and in the world,' she observes, 'is just another victim of British map-making, American business interests and the seedy intersection of these forces.' This pithy statement of fact introduces a reading of the colonial legacy as historical curiosity – for that colonial history is now militantly wedded to contemporary American imperialism. 'For centuries, the British have supported the Al Khalifa Sunni tribe – a family originating in the Saudi peninsula – as rulers of Bahrain, inserting themselves into any possibility of the Al Khalifa family aligning itself with Iran, or with the interests of the Bahraini people over and above the interests of business and power.'[1] In other words, lingering colonial interests combine with expanding American imperial designs to manufacture a geopolitics

---

1. Shirin Sadeghi, 'Intricacies of Bahrain's Shia–Sunni Divide,' Al Jazeera, 2 September 2011, http://english.aljazeera.net/indepth/opinion/2011/08/2011829104128700299. html.

in the region that systematically alienates the ruling regimes from their own people and incorporates them into the imperial modus operandi that serves oil companies and other corporate interests.

As Sadeghi points out, the ruling regime in Bahrain has done precisely what it was required to do by the British and American colonial and imperial interests that had put it in power:

> For generations, the Al-Khalifa government has made it a priority to prevent large segments of the Bahraini population from having a say in their government and their military, proving that the Al-Khalifa colonial implant has been serving its purpose to a tee. Native Bahrainis of Iranian ancestry or who are Shia are prohibited from serving in the government – with the exception of a few benign ministries – and from serving in the military and security forces. They also face discrimination in education and employment opportunities– all this in a country where they are in fact the majority.[2]

This is not sectarian rule. It is tribal rule maintained in the interests of a ruling family at the service of an amorphous empire. The ruled majority happen to be Shi'a. But they could be Martians, and still the nature of the regime would be the same. As a result, Bahrain, a tiny country, is a microcosm of the entire region, where the only alternative to alienated corrupt regimes has been the ghastly prospect of an Islamist theocracy. But that was not a real alternative, hence the logic and historic force of the Arab Spring.

Sadeghi's assessment brings the weight of colonial history to bear on the contemporary predicament of Arabs and Muslims at the receiving end of American imperialism. 'As American bullets fire from the weapons of foreign security forces appropriated by foreign rulers onto Bahraini bodies, the grim reality of 21st-century colonial vestiges and imperialist policies could hardly be clearer.' What must be kept in mind is not just the colonial vestiges but the reality of postmodern imperialism: 'As the bulk of the island struggles with discrimination for being Shia or Sunni or both, Bahrain's entire southern tip is a US military base where

---

2. Ibid.

frightened young Alabamans and Iowans pace through the streets to eat at Chili's or grab a burger from Fuddruckers. They too, are pawns in a game that has no benefits for ordinary people.' From which historical facts and evidence Shirin Sadeghi concludes:

> The so-called sectarian divide of Bahrain is a manipulative simplification of a far greater divide: that of the colonially-installed government that has no connection with or compassion for the people of Bahrain.[3]

None of that wisdom and insight would be available were we to be restricted to the opinion pages of the *New York Times*, where, on the same issue of Bahrain and beyond, Seyyed Vali Reza Nasr was hauled out once again to insist on and underline (and thus exacerbate) the sectarian divide. Nasr once again presents an idea he had offered at the height of American atrocities in Iraq: that the Saudis and Iranians are vying for power, one representing the Sunni majority of Muslims, and the other the Shi'i minority. Nasr engages in the usual fear-mongering:

> The specter of protracted bloody clashes, assassinations and bombings, sectarian cleansing and refugee crises from Beirut to Manama, causing instability and feeding regional rivalry, could put an end to the hopeful Arab Spring. Radical voices on both sides would gain. In Bahrain, Lebanon, Syria and Iraq, it is already happening.[4]

Here Nasr proactively blames Muslim sectarianism for any possible future violence, just as he had done retroactively in the case of Iraq. There is not a word about the American military base, or about the Saudi intervention in Bahrain to crush the revolutionary uprising, which was launched independent of any sectarian divide. There is not a word about civil society and the moral constellation of democratic will. What we get instead is just Shi'a and Sunnis, precisely in line with Nasr's colonial predecessors during the era of British imperialism

---

3. Ibid.
4. Seyyed Vali Reza Nasr, 'If the Arab Spring Turns Ugly,' *New York Times*, 27 August 2011, www.nytimes.com/2011/08/28/opinion/sunday/the-dangers-lurking-in-the-arab-spring.html?pagewanted=all.

The spin that such military and policy analysts put on the Arab Spring on behalf of American interests – equating 'democracy with American imperial goals – is not limited to the American halls of power that Nasr frequents and serves. It is shared by the leading European media, at once baffled and called to arms in face of the Arab Spring. There is a war here in the battle of narratives: how to read the Arab Spring, how to incorporate it analytically in the dominant *régime du savoir*. Of course the cause of capitalism cannot be compromised; hence the analytical claws come out. In a lead article, *The Economist* sought to integrate the Arab Spring into the global rise of the middle class as the machinery of capitalism.[5] The only salvation from sectarian violence is middle-class morality and bourgeois triumphalism. So good old capitalism is the answer to the Muslim malaise.

The Economist followed this lead on the middle-class uprising and ran to bank with it. 'The middle class' (a euphemism for the neoliberal free-market economy) was now overcoming Islamism, with Muslims themselves in the driving seat. The first move of *The Economist*'s argument is to globalize the phenomenon and take the Arab and Muslim element out of the revolutionary surge. 'Rebellion is in the air in China, too. In mid-August one of the largest demonstrations since the Tiananmen Square protests took place on the streets of Dalian, a north-eastern boomtown.'[6] The global uprising then reaches into the farthest corners of Latin America: 'That story has some echoes in Brazil, where an orgy of ministerial sackings has been in full swing.' The discontent then extends from the rich to the poor countries: 'In rich countries the humbling of governments has been largely a result of economic slowdown, combined with problems in controlling public finances. Emerging markets, in contrast, have kept growth going, while public spending is (mostly) under control.' What has caused this malaise? 'The explanation for their political woes must lie elsewhere. The most plausible one is that India and China – and possibly other emerging markets, too – are experiencing the early stirrings of

---

5. See 'The New Middle Classes Rise Up,' *The Economist*, 3 September 2011, www.economist.com/node/21528212.

6. Ibid.

political demands by the growing ranks of their middle classes.'
So whether the middle class is rising or falling, both are good for
the cause of capitalism; hence the global uprising for (no, not less
but) more capitalism and (no, not less but) more deregulation of
the neoliberal savagery called the 'free market economy.'

The moral of the story is that this middle class is demanding the
political freedom to join the Wall Street rollercoaster – but this
was before the Occupy Wall Street movement had shown a the New
York financial district in a different light. 'According to Martin
Ravallion of the World Bank,' *The Economist* reported,

> the middle classes (defined as people earning between $2 and $13 a day)
> trebled in number between 1990 and 2005 in developing Asia to 1.5
> billion; they rose from 277m in Latin America to 362m over the same
> period; and in sub-Saharan Africa from 117m to 197m.

This middle class wants to have American- and European-style
democracy:

> Polling evidence says middle-class values are distinctive. In a survey
> of 13 emerging markets by the Pew Global Attitudes Project in Wash-
> ington, DC, the middle classes consistently give more weight to free
> speech and fair elections than do the poor, who are more concerned
> than the middle class about freedom from poverty.[7]

So, to sum up, people were either poor and Islamist (and thus
prone to sectarian violence) or else middle class and advocates of
American-style democracy.

The Economist seeks to further elucidate the Arab Spring and
related uprisings – but still in terms established by themselves
and Nasr: 'There is no single explanation for the new middle-class
activism. Given the rise in their numbers, it was probably bound to
happen at some point. The spread of micro-blogging services has
surely made some difference.'[8] So, blogging is a factor, but not labor
unions and strikes, not economic malpractice and malfunctioning.
Thus the middle class and blogging are offered as the explanation

---

7. Ibid.
8. Ibid.

for a transnational uprising that was catalyzed by a fruit peddler who set himself on fire out of economic desperation.

This is how spin doctors wish to sell the revolutionary uprisings to themselves and to whomever else will buy their tale – and by extension impose them on the unfolding revolutions: 'at the moment, middle-class activism is a protest movement rather than a political force in the broader sense.'[9] That is to say, it is a middle-class movement that has exposed and risen up against the corruption of leaders and the poverty of the Islamist poor – and these complementary ills are to be cured by globalized capitalism. They thus strive in their narratives to assimilate and thereby neutralize these revolutionary uprisings to their own liking and their own ends. It is not just the dropping of NATO bombs that would alter the historic course of these revolutions to their advantage. Analysts and commentators have also been dropping a barrage of questionable narratives of the Arab Spring into suburban New Jersey, Washington DC, Paris, and London.

The Dialogism of Open-ended Revolt

So how has the Arab Spring dodged the spin assault, the narrative barrage, sortie after sortie, focusing on what it means, where it is headed and how it is significant, and all this by those with little investment but for career advancement of one sort or another, and committed to the accommodation of power? Fortunately the once hegemonic news media have started to lose the power to represent anything, let alone reality. This is the age of WikiLeaks, Al Jazeera, the Palestine Papers, *Al-Ahram*, *Jadaliyya*, blogging, Facebook, YouTube, Twitter, and their collective, creative, critical, and even chaotic ability to preempt the Truth Squads of Big Brother. The *New York Times* is just a click away from Al Jazeera, *The Economist* two clicks away from the *Guardian*; and facing whatever they write are the alerted Arab and non-Arab scholars, intellectuals, journalists, civil rights activists, revolutionaries – a constellation of critical intelligence that the reprehensible

---

9. Ibid.

racist expression 'the Arab Street,' which native informers had
taught them, could not summon and dismiss. Tahrir Square is
the symbolic reference point of the public space that is a liberated
republic, operated by its inhabitants. If these papers and narratives
boasted that people of might and wealth read them, then Tahrir
Square cried out: 'People Demand the Overthrow of the Regime'
– a regime that was not just political, for it included the *régime
du savoir.*

No doubt such perceptions of Islamism and sectarianism as
the defining moment of the Arab Spring, and as the panacea
for middle-class anxieties and justification for the neoliberal
scourge, have their followers and adherents among Arabs and
Muslims everywhere. But can that be all there is to the Arab
Spring? Is there any evidence to the contrary? One can of course
cite the catastrophic consequences of the free-market economy
and neoliberal deregulation, not just in the Arab and Muslim
world or even in Asia, Africa, and Latin America in general, but
also in the heart of Europe and North America – including the
bankruptcy and insolvency of one European government after
another. But the problem is neither the facts on the ground nor
the outflanked narratives that used to determine how we read
the world. We need to alter the frame of reference, the analytical
apparatus, the disciplinary thinking, that we apply to these facts
and to our understanding of the Arab Spring. What imperial
analysts, Orientalists, and misguided journalists do is not just
present the facts to their benefit but, more insidiously, insinuate
and condition the discourse in which we must counter-read those
facts. We must avoid this trap and locate our readings elsewhere.
In the *ménage à trois* of journalism, imperialism, and Orientalism
we see how 'truth' is posited upon the grid of prosaic normativity,
a reading of reality by way of sustaining the power and the benefits
of imperial domination. Because these purveyors of manufactured
'truth' have access to power, their discourses assume power; but
because those corridors of power are now exposed and weakened
by the epistemic shift that originated in Tahrir Square and now
extends all the way to WikiLeaks, the compromising fact of a
regimented link between knowledge and power is exposed for

good. The barrage of disinformation has lost its effect and the weakness of the arguments can no longer hide behind the power of the podium. Only days after NATO began gloating over its Libyan victory, documents were discovered in Libya that revealed how MI6 and the CIA were involved with Gaddafi's murderous regime.[10]

The revolutionary uprisings are predicated on no fixed ideological formations and affiliated with no political parties. Islamism, nationalism, and socialism are exhausted and have been superseded, not least because the imperialism that occasioned them has dissipated into new imperial formations. Opposition to this Empire requires new forms of resistance.[11] No political parties of any significance have been allowed to develop under the tyrannical regimes. The standard clichés with which journalists, Orientalists, and US imperial policy analysts attend to these revolutions, as a result, serve to limit analysis and invariably assimilate them into false frames of references. The revolutions in fact have their roots in far deeper normative tropes of literary humanism in the Arab world, and thus require grounding in the humanities as the paramount frame of reference. A novel of Sun'allah Ibrahim, a poem by Mahmoud Darwish, or a film directed by Elia Suleiman are far more potent frames for the emotive universe of these revolutions. The primacy of a literary context over the political act, as I am suggesting here, posits a certain mode of *heteroglossia* in the social action that makes it meaningful in vastly open-ended ways. The hybrid nature of the political language we hear emanating from the Arab Spring advances a literary *polyglossia* that cannot be ideologically anchored or imperially appropriated. The relation between indexical *utterances* is predicated on literary intertextuality. In any such utterance the social actor appropriates the words of others and populates them with powerful intent.[12] For that reason, a book such as Mara Na'man's *Urban Space in Contemporary Egyptian*

---

10. See 'CIA, MI6 "aided regime",' *Independent*, 4 September 2011, www.independent.ie/world-news/cia-mi6-aided-regime-2866310.html.
11. I discuss this point in some detail in my *Islamic Liberation Theology: Resisting the Empire* (London: Routledge, 2008).
12. See M.M. Bakhtin, *The Dialogic Imagination: Four Essays* (Austin: University of Texas Press, 1975).

Literature: Portraits of Cairo (2010) or Noha Radwan's *Egyptian Colloquial Poetry in the Modern Arabic Canon: New Readings of Shi'ir al-Ammiyya* (2011) is infinitely superior for understanding the Egyptian revolution than the columns of the *New York Times* or *The Economist*.

As I have suggested in this book, the modus operandi and the engine behind the revolutionary uprisings is a mode of *delayed defiance* that results in the gradual appearance of a new imaginative geography of liberation in which ideas of freedom, social justice, and human dignity are brought forth to the collective imagination of the revolutionaries – an imagination already cultivated in literary and artistic forms. Poets, novelists, filmmakers, singers and songwriters: they are the real theorists of the Arab Spring. Reading the signs of these uprisings, predicated on the delayed defiance that is embedded in and nourished by that literary imagination, places us very much in the midst of a fertile hermeneutics of uncertainty – an uncertainty from which journalists, Orientalists, and imperial analysts retreat, but in which the rest of us thrive. On this site, we have to work with the intimation of what we are hearing before we can ascertain how the Arab Spring speaks. It is not of speech, or language, that we must think in this domain, but of indexical utterances – phrases like *Al-Sha'b Yurid Isqat al-Nizam*, 'People Demand the Overthrow of the Regime,' and *Iran shodeh Padegan, Nang bar in Qaseban!*, 'Iran Has Become a Garrison; Shame on These Usurpers.' We read these indexical utterances with hope, with commitment, investing in the future they imply.

Asked whether 'the current wave of protest in the region indicates that, in fact, the Arab masses do want democracy,' Bernard Lewis responded peremptorily:

> What does 'democracy' mean? It's a word that's used with very different meanings, even in different parts of the Western world. And it's a political concept that has no history, no record whatever in the Arab, Islamic world. ...
>
> We, in the Western world particularly, tend to think of democracy in our own terms – that's natural and normal – to mean periodic elections in our style. But I think it's a great mistake to try and think

of the Middle East in those terms and that can only lead to disastrous results, as you've already seen in various places. They are simply not ready for free and fair elections.[13]

When will 'they' be ready? When, exactly, will they be grown up and have become complete human beings? What is it about 'them' (Arabs, Muslims, Orientals) that has made them so categorically incapable of practicing democracy, the rule of law, self-respect, decency? What sort of pathological condition is it that leads a man to think so little of an entire portion of humanity, and yet spend his entire life 'studying' them? Suppose what Bernard Lewis thinks of Arabs and Muslims is indeed the case, then what? Where are these Arabs headed – towards anarchy, wishfully thinking about a word which, for them, has no history? It is imperative that discussion of this issue be liberated from the systemic mendacity of tired Orientalist clichés. We must reverse the equation: rather than allow pathological readings of the revolutions, the revolutions must learn to read the pathological nature of such observations.

So, against the grain of these readings, how are we to read and understand the revolutionary uprisings that on the surface seem to have come out of nowhere? What do these revolutions mean, and what is their direction of travel? The uprisings are not mobilized by political parties, or organized around ideological battle cries of nationalism, Islamism, or socialism – though none of these ideologies is entirely absent. In the absence of these familiar political and ideological indices, one immediate way to start thinking through the questions is obviously to look at the iconography and expressions of the uprisings and to ask how they relate to their nature and disposition. Or, how are such expressions indicative of more enduring changes in the political cultures of the region? One hurdle that we need to overcome or at least negotiate is the received European narratives on Arab and Muslim cultures – ideas such as the 'Clash of Civilizations,' and 'The End of History,' the presumption that Muslims are incapable of

---

13. See 'A Mass Expression of Outrage against Injustice,' *Jerusalem Post*, 25 February 2011, www.jpost.com/Opinion/Columnists/Article.aspx?id=209770.

democracy or of respecting rule of law, which is regurgitated Orientalist nonsense repeated ad nauseam. Yet these tasks, performed
capably already, are not sufficient. To invoke the ground zero of
these events, the indexical utterances we have heard in Iran and
the Arab world from 2009 forward are the most immediate signa-
tures of the revolutionary uprisings, idiomatic signs and signals
that are pregnant with possibility, although it is too early to figure
out their detailed particularities. The brevity, uncertainty, and
contingency of these expressions are all definitive markers of not
simply post-Islamist but also post-ideological indeterminacy. As
Alain Badiou rightly remarks, it is long since overdue for us to
'dislodge' the emblem of 'democracy' in order 'to apprehend the
reality of our societies.'[14] That 'our' is longer Western, Eastern,
Southern or Northern. It is the emerging apparition of a world
that is dawning on all of us, and none of us has a monopoly over
how to read it.

If the United States, the countries of the EU, and Israel are all
'democracies,' dare we suggest, is it not time to wonder (as does
Alain Badiou) if this word, of Ancient Greek provenance, has any
continued legitimacy as the modus operandi of world politics.
Between putative democracies (as best represented by American
imperialism and the Israeli settler colony) and dictatorships (as
best represented by Mubarak's Egypt or Ben Ali's Tunisia), how
can we begin to think a renewed pact between the civil liberties
of peoples and nations that avoids both and cultivates a different path? Would that path not go back to the ground zero of
politics, to Egyptians gathered at Tahrir Square, or to Iranians
at Azadi Square, uttering the first indexical expressions of their
will to resist power – 'Where is My Vote?' or 'People Demand the
Overthrow of the Regime!' There is a particular line of political
philosophy, from Plato to Badiou, that increasingly universalizes
its particulars to the point of becoming implicated in a routin-
ized politics of indifference, structural-functional to its analytical
bones, where it no longer matters if you do or do not vote, and
where a gargantuan military machine like the United States and

14. See Alain Badiou, 'The Democratic Emblem,' in Georgio Agamben et al., *Democracy in What State?* (New York: Columbia University Press, 2009): 6-7.

its colony Israel become the prime examples of 'democracy' – and any nation that resists their tyranny is branded as barbarian or said to be incapable of democracy. Isn't it time, perhaps, to overcome this pathology?

The pathology has anticipated and created its own antonyms in Osama bin Laden, al-Qaeda, and the Taliban, variations on the theme of violent defiance of the terrorizing banality of imperialism. The two sides – Bush and bin Laden – fed on each other. Trumping them both, Tahrir Square and Azadi Square and their indexical expressions are the start of a renewed pact of the multitude, on the cusp of discovering a new political parlance. The words are solitary, simple, spoken from the silence of ages, allowed into the poetics of a people only, as if fearful that they may say too much. These utterances speak of silence. They are just the next breath, one breath, from a volcanic silence. They are far from certain, far from certainty, ideology, conviction. They are whispers cried out loud. They are always 'In the beginning'; always indexical. They are staccato, not crescendos, not orchestral, not complete. They are rhythmic, musical, tonal, as if to help in delivering them. They are revelatory, versatile. These words are indexical, brief, pointed, and purposeful, born out of necessity, saying a lot in the shortest possible way: *Arhil*, 'Leave!'

Indexical Utterances

If we begin with this word, *Arhil*, the shortest and most indexical utterance we hear when Arabs and Iranians pour into their streets singing and dancing their revolt, we open the door to a literary proposition that will remain suggestively *indexical*, that is pointing in a general direction, like a road sign, long before the destination is in sight. In JFK International Airport lounge I read a sign on a gate that says 'Madrid,' long before and thousands of miles away from the moment that I will actually see Madrid in bricks and mortar, its art galleries and restaurants. Indexical utterances are always deferred, and in a revolutionary momentum they are signs of a deferred defiance. They are not structural-functional in relation to the status quo. They break it down, now only suggestively, but always more thoroughly in a moment yet to come.

What we are witnessing in the Arab and Muslim worlds, predicated on these indexical utterances, is the unfolding of an open-ended revolt, the conjugation of a new revolutionary language and practice, predicated on a reading of reality that is an *opera aperta* – an 'open work,' in Umberto Eco's words[15] – a self-propelling hermeneutics that mobilizes a constellation of suggestions yet to be fully assayed. The revolutionary uprisings, long in the offing, are now being delivered onto an open-ended track that will redefine the very notion of democracy and its societal foregrounding. These revolutions will never end, because, as we have observed, their modus operandi is modulated more on the textual facilities of the heteroglossia of a novel rather than on the teleological crescendo of an epic. The swift but moderate successes of the revolutions in Tunisia and Egypt of course have much more to achieve in terms of deep-rooted institutional guarantees of civil liberties and social justice. But that is so precisely because they are not following any received script, but are unfolding like an open-ended novel that keeps writing itself as it moves on. The revolutions, then, have no facile conception of 'democracy' as their projected end; they will remain open-ended, an *opera aperta*, for a span of time yet to be imagined.

On the basis of these sets of suggestions, we need to ask the crucial question: in what way and in what idiom are Arabs and Muslims in general speaking – and can the world hear them? The questioning of the possibility of the subaltern – namely the multitude that has otherwise no say in matters of state, and has limited or no access to the imperial political imaginary that sustains a state apparatus like Hosni Mubarak's Egypt or Khamenei's Islamic Republic – is predicated on a closed-circuit conception of hegemony, in which the subaltern, the person pushing and shifting the boundaries, is denied agency. But revolutionary uprisings such as those we are witnessing posit an open-ended flow of emancipation, predicated on a literary imagination that professors

15. See Umberto Eco, *The Open Work* (Cambridge, MA: Harvard University Press, 1989).

of English and comparative literature in North America have yet to deconstruct.

Vox Populi, Vox Dei

The 'openness' of the text we call the Arab Spring is a literary contingency crafted around three intentions, as Umberto Eco has outlined them: (1) the *authorial* voice of the people who have revolted; (2) the *textual* evidence of the narrative – the visual, the aural, and the indexical – or the semiotics that works at the borderline of semiosis; and (3) the care and confidence of the participant observers who choose to read the revolutionary utterance.[16]

On that triangulated hermeneutic grid, the voice of the people cannot be reduced to an abstraction, or else elevated to a mere divinity, as 'the Voice of God.' *Voice*, it is crucial to keep in mind, is not *speech*, nor is it *ideology*; it is the sense perception of the multitude, the factual evidence of revolt. Voice is *utterance* – the Bakhtinian utterance; it is made meaningful in the alternating context of the society of revolt that gives measure and momentum to it. Voice is idiomatic: its idiomaticity is societal not ideological, or even grammatological. As a signifier it signates, it does not signify. That idiomaticity is always contingent, open-ended, and as such it appropriates and refurbishes its own elemental narrativity, just as when we are reading a novel and have no idea how it will end, and quite unlike an epic that is heroically doomed. The Egyptian revolution did not come out of the blue; nor were the iconic pictures and indexical utterances we saw and heard *ex nihilo*. The idiomaticity of this revolution thus preempts theoretical articulation into the impossibility of the speech of the subaltern. Urbanity and the public space of Tahrir Square in particular are definitive of this uprising; that urbanity is as much physical as it is allegorical, and the two feed on each other and confound. In an examination of the relationship between space and national identity in Egypt through four contemporary Arabic novels, Mara Naaman has chronicled the transformations of downtown Cairo

---

16. See Umberto Eco et al., *Interpretation and Overinterpretation* (Cambridge: Cambridge University Press, 1992).

(*Wust al-Balad*) as the *locus classicus* where 'the notion of the modern Egyptian subject has evolved in direct relationship to the changes manifest in the space of the downtown. The sense of pride, ambivalence, and contest this symbolic space evokes for Egyptians is in every way linked to the project of modernity and its legacy.' Naaman's point is to demonstrate 'how the contested nature of the downtown – as an imitation of European modernity, as Egyptian public sphere, as site for the staging of the revolution, and as modernist ruin – was and continues to be central to the notion of what it means to be Egyptian.'[17] When Egyptians speak, they are indexical within this literary allusion, with an idiomaticity that will have to be understood, and is understood, in the course of the history they are making.

In the same way that the vacant center of Tahrir Square is populated by the changing multitudes that declare it a free republic as Egyptians come and instantly redefine it, so the utterances made in it are rendered meaningful by the changing contexts of their political framings. From Bakhtin we have learned the 'primacy of context over text,' or *heteroglossia*, in the generation of meaning. The hybrid nature of language, or *polyglossia*, always socially implicates the speech act. As such, utterances are not monological speeches; they are directed, purposeful, indexical, and always implicate intertextuality. Meaning is socially invested, communally anchored. Tahrir Square is thus the physical evidence of the Egyptian novel, such as Naguib Mahfouz's *Cairo Trilogy* (1956–57), as Meydan-e Azadi is pregnant with Mahmoud Dolatabadi's *Klidar* (1963–78), where the diversity of voices makes meaning possible, in between utterances. Thus, in the terms of the Bakhtinian language I propose here, these revolutions are novelistic rather than epical – and that precisely is the reason they are leaderless. Gamal Abd al-Nasser was the last epic hero of the last Arab revolution, and Tahrir Square is the ground zero of the first novelistic revolution in and for the future of Egypt and the rest of the Arab world, a revolution with multiple cadences, utterances. In the same way that for Bakhtin novels digest and subsume other genres, Tahrir Square

---

17. Mara Naaman, *Urban Space in Contemporary Egyptian Literature: Portraits of Cairo* (New York: Palgrave, 2011).

sublates all previous Arab revolutions into a novel narrative of revolt. Tahrir Square thus works in a radically different Bakhtinian 'chronotope,' (the spatial–temporal matrix), for it stages a renewed exchange between time and space, with coordinates that remain narratively open-ended.

To perceive the indexical open-endedness of these utterances we need to treat texts as fields of potential and actual meanings, shifting words away from their presumed lexical meanings and towards the context in which they become meaningful utterances. The meaning of a phrase like *al-Sha'b Yurid Isqat al-Nizam* thus becomes an always-deferred act of defiance that oscillates between the moment of its expectation and the anteriority of its delivery. That deferred defiance, if we extend Umberto Eco's hermeneutics, is always somewhere in the triangulated frame of *intentio operis*, the intention of the text (the revolution); *intentio auctoris*, the intention of the author (the revolutionaries); and *intentio lectoris*, the intention of the reader (we who read the revolution and the revolutionaries). Through these indexical utterances, thus triangulated, the voice of the people becomes the voice of transcendence, of self-transcendence, thus of dignity, the voice of the unseen, announcing the hermeneutics of the voice of the visible, the people, the multitude, spoken open-endedly. One can and must interpret it, but it remains open-ended. If we shift to C.S. Peirce's semiology, the Bakhtinian utterance is neither a stable *icon*, semiotically fixated in its correspondence to a reality (as a red light while driving means stop), nor an *index*, identitarian in its relationship to reality (as a scream is to fear), but more in the realm of a *symbol*, where the sign is located within an interpretative circle, like the word 'revolution' in the English language. But somewhere between index and symbol, these utterances assume their renewed and open-ended meanings. These evasive patterns of signification of a revolutionary cry as an utterance make it impossible for the postcolonial deconstructionist to suggest that the subaltern cannot speak – for that very proposition is triangulated within a radically depoliticized lexicon.

The voice of the people as a constellation of utterances, as signs, is indexical, both for performative reasons and due to their political open-endedness. That takes the revolutionary realm in neither an ideological nor a hermeneutic direction but in a semiotic direction, towards a semiosis, where signs and signers enter an open-ended semiological chain reaction of meaning that no political order can control – thus *al-Sha'b Yurid Isqat al-Nizam* is atemporal, an indexical expression that remains open-endedly valid.

CONCLUSION

The People Demand
the Overthrow of the Regime

Marx once famously said we should stop interpreting the world and start changing it. That I believe is a false binary. Interpreting the world is changing it. This book is an act of advocacy by way of proactively interpreting an unfolding historical event. Interpreting the Arab Spring in the way I have doesn't just mark but in fact effects an alteration of the world we have inherited from our parents and hope to hand on to our children in a better shape. This book, from beginning to end, is my way of joining Egyptians and other Arabs from Morocco to Syria, from Bahrain to Yemen, crying out loud (with my pronouncedly Persian accent): *al-Sha'b Yurid Isqat al-Nizam.*

I wrote this book as the dramatic events code-named 'the Arab Spring' unfolded, with the urgency of reportage, the necessity of historical panorama, and the overriding theoretical imperative to make sense of events beyond the speed of their reporting. I wrote with the conviction that we – Arabs and non-Arabs – have to fight for the Arab Spring in the realm of ideas with the same vigor and determination as we do in the squares and streets. The regime of knowledge we have inherited, not just from the colonial world but even more so from the postcolonial interlude, must be dismantled with the selfsame determination that has ensured that the political regimes are overthrown. As Mubarak, Ben Ali, and Gaddafi were dragged down from their thrones in Cairo, Tunis, and Tripoli, so must the ruling regimes of knowledge production about the Arab and Muslim world be dismantled in Paris, London, and New York. We too are the *al-Sha'b*, we too *Yurid*, to *Isqat* the *Nizam*. In that very Arabic phrase I have just written in English, in the English sentence I have Arabized, dwells the task of the revolutionary vanguards of the Arab Spring. Fake French philosophers, militant octogenarian Orientalists, depleted European intellectuals, and baffled pro-Israel retired journalists have come together to attempt to rob Arabs of their revolutionary Spring. We must oppose and end their systemic mendacities with the same diligence that Tunisians and Egyptians brought down their tyrants.

Writing as an Act of Solidarity

I wrote this book, then, while deeply engrossed in the dramatic unfolding of the Arab Spring, just as I wrote my book on the Green Movement in Iran while mesmerized by the rise of the massive civil rights movement there. The two events are, I believe, integral to each other, as indeed they are to the dramatic labor, student, and antinuclear protests taking place from Greece to Spain to Britain to Wisconsin, and all the way to Japan, where the antinuclear protests surely have far-reaching implications. Writing a book while a massive transnational uprising is taking place has many disadvantages, but certain advantages too. Watching a revolution unfold is like being witness to childbirth. As you observe the minute details of birth and the breathing of a miracle, your mind runs ahead of the instant to what you and your partner plan and envision for your child. The two components of the event – the material and the imaginative – are a dialectic: they inform and form each other. There is no parenting without the nitty-gritty of nature's course; and there is no parenting without envisioning the future for your child. This metaphor has its limitations – for revolutions parent humanity as much as the revolutionaries have parented them. But, as they say, children become the best parents of their parents: they teach us how they are to be taught. And so with revolutions: we as ordinary people make revolutions, as the revolutions remake us.

I have scarce hidden my absolute sense of joy, excitement, happiness, and aspirations for the Arab Spring, or for the Green Movement – for the young and old, religious or otherwise, men and women who have poured into the streets, alleys, and squares of their destiny and cried freedom. There are forces practicing brutality, hungry for power, and blind to the innocence of these cries – forces that have visited vengeance upon our peoples. Many traps, atrocities, and diversions are on the way. This is a historic battle – and the world is watching. What I have written in this book is necessarily limited by its immediacy to the unfolding drama, as it is also braced by the excited imagination of insights that must in time acknowledge their blindness. The two – blindness and insight – will always go together and make each other possible: not just now, in the midst of the Arab Spring, but a hundred years from now when the frame of reference will be far wider

Open-ended Revolutions

The principal ideas I have put forward in this book are built around the unfolding drama of an open-ended set of revolutionary uprisings that, I suggest, declare an end to the condition of postcoloniality, that false dawn of nations liberated from the decades of European colonialism and the waning of the Ottoman Empire. Two vast and competing empires – the Soviet and the American – contested each other's domination around the globe during the Cold War period, which included the control of oil and the strategic map of what both parties called 'the Middle East.' The lived experiences of people struggling against domestic tyranny and foreign domination alike, however, taught them the hollowness of this particular geopolitical designation: for they didn't feel they were in the middle of anything. At the tail end of this condition of 'postcoloniality,' as the Israeli colonial settlement stared at the reality of the word, and precisely at a time when a strand of Marxist theory held that the period of classical imperialism had ended and we had entered a period of Empire, George W. Bush launched two very old-fashioned imperial invasions and occupations, in Afghanistan and Iraq; while at the very same time Israel was acting like a mini-empire of its own, while serving as the largest US aircraft carrier, armed with weapons of mass destruction, in the Mediterranean. The open-ended succession of revolutions that occurred in the region has now put an end to that realpolitik, and in doing so has changed the very DNA of the political culture that frames and informs our understanding of events.

The democratic uprisings demonstrate a number of key characteristics. They are more socially based and economically predicated than simply politically driven. They are nonviolent: their political actions are not informed by militant ideologies. They are post-ideological, in the sense that they have occurred in the aftermath of the exhaustion of the ideological formations conditioned by the period of postcoloniality and expressed in Islamist, socialist, and nationalist terms. They are predicated on the factual evidence of the economic malaise, social alienation, political corruption, and cultural anomie that characterized the last half-century of the postcolonial period, and as such three major social formations define them: labor unions, women's right organizations, and student assemblies, in the widest sense of these movements. All of these factors come together as a categorical denunciation of the neoliberal economic model that is the source of the sickness around the globe – and that cannot therefore be part of the cure. Women have a central role to play in the uprisings because patriarchy and misogyny have been definitive of both colonial conditions and postcolonial false dawns. The younger generation has a disproportionate role to play, due to the simple demographic fact that while infant mortality has fallen in these societies, standards of living and life expectancy have not increased proportionately; thus the young must either stay and fight for liberty, dignity, and social justice or else join the 300 million roaming around the globe, many in search of work in the north and facing the vicious racism of European societies. These are open-ended revolutions, then, precisely because of their deep-rooted historical underpinnings – which will not be resolved simply by the toppling of a Mubarak here or a Gaddafi there.

This is why I have argued that these revolutions unfold more like a novel than an epic. No hero – no Gamal Abd al-Nasser, say – is on the horizon: *shabab*, 'the young ones,' are the anonymous heroes of these revolutions. This is not to infantilize the revolutions (the French, Russian, and Iranian revolutions were not exactly the work of octogenarians – all revolutions are carried out by young people), but to acknowledge a demographic fact. These open-ended revolutions do not, fortunately, fit a closed-circuit history of corruption–revolt–corruption. There is a self-cleansing mechanism to them. They are expanding the public space they form as the modus operandi of the democracy they are demanding; this is not about the creation of an open market economy as the manifestation of democracy as we know it in North America and Western Europe. This does not mean that the uprisings are the work of socialist revolutionaries, but that paramount on the agenda is public space, not private property.

There is a renewed worldliness about these revolutions that affirms Gramsci's correcting of Kant's universalism, coming as they do at the end of the exhausted project of European modernity and the cul de sac of postmodernity. To be sure, there will be severe and prolonged resistance to these revolutions: by local elites, mini-Mubaraks, the United States, Israel, Saudi Arabia, the Islamic Republic, Hezbollah, Syria. This is an odd band that will come together in one way or another to stop the democratic uprisings because in one way or another they are all threatened. Will they be joined, in effect, by 'the left,' which if it does not join the revolutionary uprisings and chooses further fossilization will be added to that ignominious list of counter-revolutionary forces? The renewed worldliness of these uprisings demands fresh minds that are willing to abandon their instrumental reasoning and learn from – rather than trying to teach – these revolutions.

Such counter-revolutionary forces will not slow the uprisings: they will in fact ground and strengthen them, rendering the changes they initiate more enduring. The time span required by what is unfolding is unknowable, and would be counterproductive to anticipate. The revolutions will require constant vigilance from the people, the *vox populi*, who initiated them. Such attention is intuitive. The revolutions, as a result, may indeed be anarchic in their political dispositions, which gives them room to consolidate their gains in societal terms embedded in voluntary associations: labor unions, women's rights organizations, student assemblies. The barely functional state apparatus will remain tangential, its use of (what Weber theorized as 'legitimate') violence suspect, until these voluntary associations are institutionalized, at which time the state will be able to build itself again on a societal foundation, and hence will have legitimacy. Until the formation of these voluntary societal associations, any emerging state will be vulnerable to imperialist infiltration – hence my proposition that these are not total but open-ended revolutions.

Dismantling the Regime of Knowledge

The open-ended nature of the revolutions also accommodates the historic necessity of a sustained and systematic production of knowledge about the events that will first and foremost dismantle the *régime du savoir* we have inherited from both colonial and the postcolonial history. When the French Revolution occurred the ideas of Jean-Jacques Rousseau and Immanuel Kant were radically revived to read the cataclysmic event for posterity – and in fact to lay the theoretical foundations of what today we call 'revolution.' When the American Revolution occurred, Alexis de Tocqueville visited the United States and wrote *Democracy in America*, which remains to this day a cornerstone of our understanding of that world-historic event and its consequences. When the European revolutions of 1848 (dubbed the Spring of Nations and Springtime of the Peoples) erupted, Karl Marx was there to write on their causes and consequences. Lenin and Trotsky led and wrote about the Russian Revolution of 1917. The Algerian Revolution was theorized by Frantz Fanon. When the May 1968 social movement took to the streets in France, Jean-Paul Sartre and Michel Foucault were there to pull and push it in divergent directions. The First and Second Palestinian Intifadas had Edward Said to unpack and bring them to global attention. When the Eastern Bloc collapsed Francis Fukuyama and Samuel Huntington were there to twist and turn the moment to the advantage of the American empire. Revolutions need reading – interpreting them is integral to the way they change the world.

What about the Arab Spring? Will the revolutionary uprisings simply be assimilated into our current regime of knowledge, in the way innovative neoliberal Americans seek to incorporate their political tremors into global capitalism? What about the radical thoughts pertinent to these revolutionary uprisings? The task of becoming attentive students of the uprisings and seeing to it that they generate their own knowledge are tasks no less urgent than the revolutions themselves. To be sure, we are fortunately no longer in the age of grand-narrative-based universalist philosophies and sweeping theorizations. Whereas the Left Kantians' longing for 'total revolution' following the French Revolution ended up producing 'prophets of extremity' in Nietzsche, Heidegger, Foucault and Derrida, I have opted for the idea of open-ended revolutions, work-in-progress, an *opera aperta*, as a working idea to keep the tenacity of these revolutions alive theoretically.

In terms of the search for a new mode of compatible knowledge, the left is part of the problem, not the solution. The Arab and non-Arab left must shape up and join the revolutions, and cease being an obstacle to them. Of course the US, NATO, and the oil companies will do their utmost to derail the revolutions. How will the left respond? It must do more than write articles for the *London Review of Books* dismissing them all as a false dawn. For the genuine dawn of a new politics of hope and liberation is now fast upon us. What remains of the left is so petrified of catching neoliberal pneumonia and expiring that it indulges in the most fantastical explanations for its support – passive or active – of murderous tyrants like Bashar al-Assad. As Fawwaz Traboulsi, the leading Lebanese public intellectual, and one of the most seasoned Marxist historians of his generation, succinctly puts it:

> Contrary to the rhetoric of Syria being an anti-imperialist force (*mumana'a*) in the region, the Syrian economy under Bashar al-Assad has been rapidly neoliberalized and in the worst kind of way, with high levels of corruption and monopolistic control. Productive industries that usually provide work for young people have declined and the

economy has been transformed into a rentier economy. Layers of the bourgeoisie have undoubtedly benefited and some wealth has trickled down to segments of the middle classes, but on the flip side there has been a steady rise in poverty and a marginalization of the countryside and the agricultural sector. That's why the poorer regions across Syria were prepared to mobilize immediately.

Asked point blank, 'can the wave of popular uprisings inspire the Arab left to envision democratic possibilities that do not end with imperial subordination as well as strategies of resistance that are not anchored in authoritarian populism?,' Traboulsi responds:

> The left has a long tradition of being in love with dictators – legitimized by notions like the 'dictatorship of the proletariat', etc. – and I think we have not really been cured of this. The Arab left has made alliances with repressive regimes in the past. For long, the Syrian regime was looked at as one that represented steadfastness and resistance, the only country where communist parties are tolerated (of course, under heavy restrictions). So, there is a long tradition of imagining socialism as being non-democratic. Plenty of people on the left have not overcome this history. Some don't want democracy, dismissing it as 'bourgeois' and a form of U.S. control. Instead, they want something resembling Soviet democracy, but they want someone to give it to them. Others believe democracy can be achieved by foreign intervention or by simply a few constitutional changes. Democracy is a revolutionary process. You cannot export democracy; you either make it or you don't. We see proof of this across the Arab world, where people have been paying a heavy cost for basic democratic or anti-authoritarian gains, like toppling age-long presidents and putting them on trial. ... So people who want democracy to be delivered, or else remain supporters of authoritarian regimes, well, let them wait. Democracy is a historical process that will take years.[1]

One need not agree on every point with Fawwaz Traboulsi to admire his steadfast tenacity to see through the banalities of the left and have hope for the future through a detailed and painstaking encounter with history.

---

1. See 'Escaping Mumana'a and the US–Saudi Counter-Revolution: Syria, Yemen, and Visions of Democracy (Interview with Fawwaz Traboulsi),' *Jadaliyya*, 2 September 2011, www.jadaliyya.com/pages/index/2544/escaping-mumanaa-and-the-us-saudi-counter-revoluti.

It is not just the left, or for that matter the even more bankrupt right, that struggles to see the potential in the Arab Spring; Islamism, too, is integral to this faulty regime of knowledge. This does not mean that Islam's day is over or that Muslims will cease to have a significant political role to play. But it is the case that as a political ideology Islamism has exhausted itself. For some time now, scholars like Asef Bayat have been talking about 'post-Islamism.' This 'post-Islamism' is altogether post-ideological, and thus marks the end of postcoloniality as a condition of knowledge and ideology production. Islamism has had a distorted and prolonged lifespan contingent on (1) the Jewish state, (2) Euro-American Islamophobia, (3) self-righteous secularism, and (4) the combined scourge of neoliberalism and neoconservatism and the empire they would erect. False binaries – of which Islamism and secularism are but two examples – have a limited lifespan.[2] Islamism was formed by Westernism. Westernism has now imploded and with it the Islamism it inaugurated. Islamism eradicated Islamic cosmopolitanism, which had been predicated on a historical worldliness. Now, in the wake of the Arab Spring, a new cosmopolitanism will emerge.

Dismantling the regime of knowledge production we have inherited will be a long task, but the Arab Spring will produce its own leading ideas, concepts, tropes and metaphors.

Things Not Dreamt in Their Philosophy

The emerging understanding of the Arab Spring has much to learn from previous revolutionary circumstances in a comparative and transnational context. In his study of the philosophic sources of social discontent from Rousseau to Marx and Nietzsche, Bernard Yack identifies the central contradictions involved in asking for, or

---

2. The secular fundamentalists remain a key source of distortion on the Arab Spring, hunting for the slightest suggestion of anything 'religious' to peddle their fear-mongering. For a series of precise and exquisite observations about the bugbear of 'secularism,' read the interview that Talal Asad, the eminent anthropologist of the Muslim world, gave to Nathan Schneider following a visit to Egypt: 'The Suspicious Revolution: An Interview with Talal Asad,' SSRC: The Immanent Frame, August 2011, http://blogs. ssrc.org/tif/2011/08/03/the-suspicious-revolution-interview-with-talal-asad.

'longing for,' as he puts it, 'total revolutions.' Yack traces a current of thought from Rousseau down to what he terms 'the Kantian Left' (from Schiller to the young Hegel) and then to Nietzsche and Marx in which the 'dehumanizing' institutions of modern society are read as obstacles to the achieving of full humanity. The young Hegel saw this as a cul de sac, because for us to become fully human meant ceasing to be human. But Nietzsche and Marx thought that they had overcome that idealist obstacle by longing for a 'total revolution.' But that, asserts Yack, in fact further exacerbated the condition of the institutions. 'Their claims,' Yack suggests, 'represents little more than the expression of a need for an argument that has been remarkably successful at masquerading as the argument itself.'[3]

Viewed from the vantage point of the world outside Europe, to which much of this provincial discussion is limited, the philosophical contradiction that Yack detects at the heart of European revolutionary modernity through an analytic of philosophical positioning was in fact embedded in the nature (blood and bone) of the colonial and postcolonial conditions the world had experienced at large. The colonized people were told they were free to think themselves out of the darkness at exactly the moment when the gun of colonialism was put to their head, and then subsequently when they sought to liberate themselves in terms determined by the inner dialectic of colonialism and anti-colonialism in what has been termed 'postcolonialism.'

At the heart of Yack's argument, then, dwells the trope and predicament of European modernity – the project that, having visited the Holocaust upon Europe, ultimately sought to resolve and absolve itself in postmodernity. That modernity has never been the issue for a world at the receiving end of colonialism. Modernity was never either a problem or a solution for people living in the extended fields of European colonialism. Modernizing Egypt, as Timothy Mitchell has demonstrated in his *Colonizing Egypt* (1991), meant colonizing it on the model of European modernity

---

3. See Bernard Yack, *Longing for Total Revolutions: Philosophic Sources of Social Discontent from Rousseau to Marx and Nietzsche* (Princeton NJ: Princeton University Press, 1986): ch. 5, 30.

– carving, ordering, regimenting, and cutting and pasting it to the colonizers' desires. A colonial modernity was thus force-fed to Egyptians, against which they could only assert their humanity by way of an anticolonial modernity – a modernity thrown back at European colonialism by way of a revolutionary reason (neither a public nor an instrumental reason) that defined the disobedient world as it refused to yield to the rule of capital and its colonels. Modernity was a European problem that kept contradicting itself all the way to the European concentration camps and, ultimately, the Holocaust (for which the Palestinians have been made to pay). Postmodernity ended a European problem (by turning people into things, and things into instruments and objects of commodity production) but has meant nothing for the world at large. This is also true of the crisis of humanism and post-humanism. While Europeans were paving the way to the Holocaust, they destroyed, robbed, and distorted the world outside Europe.

Overcoming the condition of postcoloniality announces the end of 'the West' that had conditioned it and of the 'Rest' that was narrated in opposition to that 'West.' The Arab Spring is the inaugural moment of retrieving the world that this 'West' (the racialized code-name for predatory capitalism) had destroyed and distorted. The idea of open-ended revolutions that I have put forward here in opposition to the notion of 'total revolutions' is predicated on sustained sites of specific resistance to amorphous capital and the Empire that serves it. The more amorphous the Empire the more specific must be the site of resistance to it. But the amorphous Empire is the postmodern take on the modern will to dominate – after the end of ideologies. In order to resist the Empire we must always remain territorially site-specific, conceptually light-footed, and mimetically intransigent. Thus Elia Suleiman and Abbas Kiarostami survive the end of postcoloniality – while Mahmoud Darwish, Nazem Hikmat, Faiz Ahmad Faiz, Ahmad Shamlou, Vladimir Mayakovsky, and Pablo Neruda (the prophets of extremity) will become the signposts of a cherished but overcome topography. They were the product of colonialism and heroes of the postcolonial age.

If we navigate on the plain of the paradox that Yack maps out, Hannah Arendt can be considered the first 'post-Kantian Left' theorist of revolution who adopted a critical distance from the idea of 'total revolution,' distinguishing between the French Revolution (where, for her, social matters had become inappropriately dominant) and the American Revolution (where, in her view, political issues had correctly remained paramount), and posited the public domain as the *nexus classicus* of the political – a space in which freedom from fear and the liberty to exercise democratic rights is realized. In European political thought from Rousseau and the 'the Kantian Left' to Karl Marx the idea of a 'total revolution' predominates. Written in the shadow of the European Holocaust and the American dropping of the nuclear bomb on Japan, Hannah Arendt's critical intervention in the 1960s has hitherto had no historical revolutionary testing ground. The Arab Spring now makes it possible for us to rethink the very idea of revolution, in line with a critical strand that extends from 'the Kantian Left' to Hannah Arendt: we can move away from the idea of a total, sudden, and final revolution/resolution – a metanarrative of emancipation that further implicates the knowing subject as its agent in a self-defeating project. Thinking through Hannah Arendt's critical stand vis-à-vis Marx, and by extension 'the Kantian Left,' we are able to think through the idea of an 'open-ended revolution' by way of bringing Trotsky closer to Arendt than to Marx and Lenin – a proposition suggested in a leading slogan of the Arab Spring *al-Thwarah al-Mustamarrah*, 'Permanent Revolution.' The terror of the Jewish Holocaust in Europe, the American nuclear holocaust visited on Japan, and the Gulag in the Soviet Union, are paramount in Arendt's articulation of politics as a domain that protects the citizen against state violence. Protection and expansion of the public space (Tahrir Square writ large) is only possible through the means of an open-ended revolution.

It was initially Marx and Engels who, in the aftermath of the 1848 revolutions, developed the idea of 'permanent revolution,' meaning a revolutionary condition sustained until such time that the propertied class is deposed and the proletariat gains state power. Subsequently Trotsky extended an idea of Georgy Plekhanov's, and suggested that bourgeois democratic revolutions are weak and incomplete and as such cannot be brought to fruition by the bourgeoisie itself, which is unable and unwilling to go all the way and give land to the peasantry, the factories to the workers, rights to minorities, and put an end to foreign domination. In short, Trotsky can be seen as Arendt's nightmare, and vice versa. In the rapprochement I suggest here, the formation of independent labor unions, women's rights organizations, and student assemblies is the key conceptual mechanism for securing civil liberties (key for Arendt); thus matters of social justice (paramount for Trotsky) would be secured from the bottom up and not imposed from the top down by way of gaining state control. Though she preferred the American Revolution to the French, Arendt was still critical of the American model for the relative lack of political participation and the perfunctory character of the electoral process that effectively preempts the political expansion of the public sphere. That ever-expanding public space and political participation are precisely what inform my idea of open-ended revolution, in which the distinction no longer exists between the French (social) and American (political) model, in Arendt's terms. But in fact the fusion of the two will have created a third model, closer to what Trotsky meant by 'permanent revolution' (and that we hear in the Egyptian slogan *al-Thwarah al-Mustamarrah*), but this time in a more gradual, systematic, and grounded manner in which not just the working class but also women and students – that is, the two social formations that expand the economic into public space – will be integral to the revolutionary unfolding.

When in reading the Green Movement in Iran I called it (as I still call it) a 'civil rights movement,' I had in mind precisely the same idea of an open-ended revolt, in which not just the ruling regime but also any other regime that may succeed it will remain subject to the expansive unfolding of the public space and the consolidation of social justice from the ground up – by way of voluntary associations (Tocqueville) demanding and exacting them by virtue of their revolutionary occupation of the public space (Arendt). In other words, state formation in my judgment is the last thing that should concern the revolutionary unfolding we are witnessing. I have always been and remain suspicious of all state formations – of left, right, or center – while the ideological underpinnings of that state are still imagined and articulated in the catastrophic history of postcolonialism. If this sounds like anarchism, then I suggest that anarchism is in fact embedded in Hannah Arendt's dismissal of the revolutionary process in both French and American cases. She was more approving of the American model not just because it had paid more attention to political liberty than to social justice, but because for her that liberty was definitive of the very notion of politics. That liberty is liberty from state coercion, from tyranny; for today I cannot think of any state formation globally where the state is not either a central focus of corruption and tyranny or else an international gangster 'legalized' via the machinations of the UN, the IMF, and the World Bank.

I thus take as my point of departure in reading the Arab Spring Hannah Arendt in her reading of politics as a space protected from pre-political violence, which links her to Hobbes and Rousseau, and on the opposite side to Marx, Sorrel, and Weber, who saw politics as the space for exercising a claim over 'legitimate violence.' Given that in the postcolonial world the state has been the principal source and site of violence with barely any reference to legitimacy, and given the equally compelling fact that even in countries with a long tradition of democratic institutions all it takes is one terrorist attack to throw the entire foundation stone of habeas corpus and related civil liberties out of the window, the formation of voluntary associations is vital to protect the individual citizen from state coercion. Hence my insistence on the active formation of labor unions, women's rights organizations, and student assemblies as the crucial buffer zone between the atomized individual citizen (Agamben's 'bare life') and the totalitarian tendencies of the state. Arendt's position on revolution is in fact deeply rooted in Tocqueville's reading of the manner in which American democracy operates and preempts totalitarianism by virtue of the voluntary associations it enables. But if we consider Agamben's exquisite insight into the exposing of the citizen's 'bare life' as *zoë* and stripped of his or her *bios*, the fear of the totalitarianism of contemporary states is far more serious than the possibility of anarchy. Today – after the experience of the European Holocaust, and after US President George W. Bush's

'War on Terror' – we see clearly the criminally insane proclivities of states to devour their own citizens or else expose them as raw meat to what Agamben rightly calls a 'juridico-political killing machine.'[4]

Re-Orienting the World

The paramount issue for us today is no longer the necessity to critique the act and process of de/subjection to which we as 'Orientals' have been subjected in the course of European modernity. That has been achieved, beginning with the sociology of knowledge that preceded by more than a century Edward Said's *Orientalism*, taken forward powerfully in that seminal text by Said, and then duly built on in work, largely inspired by Said, over the past half-century. We are marching (and I use that 'we' confidently in the way José Martí wrote 'Nuestra América' in 1891) – and the singular site of our historic agency is precisely the hallowed ground where the people are marching. The question today is, how does that transgressive space of revolutionary defiance enter the global domain? There is no reason to believe that because these 'Orientals' have been posited narratively as such that they have no other (historically rooted) way of imagining or asserting themselves. Even in an Islamic context (to which even Muslims cannot be reduced), the nomocentric, logocentric, and homocentric terms of the discursive constitution of the knowing subject have been consistently valid in subjecting Muslims qua Muslims. In literary humanism, where 'humanity' is posited as a fragile and evasive subject, that subjection is even more supple, evasive, and uncertain. Over the last two hundred years, and in the face of European colonialism, all these discursive means have been glossed over by the transmutation of 'Islam' into an ideological contestation against 'the West.' So while 'the West,' through the mechanism of colonialism, has presented Muslims as 'Orientals,' and while we too (whether by negation or confirmation) have turned ourselves into 'Orientals,' we have glossed over those discursive presentations of us. Every

---

4. See Giorgio Agamben, *State of Exception* (Chicago: University of Chicago Press, 2005).

revolution is a retrieval, not a return. What is being retrieved
here is a cosmopolitan worldliness to which Islam is integral but
not definitive.

From Tahrir Square we will start 'worlding' the world by
re-Orienting it, laying a discursive claim on it. In the body of
Gadamer's hermeneutics is already evident the manner in which we
can recognize the linguisticality of not just one but multiple worlds
by virtue of which they generate and sustain their identity, alterity, and above all plurality. European colonialism and American
imperialism, with their respective retinues of Orientalists, have
historically preempted our world by seeking to understand us: they
have done so by digesting us in their own *régime du savoir*, for
their mode and manner of subjection were world-devouring. The
alterity of the Muslim, as the alterity of all others thus othered by
the entirely autonormative 'West,' is contingent on centuries of
self-transmutations. That autonormativity is evident, for example,
in the manner in which Max Weber posed the question asking why
capitalism developed here and not there – precisely at a time when
there was no longer a here and there to capitalism. Even Weber
himself recognized imperialism as predatory capitalism. By the
time of his insight capitalism was already global. The sociology
of knowledge that pre-dates Edward Said became definitive of
the manner in which Karl Mannheim and after him Paul Ricoeur
asked their question regarding the difference between ideology
and utopia. Precisely through that analytic bifurcation, 'the West'
sought to be self-evident by generating its own alterities, and thus
'the West' was transmuted into 'the world,' preempting all its
others. This was structural-functional not just by way of imperially worlding the world, but also to knowing the world, so that
this world (thus colonially narrated) would be preserved forever.
From Antonio Gramsci to Walter Benjamin, Theodor Adorno, and
Manfredo Tafuri, however, we have a sustained critical current
of thought in which that paradox of Being (of the Self) at the
expense of non-Being (of Others) was systematically exposed by
Marxists and non-Marxists as the supreme mode of alterity within
the system. But even they, up to and including Michael Hardt and
Antonio Negri, are limited in their conceptions: self-contained

within the system, within the matrix of 'the West,' the world they have inherited, worlded, and even critiqued, they are unable to see the existence or the rise of other worlds.

To world the world it has now claimed, the Arab Spring is in urgent need of theorization – multiple, varied, contested, and critical. This magnificent succession of social uprisings demands, and will soon have achieved, a whole new intellectual renaissance that must be actively conversant with the world at large, saving Europe from its provincialism, the United States from its Tea Party, and pulling both of these outdated, tired, and militant sites into the fold of humanity. Tahrir Square has become an extended metaphor. We need to extend it further into our theoretical conversations. With a steadfast determination matching the gatherings at Tahrir Square and the heroic marches of Syrians in their cities we need to think through the future of the Arab Spring, for it has to succeed not just in the battlefields of Tripoli, the streets of Damascus, the boulevards of Tunisia, and in Tahrir Square. It must be equally, if not more, successful in the language of writing about the Arab Spring, in inaugurating modes of knowledge beyond our received and dead certainties. We are at the inaugural moment of the suspension of all *régimes du savoir*. No lesser battle thus needs to be fought against manners and modes of inherited knowledge that have been coterminous with the politics of despair we have lived for the last two centuries. Our interlocutor is no longer 'the West,' for 'the West' is dead.

The rise of the Arab Spring has not just brought down the curtain on the era we call postcolonialism. It has also ended the Foucauldian reading of power and the politics of despair he theorized in his reading of governmentality – dispersed and decentered within the very body and soul of humanity. Look at the delusional banality with which the Project for a New American Century went about planning to rule the world. They created the amorphous figment of al-Qaeda to spread their own imperialism; the neocons were radicalized conservatives that pushed liberals into conservative positions and dubbed their militarism 'humanitarian intervention.' The enthusiasm of Obama's election was a catalytic moment internal to the US – to bring the history of racism to a close; but the election to office of a black president did not mean that either racism or imperialism was over.

The Arab Spring is not a fulfillment but a delivery. This is what I mean by its being the end of postcolonialism: the Arab Spring is not the final fulfillment of a set of ideologies but the exhaustion of all ideologies, a final delivery from them all. Thus the entire *régime du savoir* we have inherited is useless and counterproductive. We are not in 1789 when Kantian thoughts were set in motion. This is more like 1968 when revolutions posited epistemic exhaustion and Sartre's existentialism yielded to Foucault's poststructuralism – the systematic exposure of knowledge as coded power, of knowledge as power in discourse, of governmentality. The same period pushed the epistemic motions of structuralism to poststructuralism, of modernism to postmodernism, and, most pertinent to the world at large, the transmutation of the generation of Frantz Fanon's critic of colonialism into Edward Said's foundation of the postcolonial mode of counter-knowledge production. So, not a fulfillment but a delivery means we are in a momentous vacuum – for here, after grammar and logic and rhetoric, we have completed the *trivium* and must begin with a new language for which we will have to discover a new logic and a new rhetoric. So we cannot go back and read any revolutionary thinkers – from Rousseau to Marx, or even from Fanon to Said – to see how has this happened, for the world of all of those revolutionary thinkers came to an end when we saw Hosni Mubarak in a cage in a Cairo court awaiting justice and Gaddafi running for his life in the desert between Libya and Niger.

The end of postcoloniality means the commencement of a negative dialectic within the amorphous condition of globalized capital and its military logic of vicarious domination coded and colored as 'liberation' or 'human rights.' The answer to the use and abuse of the human rights discourse to dominate, a new version of *mission civilisatrice*, bombing in order to bring peace, terrorizing to end terrorism, stripping humanity of its human rights, is not to succumb to it or to dismiss it altogether, but to overcome it by way of a negative dialectic that does not allow for integration into the dominant ideas. As capitalism has become amorphous, and the industrial working class is dispersed into large-scale labor migration, the dialectic of emancipation must retrieve its absolute negativity on the condition of a coloniality that has now overcome itself. This is the first and final lesson that we can learn from the extension of the logic of Adorno's *Negative Dialectics* (1966) to the postcolonial scene and beyond.

The Arab Spring has made it clear that the critique of totalism and teleological thinking must become paramount and permanent, and that the idea of total revolution has morphed into open-ended revolution, *al-Thwarah al-Mustamarrah*. On this plane, thought is not a precursor of revolutionary action; revolutionary action is coterminous with its own philosophical thinking. Ideas of resistance never become systematized and so run no risk of becoming coopted. Revolutionary thought, thus posited, will stop being domineering, all conquering, eliminating resistances and alterities. There is no trusting of an all-knowing subject, no presumption of an identity between a subject and its object of knowledge. In fact the alterity of the subject remains separate from its knowing world; not identity but difference – ideals are not achieved, they are deferred. No metaphysics will emerge from this counter-metaphysics of resistance to power. Instead of revolutionary negation partaking in Islamic absolutism, Islamic metaphysics partakes in the metaphysical uncertainty of its worldliness and thus alterity and difference, which leads any remaining theological proclivity towards a liberating theodicy. The individual subject is no longer the focus of knowing but is integrated into the revolutionary difference. The only way that neoliberal individualism can be resisted in this struggle is through the dissolution of the subject via the dismantling of the *régime du savoir*. We will thus dwell momentarily on that liberating moment, anticipated in this statement by a number of already liberated Israelis – the first and the last people to be liberated by the Arab Spring:

> We are Israelis, the children and grandchildren of Jews who lived in the Middle East and North Africa for hundreds and thousands of years. Our forefathers and mothers contributed to the development of this region's culture, and were part and parcel of it. Thus the culture of the Islamic world and the multigenerational connection and identification with this region is an inseparable part of our own identity. We are a part of the religious, cultural, and linguistic history of the Middle East and

North Africa, although it seems that we are the forgotten children of its history: First in Israel, which imagines itself and its culture to be somewhere between continental Europe and North America. Then in the Arab world, which often accepts the dichotomy of Jews and Arabs and the imagined view of all Jews as Europeans, and has preferred to repress the history of the Arab-Jews as a minor or even nonexistent chapter in its history; and finally within the Mizrahi communities themselves, who in the wake of Western colonialism, Jewish national-ism and Arab nationalism, became ashamed of their past in the Arab world.... We wish to express our identification with and hopes for this stage of generational transition in the history of the Middle East and North Africa, and we hope that it will open the gates to freedom and justice and a fair distribution of the region's resources. We turn to you, our generational peers in the Arab and Muslim world, striving for an honest dialog which will include us in the history and culture of the region. We looked enviously at the pictures from Tunisia and from Al-Tahrir square, admiring your ability to bring forth and organize a nonviolent civil resistance that has brought hundreds of thousands of people out into the streets and the squares, and finally forced your rulers to step down. ... We now express the hope that our generation – throughout the Arab, Muslim, and Jewish world – will be a generation of renewed bridges that will leap over the walls and hostility created by previous generations and will renew the deep human dialog without which we cannot understand ourselves: between Jews, Sunnis, Shias, and Christians, between Kurds, Berbers, Turks, and Persians, between Mizrahis and Ashkenazis, and between Palestinians and Israelis. We draw on our shared past in order to look forward hopefully towards a shared future.[5]

---

5. 'Young Mizrahi Israelis' Open Letter to Arab Peers,' +972, 24 April 2011, http://972mag.com/young-mizrahi-israelis-open-letter-to-arab-peers. Sharing this spirit of optimism and hope does not mean ignoring the factual evidence that points to much hardship ahead. As the Palestinian Authority was getting ready to bid for Statehood at the UN in mid-September 2011, the distinguished Palestinian analyst and human rights activist Omar Barghouti wrote a detailed critique of the bid and its fundamental flaw in leaving aside the question of Palestinian refugees. See Omar Barghouti, 'Virtual Statehood or the Right of Return,' Al Jazeera, 14 September, 2011, http://english.aljazeera.net/indepth/opinion/2011/09/201191394042383843.html. For an equally informed and principled intervention on Palestinian statehood, see Joseph Massad, 'State of Recognition,' Al Jazeera, 15 September 2011, http://english.aljazeera.net/indepth/opinion/2011/09/2011915842793948I.html.

Bibliography

Abrahamian, Ervand, *Tortured Confessions: Prisons and Public Recantations in Modern Iran* (Berkeley CA: University of California Press, 1999).

Abramowitz, Michael, 'Israeli Airstrikes on Gaza Strip Imperil Obama's Peace Chances,' *Washington Post*, 28 December 2008, www.washingtonpost.com/wp-dyn/content/article/2008/12/27/AR2008122700962.html.

Abu Lughod, Ibrahim, *The Arab Rediscovery of Europe: A Study in Cultural Encounters*, with Introduction by Rashid Khalidi (Princeton NJ: Princeton University Press, 1963).

Abu-Lughod, Lila, 'Do Muslim Women Really Need Saving? Anthropological Reflections on Cultural Relativism and Its Others,' *American Anthropologist*, vol. 104, no. 3, September 2002.

Afary, Janet, *Sexual Politics in Modern Iran* (Cambridge: Cambridge University Press, 2009).

Agamben, Giorgio, *Homo Sacer: Sovereign Power and Bare Life* (Stanford CA: Stanford University Press, 1998).

Agamben, Giorgio, *State of Exception* (Chicago: University of Chicago Press, 2005).

Agamben, Giorgio, 'Introductory Note on the Concept of Democracy,' in Georgio Agamben et al., *Democracy in What State?* (New York: Columbia University Press, 2011).

Al Jazeera 'African Migrants Targeted in Libya,' Al Jazeera, 28 February 2011, http://english.aljazeera.net/news/africa/2011/02/20112286581437854l.html.

Al Jazeera, 'Nasrallah Calls on Syrians to Support Assad,' Al Jazeera, 25 May 2011, http://english.aljazeera.net/news/middleeast/2011/05/2011525174748827942.html.

al-Anani, Khalil, *The Muslim Brotherhood in Egypt: Gerontocracy Fighting against the Clock* (Cairo: Shorouk Press, 2008).

Al-Arabiya, 'Qardawi Says Bahrain's Revolution Sectarian,' *Al-Arabiya News*, 19 March 2011, www.alarabiya.net/articles/2011/03/19/142205.html.

Andoni, Lamis, 'How the Arab World Lost Southern Sudan,' Al Jazeera, 14 July 2011, http://english.aljazeera.net/indepth/opinion/2011/07/20117 13135442172603.html.

Anidjar, Gil, 'Secularism,' *Critical Inquiry*, vol. 33, no. 1 (Fall 2006).

Antoon, Sinan, 'The Arab Spring and Adonis's Autumn,' *Jadaliyya*, 11 July 2011, www.jadaliyya.com/pages/index/2047/the-arab-spring-and-aduniss-autumn.

Arendt, Hannah, *On Revolution* (London: Penguin, 1990 [1963]).

Asad, Talal, 'Afterword: From the History of Colonial Anthropology to the Anthropology of Western Hegemony,' in George Stocking (ed.), *Colonial Situations: Essays on the Contextualization of Ethnographic Knowledge* (Wisconsin MN: University of Wisconsin Press, 1993).

Asad, Talal, *Anthropology and the Colonial Encounter* (New York: Prometheus Books, 1995).

Assaf, Simon, 'Taking Sides in Syria,' *Socialist Review*, July–August 2011, www.socialistreview.org.uk/article.php?articlenumber=11719.

Badiou, Alain, 'The Democratic Emblem,' in Georgio Agamben et al., *Democracy in What State?* (New York: Columbia University Press, 2011).

Barghouti, Omar, 'Virtual Statehood or the Right of Return,' Al Jazeera, 14 September 2011, http://english.aljazeera.net/indepth/opinion/2011/09/201191394042383843.html.

Bayat, Asef, 'Egypt, and the Post-Islamist Middle East,' *Open Democracy*, 8 February 2011, www.opendemocracy.net/asef-bayat/egypt-and-post-islamist-middle-east.

BBC News, 'African Viewpoint: Colonel's Continent?' BBC News online, 25 February 2011, www.bbc.co.uk/news/world-africa-12585395.

BBC News, 'Migrants Fleeing North Africa Turmoil Land on Lampedusa,' BBC News online, 7 March 2011, www.bbc.co.uk/news/world-europe-12662756.

BBC News, 'Egypt Uprising: Islamists Lead Tahrir Square Rally,' BBC News online, 29 July 2011, www.bbc.co.uk/news/world-middle-east-14341089.

Beinart, Peter, 'Israel's Palestinian Arab Spring,' *The Daily Beast*, 15 May 2011, www.thedailybeast.com/articles/2011/05/16/israels-palestinian-arab-spring-jews-and-americans-losing-ability-to-shape-mideast.html/.

Bikiya Masr, 'Labor Day in Tahrir: New Freedom and Challenges Ahead,' *Bikiya Masr*, 2 May 2011, http://bikyamasr.com/wordpress/?p=33320.

Bishara, Marwan, 'A Rude Arab Awakening,' Al Jazeera, 1 August 2011, http://english.aljazeera.net/indepth/opinion/2011/08/20118113175178545.html.

Blumenberg, Hans, 'After the Absolutism of Reality,' in *Work on Myth*, trans. Robert M. Wallace (Cambridge MA: MIT Press, 1990): 3–33.

Butler, Judith, *Gender Trouble: Feminism and the Subversion of Identity* (New York: Routledge, 1999).

Césaire, Aimé, *Discourse on Colonialism* (New York and London: Monthly Review Press, 2001).

Chatterjee, Partha, 'Empire After Globalization', *Economic and Political Weekly*, 11 September 2004.

Cockburn, Patrick, 'Bahrain Is Trying to Drown the Protests in Shia Blood,' *Independent*, 15 May 2011, www.independent.co.uk/opinion/commentators/patrick-cockburn-bahrain-is-trying-to-drown-the-protests-in-shia-blood-2284199.html.

Cohen, Roger, 'Iran Without Nukes,' *New York Times*, 13 June 2011, www.nytimes.com/2011/06/14/opinion/14iht-edcohen14.html.

Cole, Juan, 'An Open Letter to the Left on Libya,' *The Nation*, 28 March 2011, www.thenation.com/article/159517/open-letter-left-libya.

Cole, Juan, and Shahin Cole, 'An Arab Spring for Women,' *The Nation*, 26 April 2011, www.thenation.com/article/160179/arab-spring-women.

Czajka, Agnes, 'Orientalizing the Egyptian Uprising, Take Two: A Response to Rabab el-Mahdi and Her Interlocutors,' *Jadaliyya*, 1 July 2011, www.jadaliyya.com/pages/index/2016/orientalising-the-egyptian-uprising-take-two_a-res.

Dabashi, Hamid, *Theology of Discontent: The Ideological Foundations of the Islamic Revolution in Iran* (New Brunswick NJ: Transaction, 1993/2005).

Dabashi, Hamid, *Iran: A People Interrupted* (New York: New Press, 2007).

Dabashi, Hamid, *Islamic Liberation Theology: Resisting the Empire* (London: Routledge, 2008).

Dabashi, Hamid, *Makhmalbaf at Large: The Making of a Rebel Filmmaker* (London: I.B. Tauris, 2008).

Dabashi, Hamid, *Post-Orientalism: Knowledge and Power in Time of Terror* (New Brunswick NJ: Transaction, 2008).

Dabashi, Hamid, 'The Arab Roaming the Streets of Tehran,' Tehran Bureau, 7 July 2009, www.pbs.org/wgbh/pages/frontline/tehranbureau/2009/07/the-arab-roaming-the-streets-of-tehran.html.

Dabashi, Hamid, 'The Left is Wrong on Iran,' *Al-Ahram Weekly*, 22 July 2009, http://weekly.ahram.org.eg/2009/956/op5.htm.

Dabashi, Hamid, 'Middle East is Changed Forever,' CNN, 20 July 2009, http://articles.cnn.com/2009-07-20/world/dabashi.iran.domino_1_geopolitics-iran-middle-east?_s=PM:WORLD.

Dabashi, Hamid, *Iran, the Green Movement, and the USA: The Fox and the Paradox* (London: Zed Books, 2010).

Dabashi, Hamid, *Brown Skin, White Masks* (London: Pluto, 2011).

Dabashi, Hamid, *The Green Movement in Iran*, ed. with an Introduction by Navid Nikzadfar (New Brunswick NJ: Transaction, 2011).

Dabashi, Hamid, *Shi'ism: A Religion of Protest* (Cambridge MA: Harvard University Press, 2011).

Daily Mail, 'Obama Administration Approved $40 Billion in Private Arms Sales to Countries including Libya and Egypt,' *Mail Online*, 12 March 2011, www.dailymail.co.uk/news/article-1365523/Obama-administration-approved-40billion-private-arms-sales-countries-including-Libya-Egypt.html.

Daily Mail, 'The "Dirty Secret" of British Arms Sales to Libya Just Months before Gaddafi Slaughtered Pro-democracy Protesters,' *Mail Online*, 5 April

2011, www.dailymail.co.uk/news/article-1373444/Libya-The-dirty-secret-UK-arms-sales-Gaddafi.html.

Daily Star, 'Nasrallah: U.S. Keen to Hijack Arab Revolts,' *Daily Star*, 7 June 2011, www.dailystar.com.lb/News/Politics/2011/Jun-07/Nasrallah-US-keen-to-hijack-Arab-revolts.ashx#axzz1OsFyC37F.

Daily Telegraph, 'Libya: LSE "should strip Gaddafi's son of PhD",' *Daily Telegraph*, 28 February 2011, www.telegraph.co.uk/news/worldnews/africaandindianocean/libya/8350867/Libya-LSE-should-strip-Gaddafis-son-of-PhD.html.

De Genova, Nicholas, 'The Stakes of an Anthropology of the United States,' *CR: The New Centennial Review*, vol. 7, no. 2 (Fall 2007): 231–77.

Democracy Now, 'California Professor Beaten by Pro-Mubarak Forces Minutes after Interview on Democracy Now!' www.democracynow.org/appearances/noha_radwan.

Dirks, Nicholas B., *Castes of Mind: Colonialism and the Making of Modern India* (Princeton NJ: Princeton University Press, 2001).

Djebar, Assia, *Women of Algiers in their Apartments* (Charlottesville VA: University of Virginia Press, 2002).

Eco, Umberto, et al., *Interpretation and Overinterpretation* (Cambridge: Cambridge University Press, 1992).

Economist, The, 'The New Middle Classes Rise Up,' *The Economist*, 3 September 2011, www.economist.com/node/21528212.

El-Mahdi, Rabab, 'Orientalizing Egyptian Uprising,' *Jadaliyya*, 11 April 2011, www.jadaliyya.com/pages/index/1214/orientalising-the-egyptian-uprising.

Ferguson, Niall, *Civilization: The West and the Rest* (London: Penguin, 2011).

Fisk, Robert, 'Why I Had to Leave The Times,' *Independent*, 11 July 2011, www.independent.co.uk/news/media/press/robert-fisk-why-i-had-to-leave-the-times-2311569.html.

Flock, Elizabeth, 'Women in the Arab Spring: The Other Side of the Story,' *Washington Post*, 21 June 2011, www.washingtonpost.com/blogs/blogpost/post/women-in-the-arab-spring-the-other-side-of-the-story/2011/06/21/AG32qVeH_blog.html.

Foucault, Michel, *Madness and Civilization: A History of Insanity in the Age of Reason* (New York: Vintage, 1994).

Foucault, Michel, *The Order of Things: An Archaeology of the Human Sciences* (New York: Vintage, 1994).

Friedman, Thomas, 'I Am a Man', *New York Times*, 14 May 2011, www.nytimes.com/2011/05/15/opinion/15friedman.html?_r=3.

García Márquez, Gabriel, *The Autumn of The Patriarch* (New York: Harper Perennial, 1999).

Goha, 'Counter-Revolution,' *Jadaliyyah*, 28 February 2011, www.jadaliyya.com/pages/index/759/the-counter-revolution.

Gourgouris, Stathis, 'Democratic Dreams Rage in Athens,' *Al Jazeera*, 21 July 2011, http://english.aljazeera.net/indepth/opinion/2011/07/20117198533565864.html.

Green Voice of Freedom, 'Muslim Brotherhood Rejects Khamenei Calls for Iran-style Islamic State,' *The Green Voice of Freedom*, 4 February 2011, http://en.irangreenvoice.com/article/2011/feb/04/2724.

Haaretz, 'IDF on High Alert as Palestinians Prepare for Naksa Day,' *Haaretz*, 5 June 2011, www.haaretz.com/print-edition/news/idf-on-high-alert-as-palestinians-prepare-for-naksa-day-1.365945.

Haaretz, 'Netanyahu Warns Outcome of Egypt Revolution Could be Like Iran's,' *Haaretz*, 31 January 2011, www.haaretz.com/news/diplomacy-defense/netanyahu-warns-outcome-of-egypt-revolution-could-be-like-irans-1.340411.

Hardt, Michael, and Antonio Negri, *Empire* (Cambridge MA: Harvard University Press, 2000).

Hashemi, Nader, and Danny Postel, eds, *The People Reloaded: The Green Movement and the Struggle for Iran's Future* (New York: Melville House, 2011).

Hegarty, Stephanie, 'Ramy Essam: Singer Catapulted to Fame on Tahrir Square,' BBC News online, 11 July 2011, www.bbc.co.uk/news/world-middle-east-14254564.

Hitti, Philip, *History of the Arabs* (New York: Palgrave, 2002).

Holt, P.M., and M.W. Daley, *A History of the Sudan: From the Coming of Islam to the Present Day* (New York: Longman, 2000).

Hourani, Albert, *A History of the Arab Peoples* (Cambridge MA: Belknap, Harvard University Press, 2003).

In These Times, 'Beyond the Media Radar, Egypt's Arab Spring Pushes Forth,' *In These Times*, 4 May 2011, www.inthesetimes.com/working/entry/7269/beyond_the_media_radar_egypts_arab_spring_pushes_forth/.

Independent, 'CIA, MI6 "aided regime",' *Independent*, 4 September 2011, www.independent.ie/world-news/cia-mi6-aided-regime-2866310.html.

Jackson, Thomas F., *Civil Rights to Human Rights: Martin Luther King, Jr., and the Struggle for Economic Justice* (Philadelphia: University of Pennsylvania Press, 2006).

Jadaliyya, 'Escaping Mumana'a and the US–Saudi Counter-Revolution: Syria, Yemen, and Visions of Democracy (Interview with Fawwaz Traboulsi),' *Jadaliyya*, 2 September 2011, www.jadaliyya.com/pages/index/2544/escaping-mumanaa-and-the-us-saudi-counter-revoluti.

Kant, Immanuel, *Fundamental Principles of the Metaphysics of Morals* (New York: Prentice Hall, 1949).

Kant, Immanuel, 'Idea of a Universal History with a Cosmopolitan Purpose,' in Garrett Wallace Brown and David Held (eds), *The Cosmopolitanism Reader* (Cambridge: Polity Press, 2010): 17-26.

Khalidi, Rashid, *Sowing Crisis: The Cold War and American Dominance in the Middle East* (Boston MA: Beacon Press, 2010).

Khalidi, Rashid, 'Preliminary Historical Observations on the Arab Revolutions of 2011,' *Jadaliyya*, 21 March 2011, www.jadaliyya.com/pages/index/970/preliminary-historical-observations-on-the-arab-re.

Khouri, Nourma, *Forbidden Love: A Harrowing Story of Love and Revenge in Jordan* (New York: Bantam Books, 2003).

Koppel, Ted, 'The Arab Spring and U.S. Policy: The View From Jerusalem,' *Wall Street Journal*, 29 April 2011, http://online.wsj.com/article/SB100 01424052748704330404576291063679488964.html.

Levy, Gideon, 'Israeli Protesters Must Remain in Tents until Time is Right,' *Haaretz*, 31 July 2011, www.haaretz.com/print-edition/news/gideon-levy-israeli-protesters-must-remain-in-tents-until-time-is-right-1.376113.

Los Angeles Times, 'Iran's Supreme Leader Calls Uprisings and Islamic "Awakening",' *Los Angeles Times*, 4 February 2011, http://articles.latimes.com/2011/feb/04/world/la-fg-khamenei-iran-egypt-20110205.

Lutz, Catherine A., and Jane L. Collins, *Reading National Geographic* (Chicago: University of Chicago Press, 1993).

Mahdavi, Pardis, *Passionate Uprisings: Iran's Sexual Revolution* (Stanford CA: Stanford University Press, 2008).

Mamdani, Mahmood, *When Victims Become Killers: Colonialism, Nativism, and the Genocide in Rwanda* (Princeton NJ: Princeton University Press, 2002).

Mannheim, Karl, *Ideology and Utopia*, trans. Louis Wirth and Edward Shils (New York: Harcourt Brace Jovanovich, 1936 [1929]).

Marx, Karl, 'For a Ruthless Criticism of Everything Existing,' in *The Marx–Engels Reader*, ed. Robert C. Tucker, 2nd edn (New York: W.W. Norton, 1978).

Massad, Joseph, *Colonial Effects: The Making of National Identity in Jordan* (New York: Columbia University Press, 2001).

Massad, Joseph, *The Persistence of the Palestinian Question: Essays on Zionism and the Palestinians* (London: Routledge, 2006).

Massad, Joseph A., *Desiring Arabs* (Chicago: University of Chicago Press, 2007).

Massad, Joseph, 'Are Palestinian Children Less Worthy?', Al Jazeera, 30 May 2011, http://english.aljazeera.net/indepth/opinion/2011/05/201152911 579533291.html.

Massad, Joseph, 'Under the Cover of Democracy,' Al Jazeera, 8 June 2011, http://english.aljazeera.net/indepth/opinion/2011/06/2011689456174295.html.

Massad, Joseph, 'State of Recognition,' Al Jazeera, 15 September 2011, http://english.aljazeera.net/indepth/opinion/2011/09/2011915842793948.html.

Menke, Christoph, *The Sovereignty of Art: Aesthetic Negativity in Adorno and Derrida*, trans. Neil Solomon (Cambridge MA: MIT Press, 1998).

Miami Herald, 'In Bahrain, a Candlelight Vigil Can Land You in Jail,' *Miami Herald*, 25 May 2011, http://article.wn.com/view/2011/05/30/Bahrains_official_tally_shows_cost_to_Shiites_of_crackdown/.

Middle East Online, 'Hezbollah Urges Syrians to Back Assad Regime,' *Middle East Online*, 25 May 2011, www.middle-east-online.com/english/?id=46327.

Milani, Abbas, 'A Note of Warning and Encouragement for Egyptians,' *The New Republic*, 30 January 2011, www.tnr.com/article/world/82450/egypt-riots-iranian-revolution-1979.

Mitchell, Timothy, *Colonising Egypt* (Stanford CA: University of California Press, 1991).

Mitchell, Timothy, *Rule of Experts: Egypt, Techno-Politics, Modernity* (Stanford CA: University of California Press, 2002).

Mohanty, Chandra Talpade, *Feminism without Borders: Decolonizing Theory, Practicing Solidarity* (Durham NC: Duke University Press, 2003).

Naaman, Mara, *Urban Space in Contemporary Egyptian Literature: Portraits of Cairo* (New York: Palgrave Macmillan, 2011).

Nandy, Ashis, *The Intimate Enemy: Loss and Recovery of Self Under Colonialism* (Oxford: Oxford University Press, 1989).

+972, 'Young Mizrahi Israelis' Open Letter to Arab Peers,' +972, 24 April 2011, http://972mag.com/young-mizrahi-israelis-open-letter-to-arab-peers/.

Reza Nasr, Seyyed Vali, 'If the Arab Spring Turns Ugly,' *New York Times*, 27 August 2011, www.nytimes.com/2011/08/28/opinion/sunday/the-dangers-lurking-in-the-arab-spring.html?pagewanted=all.

Right to Work, 'May Day in Tahrir Square,' *Right to Work*, 1 May 2011, http://righttowork.org.uk/2011/05/may-day-in-tahrir-square/.

Rosenberg, Paul, 'Bottom-up Revolution,' Al Jazeera, 17 June 2011, http://english.aljazeera.net/indepth/opinion/2011/06/2011616114013236175.html.

Sadeghi, Shirin, 'Intricacies of Bahrain's Shia-Sunni Divide,' Al Jazeera, 2 September 2011, http://english.aljazeera.net/indepth/opinion/2011/08/2011829104128700299.html.

Sadiki, Larbi, 'Psychosis of the Arab Revolution,' Al Jazeera, 11 July 2011, http://english.aljazeera.net/indepth/opinion/2011/07/20117118716678870.html.

Said, Edward W., *Orientalism* (New York: Vintage, 1979).

Said, Edward, 'Representing the Colonized: Anthropology's Interlocutors,' *Critical Inquiry*, vol. 15, no. 2 (Winter 1989).

Said, Edward, *The Question of Palestine* (New York: Vintage, 1992).

Scahill, Jeremy, *Blackwater: The Rise of the World's Most Powerful Mercenary Army* (New York: Nation Books, 2007).

Schwab, Raymond, *The Oriental Renaissance: Europe's Rediscovery of India and the East, 1680–1880* (New York: Columbia University Press, 1987).

Schwedler, Jillian, Joshua Stacher, and Stacey Philbrick Yadav, 'Three Powerfully Wrong – and Wrongly Powerful – American Narratives about the Arab Spring', *Jadaliyyah*, 10 June 2011, www.jadaliyya.com/pages/index/1826/three-powerfully-wrong_and-wrongly-powerful_americ.

Selim, Samah, *The Novel and the Rural Imaginary in Egypt, 1880–1985* (London: Routledge, 2004).

Smith, Adam, *The Wealth of Nations* (1776): Book I, ch. 8, 'Of the Wages of Labor'; available at: www.fordham.edu/halsall/mod/adamsmith-summary.html.

Soueif, Ahdaf, 'Egypt's Revolution Is Stuck in a Rut, but We Still Have the Spirit to See It Through,' *Guardian*, 12 July 2011, www.guardian.co.uk/commentisfree/2011/jul/12/egypt-revolution-rut-military-obstacles?intcmp=srch.

Steet, Linda, *Veils and Daggers: A Century of National Geographic's*

Representation of the Arab World (Philadelphia PA: Temple University Press, 2000).

Suhrawardi, Sheikh Shihabuddin Yahya, *The Mystical & Visionary Treatises of Suhrawardi*, trans. W.M. Thackston, Jr. (London: Octagon Press, 1982).

Telegraph, 'Saudi Troops Sent to Crush Bahrain Protests "had British training",' *Telegraph*, 25 may 2011, www.telegraph.co.uk/news/worldnews/middleeast/saudiarabia/8536037/Saudi-troops-sent-to-crush-Bahrain-protests-had-British-training.html.

Tolan, Sandy, 'Visions Collide in a Sweltering Tahrir Square,' Al Jazeera, 30 July 2011, http://english.aljazeera.net/indepth/opinion/2011/07/2011 73014265130218.html.

UN Human Rights Council, 'United Nations Fact Finding Mission on the Gaza Conflict,' UN Human Rights Council, www2.ohchr.org/english/bodies/hrcouncil/specialsession/9/factfindingmission.htm.

Walberg, Eric, *Postmodern Imperialism: Geopolitics and the Great Games* (New York: Clarity Press, 2011).

Weber, Max, 'Politics as a Vocation,' in Hans Gerth and C. Wright Mills (eds), *From Max Weber: Essays in Sociology* (Oxford: Oxford University Press, 1946): 77-128.

Wolf, Naomi, 'The Middle East Feminist Revolution,' Al Jazeera, 4 March 2011, http://english.aljazeera.net/indepth/opinion/2011/03 201134111445686926.html.

Yack, Bernard, *Longing for Total Revolutions: Philosophic Sources of Social Discontent from Rousseau to Marx and Nietzsche* (Princeton NJ: Princeton University Press, 1986).

Yaghmaian, Behzad, *Embracing the Infidel: Stories of Muslim Migrants on the Journey West* (New York: Delacorte Press, 2005).

Yaghmaian, Behzad, 'The Specter of a Black Europe,' *Counterpunch*, 23 February 2011, www.counterpunch.org/behzado2232011.html.

Index

About Zed Books

Zed Books is a critical and dynamic publisher, committed to increasing awareness of important international issues and to promoting diversity, alternative voices and progressive social change. We publish on politics, development, gender, the environment and economics for a global audience of students, academics, activist and general readers. Run as a co-operative, we aim to operate in an ethical and environmentally sustainable way.

Find out more at
www.zedbooks.co.uk

For up-to-date news, articles, reviews
and events information visit
http://zed-books.blogspot.com

To subscribe to the monthly Zed Books e-newsletter
send an email headed 'subscribe' to marketing@zedbooks.net

We can also be found on Facebook, ZNet,
Twitter and Library Thing.